# FROM SHELDON TO SECKER

THE FORD LECTURES
DELIVERED IN THE UNIVERSITY OF OXFORD
IN HILARY TERM
1958

# FROM SHELDON TO SECKER

## ASPECTS OF ENGLISH CHURCH HISTORY
## 1660–1768

BY

### NORMAN SYKES, F.B.A.

DEAN OF WINCHESTER

*Honorary Fellow of Emmanuel College Cambridge, and*
*Formerly Dixie Professor of Ecclesiastical History*

THE FORD LECTURES 1958

CAMBRIDGE
AT THE UNIVERSITY PRESS
1959

PUBLISHED BY
THE SYNDICS OF THE CAMBRIDGE UNIVERSITY PRESS

Bentley House, 200 Euston Road, London, N.W. 1
American Branch: 32 East 57th Street, New York 22, N.Y.

©

CAMBRIDGE UNIVERSITY PRESS

1959

*Printed in Great Britain at the University Press, Cambridge*
*(Brooke Crutchley, University Printer)*

ALEXANDRO HOWARD BARBER

COLLEGII REGII CHIRURGORUM ANGLIAE SOCIO

NECNON CIVILE PRO LIBERTATE

OPPUGNATORI INDEFESSO

# CONTENTS

# PREFACE

To the electors to Ford's Lectureship I owe the privilege and opportunity of giving the lectures of which this volume is an expanded version, and I desire to express to them my gratitude and appreciation of the honour done me by their invitation. To an Oxford historian the Ford Lectures are the blue riband of his profession, and the pleasure of an exile in the prospect of a series of visits to his home is tempered with apprehension lest he should fall sadly below the high standard of the foundation. When the invitation reached me in March 1957 the responsibility of writing six lectures for delivery in Hilary Term 1958 seemed to carry more of *onus* than *honor*. For, coming on the eve of the publication of what I had believed to be my *magnum ac ultimum opus*, a biography of Archbishop Wake, it found the cupboard indeed completely bare, with my note-books empty of facts and my head of ideas. In the short time available I therefore resolved to try and clear up some problems of English church history during the half-century following the Restoration of 1660, which had puzzled me often, and to ascertain, if possible, how far the faults and shortcomings of the Hanoverian church were due to the failure in 1660 and 1688 to effect the necessary reforms in the ecclesiastical constitution. The ensuing chapters represent my suggested answers.

An initial survey of the character of the Restoration Church Settlement indicated its essentially conservative nature, and emphasised the gravity of the problems with which the episcopate had to grapple along traditional lines and without the necessary revision of the Canons of 1603 and those of 1640, or without the reform of ecclesiastical administration and judicial procedure. This failure was particularly underlined by the eclipse of Convocation, thanks to the surrender of its right of taxation and its consequent decline, followed by the disputes during the reign of Anne and its suspension in 1717. The ill-effects of this suppression became clearer as my investigation proceeded. Closely associated with the conservative nature of the church settlements at the Restoration and Revolution were the fluctuating fortunes of Comprehension and Toleration, in which respect I have tried to discover the reasons for the failure to comprehend Presbyterian and Episcopalian within the re-established national church and the consequent, unexpected, triumph of Toleration and its vicissitudes between 1689 and 1719. Contemporaneously with these domestic issues, ecclesiastical union was a prominent feature of the *Zeitgeist*, and to this tendency the Caroline divines of the Church of England made a noteworthy contribution by their learned patristic studies and appeal to the primitive church, which not only earned the proud compliment *clerus Anglicanus stupor mundi*, but also led to eirenic discussion with Gallican churchmen and with foreign Protestants. Simultaneously, however the theological climate was undergoing a marked revolution as the defences of patristic orthodoxy by Bull gave place to the age of reason and the triumph of the Latitudinarians, which swept away traditional standards of belief and doctrine. Finally, a last attempt was made to effect the necessary reforms by Gibson, whose scheme of ecclesiastical reconstruction, if successful, would have remedied the omissions of 1660 and 1688 and would have equipped the *Ecclesia Anglicana* to meet the challenge of the age of reform which succeeded the Hanoverian *quieta non movenda*. With the failure of Gibson's thorough-going project, Secker strove to maintain the position of the established church by diligence and devotion to episcopal duties along conventional lines, accepting the suspension of Convocation and the impossibility of carrying through a programme of change. Surveyed as a whole, the pregnant century from Sheldon to Secker may be seen as the most influential epoch of English church history between the Reformation and the Victorian age.

I should like to express my especial thanks to His Grace The Lord Archbishop of Canterbury, Dr Geoffrey Fisher, for his ready and generous authorisation to quote from the valuable collection of manuscripts of Archbishop Secker, preserved in the archiepiscopal library at Lambeth Palace. Embracing copies in Secker's hand from various papers of Gibson hitherto unknown to me and also an Autobiography of Secker himself, this collection has furnished the greater part of what is new in these lectures; and I am most grateful to Dr C. R. Dodwell, the Lambeth Librarian, for having opened for my inspection these items, to which access had hitherto not been allowed. To many other friends and colleagues who have helped me in various ways I can offer only a general expression of thanks. To the Secretary of the University Press and his staff and to several members of the Printer's staff I am indebted for their patience and perseverance in grappling with the manuscript of a most trying and troublesome author and Syndic. To my wife I owe more than words can tell for ungrudging help in the thankless tasks of proof-reading and indexing.

A few days before the delivery of the last lecture I received the invitation to become Dean of Winchester, and it was therefore with very mixed feelings that I realised that these lectures would be my swan-song as an academic teacher. To the University of Oxford and to The Queen's College on the one hand and to the University of Cambridge and to Emmanuel College on the other hand, I owe more than I can express for the privilege of membership of their respective Societies, in which may true religion and sound learning ever flourish in accordance with their Founders' intentions.

N. S.

THE DEANERY, WINCHESTER
*Michaelmas 1958*

# I

# THE REBUILDING OF SION

'The month hath produced happy things and this is a day of joy', wrote Bishop Duppa to Sir Justinian Isham on 8 May 1660: 'for the King so long laid aside, is now proclaimed the headstone of the corner. Never was there so miraculous a change as this, nor so great things done in so short a time. But *a Domino factum est istud*: no humane wisdom can claime a share in it.' The proclamation of Charles II in London on this day seemed indeed a miracle beyond human contrivance and comprehension. Less than two months earlier, on 27 March, only two days after the City of London had formally memorialised the Council of State to invite Charles to return, Duppa had confided to his correspondent that the spring of his hopes was not 'so forward but winds and frost may blast it; and the truth is, we have been so often deluded with expectation that all storms were over, that every sunshine is suspected by me'. Now, however, the dream which he had indulged himself, 'such as David mentions when God turn'd away the captivity of Sion', had come true;[1] and on 25 May the exiled sovereign landed on British soil. Twenty years of civil strife, ecclesiastical revolution, political interregnum and constitutional chaos was about to end; and the exiles, especially the clerical exiles, who made ready to return with joy and gladness to Sion, could have had little anticipation of the storms still to burst upon the restored church and crown. Yet within a quarter of a century the Stuart house was to be in exile again, whilst William of Orange and Mary ruled in its stead; within a further quarter of a century the reign of Anne was drawing to a close amid profound uncertainty as to the security of that Protestant succession prescribed in the Act of Settlement; and even when the second miracle of the peaceful accession of the House of Hanover had been accomplished, a considerable period of unsettlement and experiment followed before the new dynasty was firmly settled on the throne.

For the Church of England which shared in the Restoration, no less than for the Protestant Dissenters who found themselves

[1] *The Correspondence of Bishop Brian Duppa and Sir Justinian Isham, 1650–1660*, ed. by Sir Giles Isham. Northamptonshire Record Society, vol. XVII (1956), pp. 180, 183.

surprisingly excluded from its expected benefits, the period was one of parallel confusion and uncertainty. To the *Ecclesia Anglicana* indeed, to which it seemed in 1660 that its warfare was accomplished, there came the shock of the secret apostasy of Charles II and the open conversion to Rome of James II with the consequent threat to its position and its very existence; and this in turn was followed by the equally disturbing experience of adjustment to the parliamentary monarchy of the Revolution and its chill ecclesiastical climate. William Sancroft, who had been deprived of his Fellowship at Emmanuel College, Cambridge, during the Protectorate and had gone into exile on the continent, was again to be deprived at the Revolution of the archbishopric of Canterbury, a dramatic turn of fortune almost without peer in the long line of successors of St Augustine. Meantime the Protestant Dissenters had been tempted by the Declarations of Indulgence proffered successively by Charles and James II, rewarded for their firmness in refusing these seductions by a legal Toleration in 1689, and again abridged of their newly-won indulgence by the Occasional Conformity and Schism Acts of the reign of Anne. Even more revolutionary were the changes in the intellectual and scientific climate, which affected profoundly religious thought and life during the latter half of the seventeenth and first half of the eighteenth centuries. 'The Restoration', as Gwatkin observed, 'is the most sudden change in English history since the Norman Conquest.... The nation went into the Civil War Protestant indeed, but otherwise less changed from the middle ages than is often supposed; and from the uneasy dreamings of the Commonwealth it awoke almost modern.'[1] Furthermore, the ecclesiastical settlement of 1662, with the minor modifications in 1689, fixed the administrative, judicial, legislative and financial structure of the established church in a mould which was to last, both for ill and for good, until the sweeping reforms of the early Victorian age. In view of the variety of these kaleidoscopic changes and of their far-reaching influence upon English religious life, little apology is needed for the choice of the pregnant century from Sheldon to Secker as the theme of a series of lectures upon this foundation.

The exultation of churchmen at the turning of the captivity of Sion was tempered shortly by apprehension, not to say suspicion.

[1] H. M. Gwatkin, *Church and State in England to the Death of Queen Anne* (1917), p. 346.

From his retreat at Richmond, Duppa wrote anxiously to Gilbert Sheldon on 11 August 1660, voicing his fears for the ecclesiastical situation.

What may be done now that the bishop of London [the aged Juxon] is arrived, (whose absence was the only honest apology we could have that nothing was done in behalf of the Church), I know not; but if nothing be, we have lost our excuse. You are the only person about his Majesty that I have confidence in, and I persuade myself that as none hath his ear more, so none is likely to prevail on his heart more; and there never was more need of it, for all the professed enemies of our Church look upon this as the critical time to use their *dernier ressort* to shake his Majesty's constancy. . . . I shall wait upon you as soon as I hear that my coming may be in any way useful. In the meantime I am more at ease because I know you stand ready upon the place to lay hold upon all opportunities, and are diligently upon the watch *ne Ecclesia aliquid detrimenti capiat*.[1]

Dr Bosher has traced the tortuous diplomacy (not to say duplicity) by which Hyde and his clerical allies frustrated the hopes of the Presbyterians for a compromise ecclesiastical settlement by means of 'Comprehension'; and the reader may not withhold a tribute to the skill, if not the straightforwardness, of the Anglican strategy. The Presbyterians indeed were bluffed out of their senses by a series of apparently favourable portents and promises, whilst their adversaries were taking possession of the church by stealth. On the one side about ten or twelve prominent puritan divines were appointed royal chaplains, including Baxter, Manton, Bates, Calamy, Ashe and Reynolds, and were allowed to preach only, and not required to read the Liturgy; next, Presbyterian leaders were summoned to a meeting with Charles, at which they were invited to submit proposals for church government and liturgy, with the expectation that the episcopalian party would be required to do the same, and hints of preferment were judicially given; and finally the king's Declaration concerning Ecclesiastical Affairs of 25 October 1660, issued after conference at Worcester House, was speciously profuse in promises. After expressing satisfaction that the 'most able and principal assertors of the presbyterian opinions' were 'neither enemies. . .to episcopacy or liturgy, but modestly to desire such alterations in either as, without shaking foundations, might best allay the present distempers', Charles adumbrated projected changes. First, that only 'men of learning, virtue and piety' should be

---

[1] Tanner MSS. 49, f. 17, cited in R. S. Bosher, *The Making of the Restoration Settlement* (1951), p. 173.

1-2

appointed bishops, with charge to be frequent preachers throughout their dioceses; secondly that, because of the size of dioceses, suffragan bishops should be appointed 'in every diocese'; thirdly, that bishops and archdeacons should exercise their jurisdiction with the advice and assistance of a council of presbyters; fourthly, that cathedral preferments should be given to divines qualified so to assist the bishops, who should also have an equal number of elected presbyters associated with them in ordination and the exercise of jurisdiction; fifthly, that confirmation should be 'rightly and solemnly performed by the information and with the consent of the minister of the place'; sixthly, that no bishop should exercise any arbitrary power; seventhly, that 'an equal number of divines of both persuasions' should be appointed to review the Book of Common Prayer; and finally, that observance of the nocent ceremonies and the taking of the oath of canonical obedience should be waived for the time being until the revision of the Liturgy had been determined. Taken at its face value, the Declaration promised important concessions to the Presbyterians and reforms of the traditional system.

On the other side however, a Bill to give the Declaration the force of law was defeated in the House of Commons by 183 to 157 votes on November 28; and a month later on 24 December the Convention Parliament was dissolved. Meantime the personnel of cathedral chapters had been replenished with a view to the nomination of bishops to the vacant sees and their canonical election in accordance with the *congé d'élire*; so that by May 1661, Dr Bosher estimates, 'the re-establishment of the Church of England, was in all essentials, virtually complete'. With the dissolution of the Convention Parliament and after due evidence of the royalist triumph at the ensuing polls, it was thought safe and possible to allow elections to Convocation; and on 12 April 1661 the new archbishop of Canterbury, Juxon, issued his mandate to Bishop Sheldon of London for the summons of his Provincial Synod. When therefore the long-promised Savoy Conference met on 15 April, the situation was almost correspondent to that of the Hampton Court Conference in 1603. The Episcopalians were once more in possession, and the Presbyterians on the defensive. The debates were not so much designed to offer concessions by which the latter might be induced to conform, as to assert the soundness of the episcopalian platform. 'A meeting at the Savoy', wrote the historian of Nonconformity, 'between divines of the two schools in the spring of 1660, would have been different from such a meeting in the spring of 1661. Something at least like equal terms might have been secured at the former date, but it is plain that afterwards the men of Geneva stood no chance with those of Canterbury. Episcopacy and the Liturgy were in possession.'[1] The revision of the Liturgy therefore was the work of Convocation, not of the Savoy Conference, and was confirmed by Parliament. It is necessary briefly to consider the nature of the ecclesiastical settlement thus carried into effect.

Like the settlement in the state, that of the church was stamped by the increasing authority of Parliament. The High Commission Court was abolished and branded as illegal; the Canons of 1640, which had been passed by Convocation after the dissolution of the Short Parliament, were formally disallowed by statute; the use of the *ex-officio* oath, which had been a subject of contention since the primacy of Whitgift, was abandoned in the restored ecclesiastical courts; whilst even the ultra-loyal Commons of the Cavalier Parliament, in accepting without discussion the revision of the Prayer Book proposed by the Convocations, did so by the narrow margin of 96 to 90 votes and with an expressly-recorded reservation of their right to debate them if they had so desired. Furthermore, whereas the Elizabethan act of 1571 (13 Eliz. I, cap. 12) had required subscription only to the doctrinal articles of the Thirty-Nine Articles of Religion, the clergy were required henceforth to subscribe them in their entirety; and a promise of remarkable stringency was also required of them by the Act of Uniformity of 1662, in respect of the Book of Common Prayer, whereby they had to declare their 'unfeigned assent and consent to all and everything contained and prescribed in and by' the said book. Finally, the same Act not only decreed that all persons not episcopally ordained by St Bartholomew's Day, 1662, should be disqualified to hold any ecclesiastical promotion, but further prohibited any one not so ordained from presuming to 'consecrate and administer the Holy Sacrament of the Lord's Supper', thereby closing the loopholes through which before the civil wars ministers who had received presbyterian ordination abroad in the foreign Reformed churches or in the Church of Scotland, had been permitted to officiate in the Church of England and to receive institution to benefices with cure of souls. This stringency was the consequence, as Burnet averred, of the fact

---

[1] J. Stoughton, *The Church of the Restoration* (1911) (vol. III of *A History of Religion in England*), p. 160.

that 'the late war and the disputes during that time had raised these controversies higher, and brought men to stricter notions and to maintain them with more fierceness'.[1] The effect of this new temper was seen forthwith in the procedure adopted for the consecration of bishops for the Church of Scotland, to which the Restoration brought a return of episcopacy. For whereas at the consecrations in 1610 the Scottish divines had not been required first to receive episcopal ordination as deacon and priest, in 1661 two of their number who had not been episcopally ordained were privately ordained to the diaconate and priesthood before the public consecration of the entire company of four to the episcopate. In regard to the revision of the Book of Common Prayer itself, perhaps the most important characteristics were the abandonment of the 'Durham Book', a revision made by certain bishops meeting at the London residence of Bishop Matthew Wren of Ely and laid before the Lower House of Convocation, which would have brought the Order of Holy Communion much nearer to the form of the first Edwardine Prayer Book of 1549, and the resolution to make only minor, though numerous, changes in the existing rites.[2] Thereby at any rate the position of those puritan clergy already episcopally ordained or willing so to be, was not made more difficult, as would have been the case if the alternative proposals had been adopted.

Such being the framework of the ecclesiastical settlement, its operation would depend principally on the episcopate, and the personnel of the restored bench became therefore a consideration of primary importance. Apart from the advancement of Juxon to Canterbury, of Frewen to York, of Duppa to Winchester and the nomination of Sheldon to London, the chief promotions went to the returned clerical exiles, notably Morley, Cosin, Earle, and Laney— to be followed in the next decade by Carleton, Creighton and Mews. The passing-over of those bishops who had stayed behind in England was observed both by themselves and by contemporaries, nor did it pass without comment. Bishop Warner of Rochester sent to Sheldon on 12 September 1660 'a true narration of somewhat which you may have forgot and of somewhat more which perchance you never heard', namely the extent of his own services to church

---

[1] G. Burnet, *A History of My Own Time*, vol. I, p. 237 (6 vols. 1823).

[2] G. J. Cuming, 'The Making of the Durham Book' and 'The Prayer Book in Convocation, 1661', *Journal of Ecclesiastical History*, vol. VI, pt 1, pp. 60–72; vol. VIII, pt 2, pp. 182–92.

and king during the late troubles. It was a comprehensive and impressive catalogue, beginning with a sermon preached in the second year of Charles I's reign in Passion week on the text from St Matthew xxi. 28 (When they saw him, they said among themselves, 'This is the heir; come, let us kill him, and seize on his inheritance'), which 'was a full and clear prophecy of that most excellent king and glorious martyr's death, the hearing whereof at that time when preached, so startled some Lords and Commons that they earnestly moved that I might be hanged at Whitehall gate'. The rest of his record was consonant with this exordium. Warner had accompanied Charles I as chaplain on his visit to Scotland, advanced His Majesty a loan of £1500 when the Scots invaded England in 1639, attended him at his Council at York in the following year, and defended the rights of Crown and episcopacy in the Long Parliament, risking a *praemunire* in respect of the Canons of 1640. During the Civil War he had refused to pay any taxes to the Parliament, for which he was deprived of all his estate, both ecclesiastical and temporal; also he had fled into Wales for three years to avoid capture after publishing a sermon 'against the most devilish act of murdering the king', and finally for refusal to take 'their wicked oath and engagements I and no bishop else was three times banished from the place of my abode', and 'I and no bishop else was forced to pay the tenth part of my estate, real and personal'. If such had been his services to the king, not less were those rendered to the church. 'In these later times whether I lived in my house or sojourned, I read the prayers of the Church morning and evening, preached weekly, Sacrament monthly, confirmed publicly and privately in orthodox congregations.' As works of supererogation he had given £100 to Charles II in exile, in addition to divers charities to his college of St Mary Magdalen; and in summary he affirmed:

So far as I can learn, there is not a clergyman living who hath done or suffered (to put them together) more for the king, the church and the poor clergy than I have; neither can any be more ready and willing to do and suffer the like again, when justly called. Reverend Sir, if you ask me why I write all this, and why to you, know, I pray, that you may be pleased to witness for me, that though I am utterly forgotten in all, yet that I have not forgot in any kind to discharge the part of a true and loyal subject to my sovereign lord, nor of a dutiful son to my holy mother, the Church.[1]

[1] Tanner MSS. 49, f. 23.

7

Notwithstanding all which, he died still without translation in 1666, having, as George Davenport remarked, 'lived long bishop of Rochester and scarce any bishop died in that see since John Fisher'.[1]

A similar plea was sent to Sheldon by Bishop Skinner of Oxford on 17 August 1662, to the effect that

a word sticks with me (I must be plain with your lordship) which my brother of Bangor told me, which makes me fear I may suffer wherein I least imagined and wherein I least deserved. For he told me that my lord high Chancellor was pleased to say that the ancient bishops were not removed because they did not (as they were bound in duty) relieve their mother the Church when she stood in most need in point of ordination; wherein if I failed, it had been just and fit not only to have taken from me the support of my bishopric, but even bishopric and all. The truth is, I ordained priests to the number of betwixt 4 and 500 from the time we were prohibited by their sacrilegious ordinance to the time of his majesty's blessed restoration; and not one of them all but subscribed to the Articles and took the oath of allegiance, even in the days when upon discovery I should have had my books and my bed taken from me, having little else left me. Nay, but I will tell your lordship more. Dr Lamplugh in those dismal days rid not fewer than 300 journeys between Oxford and Launton for the work of confirmation and ordination; so that all this, I hope, will quit me of neglect in point of ordination. Cornwall and York and all foreign countries as well as the nearer will witness for me. And for preaching I never failed one Sunday for fifteen years together.[2]

Skinner likewise died in his little bishopric, for the offence of not having taken steps to ensure the apostolic succession during the Interregnum by consecrating bishops in England. Hyde had been especially exasperated by this neglect for which he held Skinner chiefly responsible; though Duppa paid no penalty for his parallel quiescence, in his resolve to 'secure myself the same way as the tortoise doth by not going out of my shell'.[3]

For the second time in its history therefore the bench was replenished from the ranks of exiles. But whereas the Germanical exiles of the reign of Elizabeth I were favourers of the puritan clergy, the Gallican exiles of Charles II were determined to be revenged upon those Presbyterians who had pulled down the walls and bulwarks of Sion. Moreover, the Caroline episcopate has evoked an unusual string of superlatives from Gwatkin.

The episcopate never stood higher than in the time of Charles II. The nine survivors of Laudian times include Juxon, Wren and Duppa; but

---

[1] Tanner MSS. 45, f. 116.

[2] *Ibid.* 48, f. 25, cited in part by Bosher, *Restoration Settlement*, p. 125, n. 2.

[3] Isham, *Duppa-Isham Correspondence*, p. 52.

their successors are a brilliant group. Learning was represented by Cosin and Sanderson, Morley, Pearson, Gunning, and Jeremy Taylor in Ireland. Sheldon also had a name for learning in his younger days in Falkland's circle at Great Tew. To these we must add the future Nonjurors, Sancroft, Ken and Frampton. For secular learning stood the astronomer Seth Ward, who nearly anticipated Newton's discovery of gravity and was further an accomplished lawyer. Then there was the universal scholar, John Wilkins who was not refused preferment for having married Cromwell's sister, and, with Sprat of Rochester, was no purely honorary member of the Royal Society.... The bench has never been more fully adorned with splendid examples of learning, of courage, of princely munificence, of true devotion.[1]

Certainly it was no monochrome episcopal college which included prelates of the theological outlook of Reynolds, Wilkins and Croft; nor such martial, ex-service bishops as Dolben, Compton, and Mews.

The Fathers of the church would assuredly have need of all these excellencies if they were to rebuild the Sion to which they now returned. For, like the Jerusalem of Nehemiah and his companions, it had suffered sore dilapidation during the Oliverian times. Bishop Sanderson's visitation of the archdeaconry of Buckingham in July 1662 presented a typical picture of the desolation to be remedied. Thirty-seven parish churches were 'out of repair', and in a score more the chancels were in need of reparation, virtually all the churches had no surplice, thirty-four had no Common Prayer Book, nine had no Communion cup and ten no carpet to cover the Holy Table.[2] Similar conditions were found to prevail in the dioceses of Exeter and Salisbury, in the latter of which Bishop Henchman's primary visitation in 1662 showed that 'the material deficiencies to be made up, or repairs to be undertaken were considerable', particularly in respect of surplices, furnishings for the Holy Table and proper Communion Vessels;[3] whilst further corroborating testimony came from the north-east, where Archdeacon Basire had returned from travels in the Middle East to find in Northumberland the 'fabrics of many churches and chapels altogether ruinous and in great decay, and cannot be gotten repaired without visitations. Besides, in many churches there be neither Bibles, Books of Common Prayer, surplices, fonts, Communion Tables, nor anything that is

[1] Gwatkin, *Church and State*, pp. 380–1.
[2] E. R. C. Brinkworth (ed.), *Episcopal Visitation Book for the Archdeaconry of Buckingham* (Buckinghamshire Record Society, 1947).
[3] Anne Whiteman, 'The Church of England 1542–1837', in *Victoria County History of Wiltshire*, vol. III, p. 44.

necessary for the service of God'.[1] Little wonder that Bishop Cosin hastened to his diocese of Durham, leaving London at the beginning of August 1660 to spend the summer holding ordinations, confirmations and synods of his clergy at Newcastle and Durham, before returning to the capital in November for the meeting of the Convention Parliament. Even greater dilapidation had fallen upon many cathedrals, whose fabric had suffered grievously during the suppression of their capitular foundations. Lichfield was almost in ruins, and the correspondence of Bishop Hacket with Sheldon reveals the indomitable courage and vigour with which the new bishop undertook the task of rebuilding; Worcester and Hereford were sorely battered; Exeter had seen an interior wall constructed to provide separate meeting places for Presbyterians and Independents; whilst at St Paul's the choir had been used for stabling Oliverian cavalry and at St Asaph the postmaster had stabled horses and oxen in the nave.

But grievous though the condition of churches may have been, still worse was the spiritual desolation of the people. For a score of years the Anglican Liturgy had been proscribed, episcopacy abolished and an end made of the traditional system of ecclesiastical administration and justice as executed by visitations and the ecclesiastical courts. To recover this leeway, attention must first be given to the personnel of the ministry. Mr A. G. Matthews' detailed investigations in *Calamy Revised* estimate that the Restoration settlement accounted for 1760 ejections of ministers in forty-one English counties, to which must be added 149 from the universities and schools, but of whom 171 later conformed.[2] The bishops accordingly held ordinations on a scale reminiscent of the beginning of the reign of Elizabeth I, as they hastened to replenish the depleted ranks of the ministry. Cosin held his first ordination at Michaelmas 1660, Gauden of Exeter on 13 January 1661, Sanderson of Lincoln on the very day of his own consecration, 28 October 1660; and Dr Whiteman's researches have shown the large numbers admitted to holy orders. Thus Gauden ordained ninety candidates between January 1661 and February 1662 and his successor in the see of Exeter, Seth Ward, eighty-four more by the end of 1663. Miss Whiteman has remarked further the natural consequence of the urgency of the times in the number of ordinations held *extra tempora* and the

---

[1] *Remains of Dennis Granville* (Surtees Society, 1861), p. 251.
[2] A. G. Matthews, *Calamy Revised* (1934), pp. xii–xiii.

ordination of some persons both to the diaconate and priesthood on the same day.[1]

Allied with this recruitment of the ministry was the question of the educational standards of the candidates. Dr C. M. Barratt's valuable (though as yet unpublished) study of *The Condition of the Parish Clergy between the Reformation and 1660, with special reference to the Dioceses of Oxford, Worcester and Gloucester* has established the conclusion that, taking the possession of an university degree as the most objective criterion for determining the education of the clergy, the sixty years from the middle of the reign of Elizabeth I to the Civil War had seen a steady rise, so that 'it seems likely that the improvements in their qualifications under Elizabeth and the early Stuarts brought the learning of the parish clergy to a higher standard than it had ever reached before'. During the Interregnum there had naturally been a sharp decline in the number of graduates; and greater importance therefore attaches to Dr Whiteman's calculation that of the candidates ordained at Exeter between 1660 and 1663, between 57 and 63 per cent were graduates, whilst a high-water mark may perhaps have been attained at Oxford when Bishop Skinner on 20 September 1663 ordained thirty-one graduates out of a total of thirty-seven persons then admitted to holy orders. In the diocese of Durham, during the long episcopate of Nathaniel, Lord Crewe from 1674 to 1721 it has been estimated 'that out of 373 clergy at least 212 were graduates of Oxford, Cambridge or one of the Scottish universities, and at least 20 held higher degrees in divinity or laws, these last being, however, mostly dignitaries'.[2] At Peterborough Bishop William Lloyd reported to Sancroft in 1681 that he had ordained four deacons and three presbyters, adding that 'the reasons why so few were ordained, together with the method I have pursued to rescue that institution from contempt and scandal, I shall transmit to Your Grace'.[3] Not all dioceses attained an equal standard; and Bishop Peter Mews, whose own distinction was martial rather than academic, reported to Sheldon concerning the clergy of his diocese of Bath and Wells on 24 July 1675 that

it is my very great unhappiness to be infested with some so grossly ignorant that they are not able to perform their duties with any tolerable reputation to the Church; and more such are daily creeping in and will

---

[1] Anne Whiteman, 'The Re-Establishment of the Church of England, 1660–1663', in *Transactions of the Royal Historical Society*, 5th series (1955), vol. v, pp. 111–31.

[2] C. E. Whiting, *Nathaniel, Lord Crewe, Bishop of Durham* (1940), p. 249.

[3] Tanner MSS. 36, f. 33.

certainly be the ruin of it, if not timely prevented. This week I had a presentation brought me by one who, when I asked him *Quo gradu Academico ornatus es?*, answered *Non sum gradus*; to a second question, *Quot annos impendisti studiis Academicis?*, he answered *Unus*. He could not compare *Multum*; but gave it *Multum, Melior, Optimus*. He could not construe a sentence of the plainest Latin imaginable; yet he hath been priest six years and was ordained by the late bishop of Bristol, Dr Ironside. I have refused him institution and expect to be called into Westminster Hall. I write this that your Grace may consider what course to take to prevent so growing a mischief, which certainly hath its rise and beginning from ordination.[1]

Perhaps the golden mean between too harsh severity and too lax leniency may be found in the practice of Bishop Frampton of Gloucester, as related by his contemporary biographer.

In dispensing of Orders he was strict but not rigorous, careful but not supercilious, never pressing any candidate with an uncommon question serving to no other end but to dash men out of countenance and make them less ready in what they did really understand. And that he might not be imposed upon by favour or affection, he invited all candidates to his house, entertained them friendly, and examined them in a familiar way to embolden them in a further trial which he did take of every one singly and apart, that one might not be discouraged by another's brighter parts, nor the weakness of any one be discovered by the rest. For if he at any time refused to admit a person he found deficient in learning (which indeed was seldom, few offering themselves but what were well qualified); but if it so fell out, he would show them their wants, direct their studies and encourage them to proceed, and in such a gentle manner dismiss them that, as they avoided being taken notice of by others, so it turned to their advantage in the future management of their lives and study.[2]

For the fulfilment of this branch of the pastoral office, the episcopate was furnished with instructions from Sheldon in 1665, requiring the strict observance of the canons concerning ordination with especial reference to the possession of letters dimissory, forbidding any bishop to ordain outside his diocese without archiepiscopal licence, and ordering an annual return of the names, titles, degrees and orders of all persons ordained. Since bishops were dependent for information about ordinands upon the veracity of letters testimonial, Sancroft issued in 1685 a particular admonition on this head to his suffragans. On receipt of these orders 'relating to the granting and admission of Certificates and Letters Testimonial', Bishop Ward observed to the primate that they were 'indeed such as might have

---

[1] Tanner MSS. 42, f. 167.
[2] T. S. Evans, *Life of Robert Frampton, Bishop of Gloucester* (1876), pp. 177-8.

prevented many great mischiefs if they had been timely prescribed and religiously observed. My trust is that almighty God by your Grace's hand will rebuild what hath been broken down and strengthen that which still remains of order in the Church.'[1] In 1685 also the bishops of the province agreed upon ten articles to govern their conduct in conferring holy orders, embracing the canonical age for ordination, the possession of an academic degree, a *bona fide* title, testimonials of good conversation, due examination and ordination only at the four embertides, and a scrupulous observance of the prohibition against conferring both the orders of deacon and priest on any candidate on the same day.[2]

Tradition, reinforced by Canon 60, required bishops to administer Confirmation during their triennial visitations; but though evidence of regular performance of the duty of visitation is extant, details concerning Confirmations are hard to discover. Cosin related how during the course of his visitation in September 1660, 'upon Sunday last I had a solemn Confirmation with a sermon to that end before it, and yesterday I had another; for the company was too great to go through with them all in one day, yet I admitted none but those who were duly examined and brought testimonies besides, subscribed by their own ministers'.[3] Bishop Hacket of Lichfield sent to Sheldon on 17 June 1665

an account of my late progress into Salopshire. I began my journey on the last of May and returned to my home on the 16th of this June. I began at Bridgnorth, so to Salop, to Elsmere, to Wenn, to Whitchurch, to Drayton in Hales, to Hadnet and to Stafford on my way home. God gave me strength to preach in all these eight market towns in the compass of those few days. I was marvellously resorted to everywhere, and in those several places I confirmed 5,384;

requiring them moreover 'not to be tumultuarily presented but with the pre-examination of their several ministers'.[4] Bishop Mews likewise informed Sheldon in 1674 that 'on Sunday last I confirmed above 500 at Shepton Mallet and as many more at Pilton a fortnight before';[5] whilst Frampton was so devoted to this branch of the

---

[1] Tanner MSS. 39, f. 92.

[2] E. Cardwell, *Documentary Annals of the Reformed Church of England* (1844), vol. II, no. CLII, p. 322; no. CLVII, pp. 342–4; no. CLXI, pp. 354–8.

[3] *The Correspondence of John Cosin*, ed. G. Ornsby (Surtees Society, 1869), vol. II, p. 31.

[4] Tanner MSS. 45, f. 13; T. Plume, *A Century of Sermons preached by Dr John Hacket: with an Account of the Life of the Author* (1675), p. xxxix.

[5] Tanner MSS. 42, f. 119.

pastoral office as to persist after his deprivation as a Non-juror, when 'for private, though sometimes numerous confirmations he continued till near the time of his death, very many for that end applying to him'.[1] In the diocese of Peterborough, Bishop Lloyd during his primary visitation in 1681 confirmed 100 persons at Towcester, 300 at Daventry, and a total of 600 at Peterborough, Oundle and Castor.[2] But the prevailing uncertainty as to the solemnity of episcopal administration of the rite was shown by the *Rector's Book of Clayworth, Notts*, during the incumbency of William Sampson; who noted the names of thirty-three persons presented by him for confirmation to Archbishop Dolben of York at Retford on 16 July 1685, and contrasted this with the visitation of Archbishop Lamplugh at the same town on 16 May 1690, when 'there was a confirmation, but so confused a thing that I could not see who of my own parish was there'. On the next occasion, the rector simply noted that on 12 May 1693 'Dr Sharp, archbishop of York made his first visitation and confirmed at Retford'; but on 5 May 1698, when Sharp again confirmed there in his visitation, Sampson recorded the names of twenty-six of his flock who received the laying-on of hands.[3] Perhaps also the edifying character of the rite was not enhanced at Wenn in 1665, whence Bishop Hacket reported that official letters announcing the naval victory won by the duke of York against the Dutch off Harwich 'were shown to me as I was busy in the chancel in Confirmation; I rose up and desired all the congregation to join with me in prayer, and I ventured upon an extemporal prayer of thanksgiving at the Communion Table, which was answered with an *Amen* like a clap of thunder'.[4] *Per contra*, even of two blackamoors of the bench, Nathaniel Lord Crewe, bishop of Durham, and Thomas Cartwright, bishop of Chester, a favourable account may be rendered in respect of their administration of Confirmation. Dr Ellison, vicar of Newcastle, preaching before Crewe in St Nicholas' church in 1701, eulogised his 'pastoral care, that you make not Confirmation an appendage to your triennial visitations, but your yearly business in some part or other of your diocese; and this year particularly your lordship was pleased to go to many small villages, as well as larger towns'. Moreover the

---

[1] T. S. Evans, *Life of Frampton*, p. 189.     [2] Tanner MSS. 36, f. 33.
[3] *The Rector's Book of Clayworth, Notts*, ed. by H. Gill and E. L. Guilford (Nottingham, 1910), pp. 72, 93, 103, 124-5.
[4] Tanner MSS. 45, f. 13. Hacket to Sheldon.

compliment was justified by Crewe's practice in holding Confirmations every year from 1674 to 1716.[1] Likewise the *Diary* of Cartwright from August 1686 to October 1687 records a Confirmation of about 300 persons at Richmond on 14 November, of about 200 in Chester cathedral on 21 December and of a further 350 there on New Year's day; of 90 at Tarvin parish church on 23 January, of 300 at Whitegate on the 25th and at Lancaster of 500, 'most of them aged people, God be praised' on 14 August 1687.[2] The extremes of contemporary practice in regard to Confirmation may be seen from the contrasting circumstances that Cartwright confirmed three candidates for holy orders on the eve of their ordination on 18 December 1686 and four more on 25 September 1687, whereas Nicholas Ferrar at the tender age of six had received the episcopal laying-on of hands twice during the same service, observing that 'it was a good thing to have the bishop's prayers and blessing twice, and I have got it'.[3]

The keystone of the arch of ecclesiastical administration however was the visitation, upon which to a considerable degree the good estate of the church depended. Alike etymologically and historically the overseeing of his flock was the primary duty of the bishop and visitation the means of its realisation. In the greater part of western Christendom the size of dioceses had resulted in episcopal visitations becoming synodal instead of parochial, and the several other avocations of medieval prelates had led to the assertion by the archdeacon of a right of visitation in his own behalf and not by virtue of delegation from the bishop. Tradition and ecclesiastical legislation therefore had settled the episcopal visitation as triennial and the archidiaconal as annual or bi-annual. The majority of Caroline bishops fulfilled this branch of their duty diligently. Cosin embarked on a visitation of his diocese in the summer of 1660 and again in 1662, which latter year saw the general resumption of episcopal visitations. The accounts sent to Sheldon by Bishops Ward of Exeter in 1662, Roberts of Bangor in 1665, Hacket of Lichfield in 1665 and again in 1666 and 1668, and Fuller of Lincoln in 1668, afford sufficient evidence of their zeal and care.[4] Compton of London, moreover,

---

[1] C. E. Whiting, *Nathaniel, Lord Crewe*, pp. 255, 288.

[2] *Diary of Thomas Cartwright*, ed. by J. Hunter (Camden Society, 1843), pp. 12, 21-2, 27-8, 72.

[3] Cartwright, *Diary*, pp. 19, 80; B. Blackstone, *The Ferrar Papers* (Cambridge, 1938), p. 10.

[4] Tanner MSS. 48, ff. 19, 45, 48; 45, ff. 13, 21, 71; 44, ff. 15, 42.

held visitations in 1677, 1685, 1690, 1693–4, 1700 and 1706; and in 1685 conducted a parochial visitation of the archdeaconry of Middlesex during the course of which he visited seventy parishes.[1] Even more diligent was the practice of Lloyd of Peterborough, who reported to Sancroft in 1681 that

the Chancellor, Archdeacon and myself have begun a parochial visitation in this diocese and have already visited 132 parishes, where we found great defects and many things out of order, so as to convince us that some of the ministers of those parishes have been very careless, and most of their churchwardens false and forsworn; for which wilful perjury I have ordered proceedings to be had against some churchwardens, hoping it may prove an effectual method to awaken others to a serious sense of their duty. What was found amiss by parochial visitation was ordered *sub poena juris* to be repaired and rectified in a convenient time, suitable to the nature and quality of the defects and dilapidations.[2]

There were indeed exceptions to this rule of good conduct. The diocese of Lincoln could hardly have failed to suffer during the long episcopate from 1675 to 1692 of Thomas Barlow, Provost of The Queen's College, 'a prodigy of learning' and notable benefactor to the college library, who nevertheless *diocesin quidem amplissimam ita administravit, ut per sedecim annos nunquam praesens visitationem celebravit aut Ecclesiam Lincolniensem umquam conspiceret; unde episcopi Buckdeniensis potius quam Lincolniensis nomine decantabatur.*[3] Much more serious was the neglect of Thomas Wood, the successor of Hacket in the see of Lichfield, concerning whose unsatisfactory behaviour as dean of that cathedral much correspondence had passed between Hacket and Sheldon. Notwithstanding which Wood was appointed to the bishopric in 1671; and already before Sheldon's death his conduct had become so scandalous as to cause the primate to draft a letter of severe censure, which however was never sent. The missive began by observing that

neither the duty you owe to your diocese as you are a bishop, nor anything that I have said to you by word of mouth, has been prevalent to carry you down to your bishopric to make your personal residence there;...but that you still remain in and about London without any just cause that you have made appear to me.

[1] E. F. Carpenter, *The Protestant Bishop, Henry Compton* (1956), pp. 216, 218.
[2] Tanner MSS. 36, f. 185, Lloyd to Sancroft, 6 December 1681.
[3] J. R. Magrath, *The Queen's College, Oxford* (1921), vol. II, pp. 34–5 n.; citing Richardson's 1743 edition of Godwin, *De Praesulibus Angliae.*

Accordingly Sheldon had decided to send this written injunction

to show you how serious I am in that particular, and to tell you once more that I do expect you should forthwith and without any delay, go down to your bishopric and make your residence there; for if you will not perform that episcopal duty that is incumbent upon you, yet I must and ought to do that which lies upon me, as I am your metropolitan; which is to see that done by you which you so grossly neglect.

In conclusion, the solemn warning was given that

albeit I should be very unwilling to take any public rigorous course with you, yet if this which I now require from you be not obeyed forthwith, you must expect to hear further from me in another way, which, if it puts you to any open shame, it is your own fault, when gentler means were used and yet could not prevail.[1]

The reason for the omission to despatch this rebuke is not known; but the letter, falling into the hands of Sancroft as Sheldon's successor in the primacy, and the conduct of the bishop not having improved, was sent by the hand of one of the archbishop's kinsmen, together with a still more blistering covering letter.

My Lord, We read in the holy story that there came a writing to King Jehoram from Elijah the prophet;[2] whereas 'tis certain that Elijah was dead some years before Jehoram reigned. Hereupon interpreters trouble themselves much, how this letter was written and how conveyed from the other world. But the most easy and natural account is that the prophet wrote it in his lifetime and left it to Elisha his successor to be delivered in due time. My lord, your adventure at present is much the same. There came lately to my hands the draught of a letter, which my immediate predecessor designed to send you some time before his death, but was prevented. But the state of the case that occasioned it is to this day so much the same, and indeed so much worse, as the shore of the east part of Suffolk is farther distant than London from the place where you should be, that I durst not detain you from a writing, which is due to you, every word of it, by all the rules of justice, both *ex congruo et condigno*. I have therefore exemplified it, word for word; and thus it is.

After having transcribed the letter in full, Sancroft continued:

This is the letter. My lord, you have long had Moses and the prophets, the laws of the Church you live and teach in, and the exhortations and remonstrances of your superiors, to remind you of your duty; And though these have had little success upon you, yet now one comes to you from the dead, perhaps you will hear him. If not, I shall consider that as the monitions of the letter belong to you, so the resolution at the next remove belongs to me, in the example of it, for the effectual prosecution whereof

---

[1] Tanner MSS. 36, f. 190.
[2] The reference is to II Chronicles xxi. 12–15.

I have his majesty's express command (as far as the utmost of my power may extend) together with his declaration that if it proves still ineffectual, he will supply it by interposing his own, which I wish heartily you may well timely consider and prevent.[1]

Sancroft's letter bearing date 14 December 1681, was delivered the following month to the bishop of Lichfield, who received it 'in a morose temper'.[2] That it failed of effect is evidenced by the fact that on 16 July 1684 the archbishop, in the presence of the bishops of Rochester and Sodor and Man and the bishop-elect of Bristol, pronounced formal sentence of suspension against Wood *pro absentia sua a sua diocesi, neglectu officii sui et caeteris criminibus contra eum allegatis et probatis*.[3]

Visitation, however, was but the first stage of the bishop's pastoral duty; for its primary objective was to inform him of the state of his diocese, and it needed to be followed by appropriate steps to correct what was amiss and supply what was lacking, both in respect of the fabric and services of the parish churches and in regard to the behaviour of both clergy and laity. So far as offending clergy were concerned, their correction in the first place might be a matter of pastoral counsel, as the practice of Bishop Frampton well illustrated; who

to prevent any scandal, usually in his charge at the visitation, reprimanded them in Latin, to hide, if possible, the faults of a brother from vulgar eyes, or at least not to press their crimes into profane ears. And if this had not the desired effect, then he would contrive to surprise the offender with a visit, and there forewarn and testify, hear what could be said, and, if occasion was, exhort and rebuke with all authority, directing their discretion, moving them to consider, if not the scandal of their own persons yet the great reproach that their order would suffer by it. And so happy was he in this method that the clergy were generally without blame for their morals.[4]

Upon occasion, however, both with clergy and laity sterner measures were necessary, and persuasion had to be supported by coercion. Together with other branches of ecclesiastical administration, the courts Christian resumed their authority and operations at the Restoration, and judicial business was transacted in the courts of the archdeacon, bishop and the various archiepiscopal courts. The traditional jurisdiction of the Church in matrimonial and testamentary causes, over breaches of the moral law and of ecclesiastical

[1] Tanner MSS. 36, f. 190, verso: in Sancroft's hand.
[2] *Ibid.* f. 215, John Brame to Sancroft, 17 January 1681/2.
[3] E. Cardwell, *Documentary Annals*, vol. II, pp. 352–3.
[4] T. S. Evans, *Life of Frampton*, p. 169.

discipline, and over defamation, was restored; and with it the customary methods of procedure, embracing the sentence of excommunication with the resultant penance or commutation, and the expedient of compurgation. Inevitably the restoration of the church courts was followed by a revival of well-known criticisms and objections, concerning the corrupt practices of minor officials, excessive fees, inordinate delays, and multiplicity of rival ecclesiastical courts and officers, whilst the use of writs of prohibition to hinder their procedure added to the delays and costs of litigation. Dr Whiteman has observed that 'nowhere is the basic conservatism of the re-establishment of the Church better seen than in the revival of its judicial authority';[1] to which may be added the complementary comment that in no sphere was the failure to effect reforms more unfortunate and far-reaching in its effects. Dr Whiteman indeed has remarked further of the courts of the diocese of Salisbury that

on their fairness it is hard to form a judgment; but the Deposition Books show that witnesses were carefully examined, and the amount of private litigation which came before the courts suggests that some people expected justice from them; on the other hand procedures like compurgation... lent an archaic air to their sessions.[2]

Burnet was perhaps too zealous a reformer to form a just estimate of the church courts; yet behind his denunciation of them as

the most corrupt courts of the nation, in which they think of nothing but of squeezing and oppressing people by all the dilatory and fraudulent ways that are possible,

there lay practical experience and an honest attempt at reform; for as bishop he

tried how to regulate his Consistorial Court, and for some years went constantly to it, but found that which is crooked cannot be made straight, all their proceedings are so dilatory and engage men into such an expense that he did not wonder to hear them so much cried out on as they were, they are a great grievance both to the clergy and laity.[3]

Unpopularity did not necessarily mean inefficiency; for both laity and clergy objected to ecclesiastical discipline of all kinds, and the more effective it was, the louder their complaints. Dr Whiteman has noted that no less a person than Edward Seymour, a future

---

[1] A. Whiteman, 'The Re-establishment of the Church of England 1660–1663', *Trans. Royal Hist. Soc.* 5th ser. (1955), vol. v, p. 117.

[2] *V. C. H. Wiltshire*, vol. III, p. 47.

[3] H. C. Foxcroft, *A Supplement to Burnet's History of My Own Time* (1902), pp. 331, 503.

Speaker of the House of Commons, appeared before the Salisbury Consistory Court in 1671; whilst Bishop Frampton in 1682 had to deal with the difficult case of two sons of Lord Wharton, whose home was outside his diocese, but who in a drunken revel had violated the parish church of Barington by night, tearing the Bible and cutting the bell-ropes. He ordered the churchwardens to make a formal presentment of the offenders, to whom he gave private admonition, and followed this by a summons to appear before himself personally as Judge in his court. Upon the receipt of a letter from the elder brother, 'full of tender expressions, representing his shame and sorrow for the fault, begging pardon and submitting himself to what I shall enjoin', Frampton resolved not to give publicity to the episode further. He submitted to the decision of Sancroft and Compton whether it would not be wiser instead to summon the chief offender 'to appear at the same place where he gave the scandal, and there, in the same church, to atone for what he hath done, and for a part of his penance I intend to enjoin him to lay down £50 for the repair of Stow church'. Second thoughts again altered his purpose; for he decided upon Stow church as the venue, instead of Barington, 'doubting that by meeting their own company there, they might harden one another and turn all to ridicule'. Accordingly the two brothers acknowledged their fault in the presence of the bishop, attended by three clergymen and three laymen, asked pardon for their offence, and gave 50 guineas by way of commutation of penance; of which sum Frampton returned 10 guineas and applied the rest to the repair of Stow church. Finally in expressing regret, the offenders said 'it was neither atheism, popery nor fanaticism that led them to it; but mere drunkenness'; whereupon the bishop dismissed them 'with many wholesome admonitions'. In face of criticism of his action in transferring the matter from public to private determination, Frampton sent to Sancroft copies of three letters written by the culprits affirming their repentance. The bishop's biographer indeed believed that 'the laity were never more strictly governed, nor more gently handled'.[1]

Three cases of clerical delinquency illustrated further the reality of Frampton's episcopal discipline. In the first, an incumbent, 'more like a libertine than a priest', after refusing to respond to fatherly admonition, was prosecuted in the bishop's court; where

---

[1] Tanner MSS. 35, ff. 73, 111, 172, Frampton to Sancroft, 24 August and 21 October 1682; and 27 January 1682–3; T. S. Evans, *Life of Frampton*, p. 165.

sentence was deferred in the hope of reformation, and when this failed, Frampton proceeded first to suspension and finally to deprivation. The second offender was a good classical scholar and excellent preacher, guilty rather of indiscretion than vice, but commonly defamed by his parishioners as drunken and incontinent. He was suspended for three years, after which, 'the storm over, he continued in reputation among them to the last'. The third episode concerned the incumbent of a chapel which was a donative in the gift of the Haberdashers' Company, and in which the cleric preached 'not only sedition but downright treason', and also 'enthusiastical rapsodys'; until at length 'for his heterodoxy in doctrine and his opposition to rubrics and neglect of holy days, in short for a very constant irregular practice, having been reproved and hardening his neck, hating to be reformed, he was put out of the chapel'.[1] Dr Whiteman has observed that 'the most convenient way of cutting short a case or bringing an offender to heel was by the direct intervention of the bishop, a frequent occurrence in both Exeter and Salisbury dioceses in the Restoration period, particularly where the clergy were concerned';[2] and her conclusion is borne out by this practice of Frampton, and illustrated further by instances of Cartwright's sitting in his consistory in Chester cathedral to determine a cause of defamation by a summary hearing, as well as in a variety of other cases.[3] Bishop Hacket's biographer indeed recorded that he would

frequently sit Judge in his Ecclesiastical Courts and hasten the despatch of all affairs, and especially if there were anything that concerned his clergy, would always be present at the hearing of those causes, that neither his clergy, nor any by them, might be wronged.

Furthermore, he received at his house complainants,

even the meanest people, who were grieved with long and tedious suits, and after hearing all they could say, would sometimes send for the Chancellor and Proctors on both sides, and that he could not redress at home he would oftentimes go to court and end there; throwing out many causes that had been long depending for trivial matters, and would not suffer any causes to be entered for defamatory words or trifles without his own knowledge first, to the end they might be composed without much vexation to the parties; by this means his lordship created to himself much trouble, which he valued not for the good he did by it.[4]

[1] T. S. Evans, *Life of Frampton*, pp. 169–76.
[2] A. Whiteman: 'The Re-establishment of the Church of England, 1660–1663', p. 120.
[3] Cartwright, *Diary*, pp. 37, 39, 83.    [4] T. Plume, *A Century of Sermons*, p. xxxvii.

These examples notwithstanding, there is reason to conclude that the ecclesiastical courts became less effective progressively as the post-Restoration period developed. The use, and abuse, of excommunication had been a constant item of puritan protest since the reign of Elizabeth I, partly because of its indiscriminate imposition in a great number of cases and its relaxation by a money payment, and partly because lay officials imposed and relaxed it instead of reserving these processes to the bishop or archdeacon. Moreover the laity had not conceived any greater respect than liking for ecclesiastical discipline during its twenty years' desuetude. Dr Whiteman has cited the comment of a Wiltshireman, Salathiel Dean of Sutton Mandeville, that 'he cared not for the Court, nor power of it, it was but Excommunication'; and this instance was paralleled by the experience of William Sampson at Clayworth, who in a dispute with some of his parishioners in 1683 about his claim to a portion of the wages paid to their servants, took a citation out of the spiritual court against individual servants, only to discover that their masters 'told them that all I could do at them, was to excommunicate them, which was only their not going to Church, etc.'; whereupon he began 'to think that to proceed with them in the spiritual court would be of small effect'.[1] There can be little doubt that the failure of the Restoration settlement to reform the ecclesiastical courts and the canon law was one of its gravest defects, from which the Church was to suffer increasing disadvantage.

Moreover there were signs of the emergence of another thief of episcopal time and energies, in the shape of the increased demands of attendance in Parliament. 'The pastoral activity of the bishops was temporarily suspended when Parliament and Convocation reconvened in London at the end of November 1661. In line with a tradition soon to be firmly established, the prelates were instructed that their parliamentary duties must have priority over all others.'[2] It was only to be expected that stress should be placed upon parliamentary attendance at the very outset of the return of the bishops to the House of Lords and the fashioning of the ecclesiastical settlement, when the king 'strictly required the personal attendance of every one of them', a mandate obeyed by twenty-three out of twenty-seven prelates.[3] But the custom once inaugurated became

---

[1] A. Whiteman, in *V.C.H. Wiltshire*, vol. III, p. 47; Gill and Guilford, *The Rector's Book of Clayworth*, pp. 60–2.
[2] Bosher, *Restoration Settlement*, p. 237.     [3] Tanner MSS. 49, f. 117.

normal, as may be seen from an injunction sent upon a later occasion by Sheldon to the bishops of his province, to the effect that

the King's most excellent Majesty having intimated his pleasure by his late proclamation that there should be a full and entire convention (if it may be) at the first opening of the parliament now approaching, I cannot but think it necessary that the several bishops of my province should be again reminded hereof, and as many as are able, advertised to give their attendance in person, or if otherwise their age or indisposition of health should detain them, that their respective proxies be sent up here and exhibited the first day of the session, that their absence may then be supplied in some sort.[1]

In reply to such overtures, the archbishop's correspondence reflected the various reactions of his suffragans to the royal and primatial commands. 'I never did, I never will draw back from anything your grace commands', wrote Bishop Hacket in 1667.

I did desire to have kept my autumn at Lichfield, and to have comforted myself in my weak langours in my own house. If I may not be suffered to cherish myself, when never-failing recurrent maladies afflict me, God's will be done, I will prepare for a most distasteful journey. It was a brave Roman's resolution, and it is mine, *vivere non est necesse, obedire est necesse*. If God assist me, I will set forward with easy journeys to be at the ensuing session of parliament about the 17th day of October: sooner I cannot make preparation, nor fit myself with beasts to draw my coach.[2]

From two successive archbishops of York came pleas for consideration of the expense and inconvenience involved in a journey from so great a distance. Frewen in December 1662 earnestly desired to be excused attendance, 'to prevent (if it may be) sundry foreseen inconveniences to my purse which must necessarily come with it', to avoid the expense of hiring 'the carrier horses for my coach, mine own not being acquainted with such service', and particularly because 'to the winter of the year, add I may likewise the winter of my age, which will be 75 complete next May'.[3] Sterne in October 1673 reported 'the ill ways, and weather and the high waters' as impediments to his journey, adding that 'I shall come with the greatest part of my family, about thirty, and therefore I would not willingly come if in vain'.[4] The bishop of Norwich in 1679 and on other occasions sent by the hand of his medical adviser a certificate that his lordship was 'not possibly able to endure the motion of a coach for a few miles,...so that it may hazard his life

---

[1] *Ibid.* 43, f. 200.  
[2] *Ibid.* 45, f. 221.  
[3] *Ibid.* 48, f. 62.  
[4] *Ibid.* 42, f. 46.

to undertake a London journey';[1] whilst Bishop Lucy of St David's in 1675 wrote that

I conceive your grace no sooner observes my name at the bottom of my letter but the subject of it is discerned; but for the fuller satisfaction it is a petition for your grace's favour to a poor old man who hath not been two miles from his house these three last years, nor able to do it. The physician said *Ars*, but I say *Via longa, Vita brevis*. If I should set out now, it were odds I should not get to London in life; truly I would ambitiously desire to be at the parliament, but cannot unless it were kept at Brecknock.[2]

Bishop Fleetwood of Worcester in 1678, whilst pleading his age and infirmities as an excuse, promised that 'if I cannot be excused, immediately upon notice of it, I will obey though it be to the hazard of my life';[3] whilst from Bishop Lamplugh of Exeter in 1675 there came a promise to be in London for 5 November, if Sheldon relied on him; 'otherwise I would beg leave to be excused, for here I find work for more bishops than one in this large diocese, and I cannot with comfort be long absent from my charge'.[4]

It may well have been the case that these replies would have been somewhat different if the English bishops had been under the same penalties for non-attendance in Parliament as were their brethren in Scotland, who by an Act of Parliament were liable to a fine of £1200 Scots if absent from its sessions after 27 May 1662 'without a lawful excuse timely represented and admitted', and to a further fine of £12 Scots for each further day's absence without leave, and even of £6 Scots if they took their seats after the calling of the roll.[5] It was true that the Scottish Parliament did not meet so regularly nor for so long periods as the English. Notwithstanding in both countries episcopal administration was seriously hampered by the duty of parliamentary attendance, whose demands increased during the half-century following the Restoration. When Burnet became bishop of Salisbury after the Revolution, he reckoned it one of the gravest obstacles to the efficient discharge of pastoral oversight. 'The attendance on parliaments is a great distraction, and puts us to a great charge, besides calling us off half the year from doing our duty';[6]

---

[1] Tanner MSS. 38, f. 23.    [2] *Ibid.* 42, f. 142.
[3] *Ibid.* 39, f. 131.    [4] *Ibid.* f. 111.
[5] T. Thomson and C. Innes, *Acts of the Parliament of Scotland, 1593–1707* (1814–75), vol. VII, pp. 371–2.
[6] Foxcroft, *Supplement to Burnet's History*, pp. 505–6. Burnet, *History of My Own Time*, vol. VI, pp. 215–16.

and both he and Archbishop Sharp protested against the novelty of annual sessions which became the norm after 1689 and further aggravated the inroads upon episcopal time. This circumstance emphasised the gravity of the failure at the Restoration to implement Charles II's promise in his Declaration concerning Ecclesiastical Affairs to appoint suffragan bishops in every diocese, whose services would have mitigated the evils of the prolonged absence of the diocesan prelates from their sees. Bishop Hacket indeed was so occupied in 'preaching daily, hearing and determining cases of conscience, judging in causes ecclesiastical, repairing and building churches', that 'all absence seemed tedious and intolerable to him abroad, so that he never slept out of his diocese in many years'. Even during Parliament time he often returned 'before the end of the session, sometime in frosty, winter weather, to be, like the good pastor, among his sheep, where they might hear his voice at Christmas and the other great feasts'.[1]

The chief problems of the re-establishment of the church, however, lay at the door of the parochial clergy, who had to contend not only with a lack of the prescribed ornaments of the church and ministers, but also with the much more serious effects of the protracted proscription of Anglican worship upon the religious habits and customs of their flocks. These results were reflected particularly in regard to the two obligatory Sacraments of Baptism and the Eucharist. Private baptisms had increased so considerably that one of the principal objectives of the restored clergy was to emphasise the duty of public baptism in church except in cases of grave emergency. Dr George Bull as a parish priest at Suddington St Mary

was always very unwilling to administer baptism in private houses, except in cases of necessity,...and therefore he not only admonished parents to bring their children to receive public baptism, but...that the performance might be more solemn, he desired it might be on Sundays or other holy days when the greater number of people were met together,

urging 'this with greater importunity upon his parishioners'. Later also as bishop of St David's

among other irregularities, which he found had prevailed in his diocese, was the general custom of administering public baptism in private houses. This he declared against as an absurd and uncanonical practice;...[and] took a great deal of pains both in his Charge to the clergy and in his discourses with them and the laity, to convince them of the unreasonableness and irregularity of that custom;

[1] T. Plume, *A Century of Sermons*, p. xxxix.

but his biographer was constrained to admit that 'his endeavours in this matter did not meet with that entire success which he expected and desired'.[1] Bull's efforts and experiences were paralleled elsewhere; for Dean Granville complained of one of his curates' 'complaisance with the rich about privately baptising', which was 'quite contrary' to his own method;[2] whilst Bishop Compton in 1683 made 'the shameful disuse of public baptism' one of the principal topics of conference with his clergy.[3] At Clayworth, William Sampson appealed to the archbishop of York for support in requiring the public presentation in church of a child privately baptised (though 'the child not sick'), before entering the baptism in the parochial register; arguing that this was in accordance with the Prayer Book rule, and adding

that if private baptism was otherwise allowed than in case of danger, or that children recovering should be registered without being brought first to Church to have it there certified in what manner they were baptised, then those who were captious and wayward to the laws of the Church would soon perceive the advantage of it, and would use private baptism upon every occasion, since that neither surplice, nor Godfathers nor Godmothers, nor the sign of the cross need be used at that office.[4]

The continuance of the practice, however, was testified by the fact that so late as 1702 the Lower House of Convocation included amongst their articles of representation to the bishops the 'great neglect of bringing such infants as have been privately baptised into the Church', and 'that the unjustifiable use of the form of public baptism in private houses...in some places hath given opportunity to persons to intrude into the administration of that holy sacrament, and occasioned those undue practices of mutilating the public form and baptising without the sign of the cross and Godfathers and Godmothers'.[5]

But the greatest neglect resulting from the Interregnum was in regard to the Sacrament of the Lord's Supper. When Ralph Josselin's *Diary* recorded his administration of the Holy Communion in his parish of Earls Colne on Easter Day 1665, he remarked that 'twelve of us received the Sacrament of the Lord's

---

[1] R. Nelson, *Life of Dr George Bull* (London, 1713), pp. 62–3, 429–30.

[2] *Remains of Dennis Granville*, pt II, pp. 159–60.

[3] *Episcopalia, or Letters of Henry Compton, Bishop of London to the Clergy of his Diocese, 1686* (ed. S. W. Cornish), p. 3.

[4] Gill and Guilford, *The Rector's Book of Clayworth*, pp. 35–6.

[5] E. Cardwell, *Synodalia*, vol. II, pp. 709–10.

Supper publicly for which I bless God; I believe its 22 or 23 years since received on that day and occasion'.[1] To recover so much lost ground was a task of great difficulty. Bull at Suddington admitted that the Holy Eucharist 'was not performed so often in this parish, as he earnestly desired, and yet oftener than is usual in little villages, for he brought it to seven times in a year'.[2] Dean Granville so exhorted his curates at Sedgefield that gradually the standard was raised from nine times per year to a monthly Sacrament;[3] whilst Sancroft's Injunctions of 1688 required that 'in greater towns the clergy should administer the Communion once every month, and even in the lesser too if communicants may be procured, or however as often as they may'.[4] Apart from the churches of London and Westminster, it is doubtful whether much improvement on Bull's standard was attained. Dr Whiteman has noticed in the diocese of Salisbury that the Holy Communion 'was seldom celebrated more than three times a year, in many places not so often. The church courts do not appear to have tried to enforce more than a general reception at Easter'.[5] In 1681 Dean Simon Patrick of Peterborough remarked that Sancroft had exhorted cathedrals to observe a weekly celebration in accordance with the rubric, although as prebendary of Westminster he did not succeed in inducing the dean there to follow this example. On the other hand John Evelyn noted from Wotton at Easter 1694 that 'unless at the four greater feasts there is no Communion hereabouts',[6] a custom most probably representative of the majority of country villages.

Perhaps the two contemporary diaries of William Sampson at Clayworth and Ralph Josselin at Earls Colne represent the extremes of Caroline churchmanship in relation both to the two incumbents and to their parishes. Josselin indeed was typical of those puritan clergymen who remained within the establishment throughout the stormy changes of the seventeenth century, being vicar of his Essex parish from 1640 to 1683. His own churchmanship was of somewhat doubtful calibre; for when in February 1640, as he recorded, 'I was ordained a minister at Peterborough by the Bishop and six ministers,

---

[1] *Diary of Ralph Josselin: 1616–83*, ed. E. Hockliffe, p. 146 (Camden Society, 3rd series, vol. xv, 1908).

[2] Nelson, *Life of Bull*, p. 62.     [3] *Remains of Dennis Granville*, pt II, pp. 129–33.

[4] Cardwell, *Documentary Annals*, vol. II, no. CLXV, p. 374.

[5] *V.C.H. Wiltshire*, vol. III, p. 45.

[6] *Diary of John Evelyn*, 6 May 1694, ed. E. S. de Beer: vol. v, p. 180 (6 vols., Oxford, 1955).

I would not bow towards the altar as others did'. He was a staunch supporter of the parliamentary cause in the civil war, becoming chaplain to Colonel Harlakenden's regiment, and remarking of the execution of Laud that 'the Archbishop, that grand enemy of the power of godliness, that great stickler for all outward pomp in the service of God, left his head on Tower Hill, London, by ordinance of parliament'. It was in keeping with such sentiments that Josselin noted receiving 'the Directory of Public Worship and an ordinance of parliament to take away the heavy burden of the Book of Common Prayer in all the parts of the same', and also accepted the Engagement. When on 6 May 1660 he remarked how 'the nation runneth unto the king, as Israel to bring back David', it was with the ominous reflection that 'ministers were pitifully put out of their livings', and that he 'heard of threatenings against' himself; whilst he saluted the Act of Uniformity in 1662 with the observations on 16 August that 'it is a sad case that men are like to be put in by this Act', and on the morrow, a week before St Bartholomew's day, that this was 'the last Sabbath of our liberty by the Act'.[1]

It was not to be expected that such a puritan would be comfortable under the restored episcopacy; and his diary recorded many anticipations of ecclesiastical censure and discipline against himself. On 10 October 1660 he absented himself from the archdeacon's visitation; on the 12th 'the Book of Common Prayer [was] laid in the desk for me; 19, laid again and used in part in the morning but in the afternoon taken away; 26, brought again, but pitched and abused'; whilst on 9 November he noticed that 'now I am left alone of the nonconformists; what God will do with me I know not'. So he continued amid rumours of suspension, maintaining a half-conformity at best. On 9 June 1664 he was 'called on again to court for not administering the Sacrament'; on 11 September 'I had some apprehension it might be my last sermon'; whilst three days later 'was the Bishop of London's primary visitation, when I, having committed myself to God, appeared and through mercy met with no rubs, but my path clear'. On 30 October he 'gave the Sacrament of the Lord's Supper, 12 present, some with great devotion and brokenness of heart'; on 7 May 1665 he 'began to expound things out of the Church Catechism for the information of youth'; and on 28 April 1667, having received notice 'I was suspended, I forbore to preach in the afternoon'. Two years later still, on 9 July 1669 he

---

[1] *Diary of Ralph Josselin*, pp. 8, 23, 25, 134-5, 140.

'rid to Court, whither summoned for not wearing the surplice, [but] dismissed without fee'; whilst on 19 September 1676 'we had a parochial visitation, some things complained of, as the want of a surplice, in other things it was well'. Again on 5 September 1677 at the visitation he 'received admonition to use all the prayers always', and on 14 May 1678 though not attending the Court, he 'came off well at present as to surplice'. Furthermore on 12 September, after complaint made against him to the bishop by his clerical brethren, the priests of Hatfield and Easthorp, he was 'but coarsely used by the Bishop'; whilst finally on 16 May 1680 he 'wore the surplice', and on the following day 'rid to Court: I avoided receiving articles through God's goodness... the matter is the surplice, which I see no sin to use and shall endeavour to live as quietly as I may to the end of my race'. Josselin was not indeed an unlearned man. He devoted himself to the study of Hebrew and Greek and amongst other works read the Magdeburg Centuries, Isaac Voss, Bellarmine, and Pearson *On the Creed*, whilst at the age of 66, on 8 April 1683 he 'preached a little more than an hour'.[1] But when twenty years were needed to bring an incumbent to conformity, what might be expected of his flock?

William Sampson of Clayworth was a man of very different stamp, having been Fellow and President of Pembroke College, Cambridge and being elected in 1694 to the Mastership, when, he added laconically, 'I excused myself to them'.[2] He was also Prebendary of Clifton in Lincoln Cathedral and was thrice elected a proctor in York Convocation. In his answers in 1676 to the visitation queries of the archbishop of York, he reported that his parish contained no popish recusants, nor 'any other dissenters which either obstinately refuse or wholly absent themselves from the Communion of the Church of England at such times as they are by law required to communicate'; and consequently the 'number of persons, young and old within the parish... being under 400, there are of them of age to communicate according to the Canon, 236, and there did actually communicate at our Easter Communnion 200, that is to say on Palm Sunday, Good Friday and Easter Day'. Moreover the communicants were 'all taken by name at the Communion Table before they received'.[3] Nor was this high proportion a flash in the pan, as was the case in the parish of Hillingdon, Middlesex, in 1683 when on Easter Day and

---

[1] *Diary of Josselin*, pp. 141, 145–7, 156, 159, 169, 171, 173–4, 178, 181.
[2] Gill and Guilford, *The Rector's Book of Clayworth*, p. 104.    [3] *Ibid.* pp. 14, 19–20.

Low Sunday '300 persons received the Communion, alarmed to their duty by an order from Henry, Lord Bishop of London'.[1] Sampson kept a yearly account of the numbers at each of the great Festivals from 1676 to 1701, and in eight of these years the Easter muster was 200 or more, only once did it fall so low as 100, whilst in seven other years it was over 150. On Christmas Day 1684 he 'added to the Communion of this day, the two Sundays next following and so resolved to do at Whitsuntide Communion, so that having three times three Communions (that is, nine in all) there might be an opportunity for all to communicate'.[2] This practice, however, seems to have been discontinued after 1690 and the former custom to have been restored; and it was during the rest of Sampson's incumbency that the Easter communicants fell below 140. He also observed the yearly Rogationtide perambulations, 'began his resolution to have public prayers on Wednesdays and Fridays throughout Lent' on Ash Wednesday 1679,[3] and made an annual entry of the number of persons baptised, married and buried. One thing he had in common with Josselin, a keen interest in the annual income of his benefice, of which full details are given year by year; for like Jonathan Swift's country parson,

> His talk was now of tithes and dues,
> He smoked his pipe and read the news.

But the dark clouds spreading over the ecclesiastical landscape during the latter years of Charles II and the short reign of James II cast lengthening shadows also over Clayworth. Neither of the sons of the royal martyr inherited his devotion to the Church of England; and during the hectic closing years of Charles the Exclusion controversy foreshadowed the crisis which was to develop rapidly during the reign of his successor. On the Sunday following the accession of James II, being the 5th after Epiphany, Sampson at Clayworth remarked that 'the Collect in the Liturgy of our Church is observable: "O Lord, we beseech Thee to keep thy Church and household continually in thy true religion, that they who do lean only upon the hope of thy heavenly grace, may evermore be defended by thy mighty power"'—a truly prophetic suffrage.[4] It is unnecessary to rehearse the thrice-told tale of James' assault upon the established church in the interests of his co-religionists. But constitutionally

---

[1] E. F. Carpenter, *The Protestant Bishop, Henry Compton* (1956), p. 226.
[2] Gill and Guilford, *The Rector's Book, Clayworth*, p. 66.
[3] *Ibid.* p. 40.  [4] *Ibid.* p. 67.

he was its Supreme Governor; and the commission which Charles II had set up in August 1681 (consisting of the archbishop of Canterbury, the bishop of London, Halifax, Hyde and Edward Seymour) to undertake the distribution of the ecclesiastical patronage of the Crown was suffered to lapse. Gwatkin indeed considered that the episcopal nominations of Charles II 'were as generally good as his successor's were generally bad'; noting specifically that 'Parker of Oxford was a controversialist of the baser sort, Cartwright of Chester a sycophant pure and simple, Watson of St David's the only English bishop deprived for gross misconduct since the Revolution'.[1] It may be remarked, however, that Cartwright's principal offence was rather political than ecclesiastical; for it was his hand which 'penned the form' of the Declaration of Indulgence. In episcopal administration during his brief tenure of his see, the evidence of his Diary suggests that he did not fall below the standards of the age in ordination, confirmation and visitation. But other aspects of his ecclesiastical conduct were open at least to misconstruction. He consented to be present at the consecration of Monsignor Dada, being 'conducted into a convenient place in St James' Chapel'; a compliment which the king returned on his visit to the bishop at Chester in August 1687 when he twice touched for scrofula in the choir of the cathedral.[2] Upon the vacancy of the sees of Oxford and Chester in 1686 indeed Sancroft had recommended the eloquent and erudite Robert South for the former, and Dr James Jeffreys, prebendary of the ninth stall in Canterbury cathedral and a kinsman of the Lord Chancellor, (whom he had already proposed for St David's) for Chester.[3] Instead the king appointed Parker to Oxford and Cartwright to Chester, as he had already nominated Watson to St David's. The northern primacy he kept vacant for two years and a half after the death of Dolben; whilst the Ecclesiastical Commission suspended Compton of London for his refusal to silence John Sharp, rector of St Giles, who was preaching anti-Roman sermons in reply to the proselytising activities of Roman priests in his parish.

Similar actions of James affected the Church of Scotland; where indeed by the Assertory Act of 1669,

the ordering and disposal of the external government and policy of the Church doth properly belong to His Majesty and his successors;...And

---

[1] H. M. Gwatkin, *Church and State in England*, pp. 371, 380.
[2] Cartwright, *Diary*, pp. 47, 52, 74–5.
[3] D'Oyly, *Life of Sancroft* (1821), vol. I, pp. 235–6.

that His Majesty and his successors may settle, enact and emit such constitutions, acts and orders as concerning the administration of the external government of the Church and the persons employed in the same, and concerning all ecclesiastical meetings and matters to be prepared and determined therein, as they in their royal wisdoms shall think fit.[1]

Accordingly Archbishop Peterson of Glasgow on 20 December 1688 explained to Sancroft that

the King's Supremacy by the first Act of Parliament of 1669, is so asserted and established, that by the words of the law, it is in the king's power not only to dispose of the persons and places of all bishops at his pleasure, by removing them from their offices and benefices (and accordingly the late King and this have been in constant possession of so doing) but even to change episcopacy itself into any other form of government.[2]

In 1686 James II deprived Bishop Bruce of Dunkeld of his see and appointed James Hamilton in his place, though in the following year Bruce was authorised to exercise his ministry and in 1688 was translated to Orkney. In 1687 also, Archbishop Cairncross of Glasgow was deprived for refusal to censure Dr James Canons for preaching against popery. In both kingdoms therefore James showed his resolution to brook no opposition to his policy.

Events moved swiftly towards the crisis caused by the royal Declaration of Indulgence and the petition of the bishops. On Trinity Sunday 1688 the rector of Clayworth remarked that 'the Declaration for Liberty of Conscience was generally (here as elsewhere) refused to be read in the church'; and that 'one of the Psalms to be read in course that day was the 52nd, which is observable, especially the first four verses; and the day following was St Barnabas, on which was read also in course the 10th of Ecclesiasticus, which was strangely predictive in the 14 first verses'.[3] The 52nd psalm, beginning with the words, 'Why boastest thou thyself thou tyrant that thou canst do mischief', expressed on the one hand 'the bitter resentment felt by the godly man towards one who had no fear of God', and on the other hand 'the doctrine of divine retribution'. The tenth chapter of Ecclesiasticus drew contrasting pictures of the wise judge and the unwise king, and remitted the defence of justice to God, who

---

[1] W. C. Dickinson and G. Donaldson, *A Source Book of Scottish History* (1954), vol. III, p. 160.

[2] W. N. Clark, *A Collection of Letters addressed by Prelates and Individuals of High Rank in Scotland to Archbishop Sancroft* (1848), pp. 93–4.

[3] Gill and Guilford, *The Rector's Book of Clayworth*, pp. 82–3.

'hath cast down the thrones of proud princes and set up the meek in
their stead'. Again on 8 June, Sampson noted that the seven bishops
in the Tower 'had divine service, where the 2nd Lesson was 2.
Corinthians, 6; and soon after, was applied to the Archbishop the
case of Eleazar, 2 Maccabees, vi. 18 to the end of the chapter'.[1] The
New Testament lection described the situation of God's ministers
'in much patience, in afflictions, in necessities, in distresses, in
stripes, in imprisonments, in tumults, in labours, in watchings, in
fastings'; yet, notwithstanding, 'as dying and behold we live, as
chastened and not killed'. In the second passage Sancroft was
likened to Eleazar, 'one of the principal scribes, an aged man', who
refused to compromise with evil in matter of religion; 'for though
for the present time I should be delivered from the punishment of
men, yet should I not escape the hand of the Almighty; wherefore
now, manfully changing this life, I will shew myself such an one as
my age requireth, and leave a notable example to such as be young,
to die willingly and courageously for the honourable and holy laws'.
A month later, on 16 July, the archdeacons were due to appear and
make a return to the Ecclesiastical Commissioners of the names of
those clergymen who had not read the Declaration; but, the time
for their appearance being extended, 'before that came, the snare
was broken and we were delivered; I mean the Ecclesiastical Commission itself was taken away by the news of the Prince of Orange's
preparations to invade the kingdom'. Finally, near the end of the
same year, on 17 December, Sampson observed that 'the Prince of
Orange sent a kind of order to the King to have him remove himself from Whitehall; on which day at the Evening service was read
in course Psalm 89, which see, verses 32–37'.[2] The verses specified
related the unfaithfulness of the later kings of the Davidic line and
their punishment, together with the faithfulness of God in maintaining his Covenant with David and preserving the throne of the
nation. 'My covenant will I not break, nor alter the thing that is
gone out of my lips.' Rarely can the *sortes liturgicae* have been more
apt or pertinent, including those from the Apocrypha which the
puritans wished to banish from the lectionary.

The rapid march of events, however, had outstripped the comprehension of a majority of churchmen. In 1688, as to some extent
in 1660, events overtook men; and the Church of England found
itself generally in a state of unpreparedness for a further crisis,

[1] *Ibid.* p. 83.  [2] *Ibid.* p. 83.

which ranked second only to the Restoration in importance. When Dr William Clagett was walking from London to Highgate with his young friend and protégé, William Wake, shortly before the invasion of William of Orange, 'he fell into discourse, I know not how, concerning the measures of civil obedience. I had never well examined that matter', Wake recorded,

but by the prejudices of my education first under my own father and then under Bishop Fell, had been accustomed to think that all princes were absolute and their subjects were not to contradict them, but merely to obey. I was startled at his discourse, when I heard him hint at something to be done to put a stop to the king's arbitrary proceedings; and began to ask, whether such an attempt could be justified, let the king do what he would? He did not enter any farther into particulars; but in general answered, that he could not tell but that in some cases such endeavours might be lawful. For which I as much wondered at him then, as I have done at my own folly and ignorance since.[1]

But amongst churchmen who were expecting radical changes, though their nature could not be foreseen, was Archbishop Sancroft himself; who, as Wake recollected, engaged several of the clergy 'to make a review of our Liturgy, to look over the daily Service and the Communion Book, and to consider what might be fit to be added to or altered in either'. At first sight Wake was surprised that such an academic exercise should be commanded

at this time, when we had so much other business against popery upon our hands. And I well remember that, intimating somewhat to this purpose to a certain bishop, he told me things could not long stand in their present posture; and when I pressed him farther, I got only this obscure, yet remarkable, answer: 'That men who rode over precipices, would in a little time either break their necks, or they would come to their journey's end.

Soon the strategy which Sancroft was following became plain.

It was said that after the civil wars, when the king returned, there was nothing in readiness; and then they were so straitened in time and hurried on by the parliament, that they neither could do all that was fitting, and considered too little of what they did. That we ought to be better provided against another time, and duly to consider how we might not only improve our own constitution, but bring over the truly honest and well-meaning Dissenters to join in Communion with us.[2]

Thus the church moved into the storms and tempests of the Revolution. During the quarter of a century since 1662, its bishops

---

[1] Wake, Autobiography, f. 30 verso.    [2] *Ibid.* f. 31 et verso.

and clergy had striven with diligence and zeal to regain the ground
lost during the Interregnum; and their efforts might have been
crowned with a greater measure of success had the administrative,
judicial and financial machinery of the church been refashioned to
meet the new situation in which perforce it found itself. In prospect
of the events of 1688, and in the light of Sancroft's foresight in preparing to meet them, it might have been hoped that the opportunity
lost at the Restoration would be recovered at the Revolution. It was
to be the great misfortune, even tragedy, of the established church
that the political issues of the deposition of James II and proclamation of William III were to frustrate both the hopes and endeavours
of Sancroft to remove those things in the ecclesiastical constitution
which were shaken, so that the things not shaken might remain.

3-2

# II

# THE ECLIPSE OF CONVOCATION

'I had some speech with [the Lord Archbishop] yesterday', reported Peter Heylyn to Sheldon on 12 April 1660,

and found him willing to defer it [the Convocation] longer than may stand with the safety of the Church; for questionless, some busy members of the House of Commons will thrust themselves into concernments of religion, when they shall find no Convocation sitting to take care thereof; and when it was replied that the intimating of a Convocation might prevent that mischief, I answered that I thought it would rather hasten it, and make them the more earnest to make use of their time before the prey would be taken out of their mouths by the actual coming together of so many divines, from whom they could not honestly pretend to extort the cognisance of those matters which belong properly to their calling. The like care must be taken to prevent the laity from bringing the clergy into taxes and payments with them, constantly practised since the first beginning of the late Long Parliament, [and] not otherwise to be prevented than by having a bill of subsidy ready to be presented to the king in the name of the clergy, and by the king to be delivered unto such of his learned council as shall be members of that house, before the Commons enter upon that consideration.[1]

Few examples of predictive prophecy, save perhaps that of Thomas Sikes of Guilsborough concerning the revival of a high doctrine of the church by the Tractarian movement, can have better claim to honour for their accuracy than Heylyn's prognosis of the rivalry between Convocation and Parliament, particularly the House of Commons. Its fulfilment constituted one of the principal causes of the failure of the ecclesiastical aspect of the Restoration settlement, and the history of Convocation during the succeeding half-century was to justify its pessimism.

The Convention Parliament was necessarily unattended by a meeting of Convocation; and it was therefore of greater importance that its successor, the Cavalier Parliament, to which was reserved the fashioning of the ecclesiastical settlement, should be so accompanied. Accordingly so soon as the results of the elections to this Parliament established the victory of the royalists, archiepiscopal

---

[1] Tanner MSS. vol. 49, f. 146, cited (in part) in Bosher, *Restoration Settlement*, p. 214.

mandates were issued on 12 April 1661 for the summons of the Provincial Convocations, to assemble on 8 May. Two particular tasks awaited their deliberation; the revision of the Book of Common Prayer and that of the abortive Canons of 1640. Royal letters of business were issued to this end on 10 October, and a joint committee of both Convocations to consider revision of the Liturgy was appointed on 22 November. The work was transacted with such expedition that the committee's report was completed within a month, and on 20 December received the approval of both Convocations. The business was then transferred to Parliament, where the Lords read the Bill of Uniformity, without debating the alterations made in the attached Book of Common Prayer and with an expression of thanks to the Convocations for their pains; whilst the House of Commons on 16 April 1662 likewise accepted the revision without debating its contents, but only by a narrow majority of 96 votes to 90 and with an express reservation of their right to such detailed discussion.[1] In respect of the Liturgy therefore a conflict had been avoided by the readiness of both Houses of Parliament to accept the revision proposed by Convocation without detailed examination of the changes, though with the significant assertion by the Commons of their rights in the matter.

Much more delicate and difficult was the issue of revision of the Canons of 1640. These canons had been passed by Convocation after the dissolution of the Short Parliament on 5 May 1640, by virtue of a special commission issued by Charles I on 12 May, authorising their continued session in accordance with the opinion of seven judges in favour of the legality of the action. When the Long Parliament met in the following November, however, the House of Commons carried a resolution declaring the canons invalid because of their alleged inclusion of 'many matters contrary to the King's prerogative, to the fundamental laws and liberties of the realm, to the right of parliaments, to the property and liberty of the subjects, and matters tending to sedition and of a dangerous consequence'. A further resolution of the same house claimed 'that the clergy of England, convented in any Convocation or Synod or otherwise have no power to make any constitution, canons or acts whatsoever in matter of doctrine, discipline or otherwise, to bind the clergy or

---

[1] *Journals of the House of Commons*, vol. VIII, p. 408. 'The Question being put, that the Amendments made by the Convocation and sent down by the Lords to this House might by Order of the House have been debated: It was resolved in the affirmative.'

laity of this land without common consent of parliament'. It may be agreed that there can be no question of the legality of the royal commission authorising the convocation to continue its sessions after the dissolution of Parliament; since the coincidence of the summons and dissolving of the two assemblies was simply a matter of custom. Nor can it be doubted that the assertion by the House of Commons of the necessity of parliamentary (as distinct from royal) assent to any canons passed by convocation was a revolutionary innovation. Notwithstanding, at the Restoration the act of 13 Car. II, cap. 12,

provided that this act, or anything therein contained, shall not extend or be construed to extend to give unto any archbishop, bishop or any other ecclesiastical judge, officer or other person or persons aforesaid, any power or authority to exercise, execute, inflict or determine any ecclesiastical jurisdiction, censure, or coercion which they might not by law have done before the year of our Lord 1639, nor to abridge or diminish the king's majesty's supremacy in ecclesiastical matters and affairs, nor to confirm the Canons made in the year 1640, nor any of them, nor any other ecclesiastical laws or canons not formerly confirmed, allowed, or enacted by parliament or the established laws of the land as they stood in the year of our Lord 1639.

Accordingly, as Edmund Gibson observed in his *Codex*, although the Canons of 1640 contain many items

of such a nature as could give no reasonable offence to the temporal legislature, relating only to the discipline of the church and clergy, and the regulation of the ecclesiastical courts,

yet

others there are, which concern the regal power, the civil establishment of the Church of England, the state of Popery and Presbytery, and the like; and

we cannot doubt but that it was with an eye to the same heads, that the parliament under Charles II in framing the present clause, guarded so diligently against the suspicion of giving credit or authority to the said Canons.[1]

In view of the equivocal authority of the Canons of 1640 it was of especial importance that the Convocation of 1661 should undertake their revision, in order to remove what might give just ground of offence and to enact those which were necessary for the restoration of ecclesiastical order and discipline. To this end the Crown authorised the Convocation to

[1] E. Gibson, *Codex Juris Ecclesiastici Anglicani*, vol. II, tit. XLI, cap. V, p. 995 footnote *p* (2 vols, 1713).

propose, confer, treat, debate, consider, consult and agree upon the exposition or alteration of any canon or canons now in force, and of and upon any such other new canons, orders, ordinances and constitutions, as they...shall think necessary, fit and convenient.[1]

Upon the receipt of this royal permission, the archbishop on 7 June 1661 admonished the Lower House to deliberate on the question of the reform of the Canons and to submit their opinions in writing to the Upper House; and on 19 June constituted a committee of twelve bishops and twenty-four of the inferior clergy to draw up a report. On 17 July the bishop of Salisbury presented certain canons in writing, which were remitted for further consideration after discussion in the Upper House. On 19 July the bishop of Gloucester further submitted *nonnullos canones conceptos et in papyro scriptos*, which after consideration were likewise returned for revision; and the same happened on 22 July in respect of other canons presented by the bishops of Bath and Wells and of Rochester. The business of revision of the Book of Common Prayer held the stage for some time, until on 8 January following the Upper House debated the revision of the actual Canons of 1640, resuming their consideration on 17 January and remitting the matter to their lordships of Bath and Wells, Oxford, St Asaph, Peterborough, Lincoln, Carlisle, Norwich and Gloucester; to whom were added on 24 January the rest of the bishops. A month later on 22 February the question was again discussed and the revision committed to the bishops of Oxford, Sarum, Worcester, St Asaph, Carlisle, Hereford and Chester; but notwithstanding these several steps taken, the revision of the Canons was not carried further.[2]

The cause of this failure is as obscure as the results were unfortunate. Dr John Barwick, Prolocutor from February 1662 to his death in November 1664,

found plainly that some whose interest it was very much, that the practice of religion should be zealously promoted, were not yet hearty enough in their endeavours to restore the decayed discipline of the Church....But who they were that prevented laying hold of an opportunity of doing the Church that service, it is not lawful to conjecture, where the case is invidious and perhaps not sufficiently known. Yet this is most certain that his sacred majesty granted this venerable assembly liberty under the broad seal to accomplish this work. Nor is it less certain that the convocation divided itself into divers colleges and committees for carrying it on, and

[1] E. Cardwell, *Synodalia*, vol. II, p. 687.
[2] *Ibid.* pp. 643, 645, 647, 649–50, 660–2, 665.

assigned to each their peculiar share therein; yet to the very great grief of all good men these preparations came to nothing. For the endeavours of many, though very hearty, were wholly frustrated by one or two, on whom this matter chiefly depended.[1]

Gibson believed that the drafts of canons presented in the Upper House of Convocation had been lost, so that their contents could not be ascertained. But a series of proposals for the reform of ecclesiastical courts from a variety of hands, including those of Sir Leoline Jenkins, are extant; from which an idea may be gained of the matters under consideration. Amongst other suggestions, the prescription of a table of fees which henceforth should be followed exactly was put forward. It was recommended that the bishop of each diocese should sit personally in his court to oversee its proceedings and add to their credit; that sentence of excommunication should be pronounced in open court by the bishop attended by some clergy either of his cathedral church or of his diocese; and that sentence of absolution from excommunication should be likewise solemnly pronounced. Furthermore it was proposed that for lesser offences, excommunication should be replaced by contumacy; and that this should involve the same penalties, save that it should not exclude the person declared contumacious from attendance upon the prayers and sermons of the church nor from receiving Christian burial. Similarly commutation of penance for a money payment should be given only when authorised by the archbishop or bishop. In conformity with this project, excommunication would be restricted to the offences of blasphemy, heresy, schism, refusal to bring children to receive baptism, refusal to receive the Holy Communion and to attend divine service, error in religion and doctrine, incontinence, usury, simony, perjury and idolatry.[2] But, notwithstanding the widespread agreement as to the necessity of reform of the courts Christian, and in particular of excommunication and absolution therefrom (the administration of which had been the subject of continual puritan criticism since the Elizabethan *Admonitions to Parliament*), no practical steps were taken to effect these changes; and especially to give greater solemnity to excommunication by freeing it from association with lesser offences for which contumacy was an easier and more appropriate sentence. In 1674 indeed

---

[1] White Kennett, *A Register and Chronicle, Civil and Ecclesiastical* (1728), p. 630: citing the *Life* of Dr John Barwick.

[2] Tanner MSS. 315, ff. 66, 80, 82, 92, 98, 102, 107, 109.

Dr Francis Turner reported to Sancroft that Bishop Morley of Winchester had heard good reports of his speech upon being admitted as Prolocutor,

because you hinted in it many excellent things in order to the restoring our discipline and maintaining our doctrine. The Canons of '40 against the Socinians are desired to be reinforced and many expedients are in the minds of our governors for the reformation of abuses.[1]

But nothing came of these, nor of many other, good designs despite the zeal of their promoters.

By this time, moreover, a further stroke of fortune had proved disastrous for the Convocation, since it had realised the second of the fears expressed by Heylin and through the agency of the very person whom he had cautioned against it. By an oral agreement reached between Archbishop Sheldon and Lord Chancellor Clarendon in 1664, the right of the clergy to tax themselves in Convocation was surrendered, and they were henceforth to be included in the money-bills of the House of Commons. Speaker Arthur Onslow related that Bishop Gibson told him 'that this was the greatest alteration ever made without an express law'.[2] The fact that no other account of the transaction than oral tradition has survived, makes it correspondingly difficult to ascertain the motive of the transfer. It seems probable, however, that the archbishop in consenting to the bargain, accepted the lesser of two evils. For the clerical subsidies voted in Convocation were based on the *Valor Ecclesiasticus* made in the reign of Henry VIII, as were also the First Fruits and Tenths paid by the clergy to the Crown. For at least a century there had been pressure from a variety of lay sources for a revaluation of ecclesiastical benefices, in order to increase the proportion of taxation paid by the clergy. So early as 1562, as Strype recorded, 'there seemed to be some that put the Queen upon taking a new survey of all ecclesiastical livings, pretending that hereby the values of First Fruits and Tenths would be considerably advanced to her, to the further oppression of the needy clergy'. Accordingly, amongst Articles laid before Convocation in that year was one, 'whether, if the writ *Melius Inquirendum* be sent forth, the likelihood be, that it will turn to the Queen's commodity?'[3] Although this attempt was frustrated, in 1572 Archbishop Parker had to intercede with Cecil

---

[1] *Ibid.* 42, f. 75 (12 January 1673–4).
[2] Speaker Onslow's Note to Burnet: *History of My Own Time*, vol. IV, p. 509.
[3] J. Strype, *Annals of the Reformation* (1709), p. 305.

to prevent a commission for a *Melius Inquirendum*, observing that 'I can say no more but *Deus misereatur nobis. Est modus in rebus.*' Two years later he renewed his appeal to the Treasurer to spare the clergy the threatened spoliation.[1] Similarly in 1584 sundry 'spiteful men shewed another instance of their goodwill to the clergy', as Strype observed ironically, by striving 'for the issuing out a commission for a *Melius Inquirendum*'; which Whitgift scotched by his *Notes de Melius inquirendo* and by his influence with the queen and Burleigh.[2] Furthermore in the case of *Rex* v. *The Bishop of Bristol and Hanley*, in 1610, Sir Edward Coke applied the principle to 'all dues and taxes paid to the King', which, he contended, should be 'assessed according to the actual value of the benefice', instead of 'by the rated value in the King's Books'.[3] Yet again in 1620, the suggestion was made to James I, 'that a new valuation should be made of all spiritual preferments (which now in the King's books passed at under-rates) to bring them up to, or near, the full value thereof'. Despite the low state of the royal exchequer, both the Treasurer, Cranfield, and the king declined to impoverish the clergy; 'and so', added Fuller, 'the project was blasted for the present, as it was when it budded again, propounded by some unworthy instrument, in the reign of king Charles'.[4]

The clergy therefore had good reason to fear the revived whispers after the Restoration of a *Melius inquirendum*; which would involve not only a higher rate of subsidy for the Crown, but also an increased payment of First Fruits and Tenths. If the choice lay between this dread measure and the surrender of their right of independent taxation, there was good ground for opting for the latter and lesser evil. Tradition related indeed that 'it was at the motion of the bishops, and that a meeting was held between some of them at Lambeth and the Chancellor, Treasurer etc. to settle the matter'.[5] Bishop Hacket of Lichfield, in answer to a request of Sheldon for his opinion 'how the clergy at present should behave themselves, if levies of money should be raised upon us by others and not by ourselves in Convocation', replied that though ignorance of details

---

[1] J. Strype, *Life of Matthew Parker* (1711), p. 406.
[2] J. Strype, *Life of John Whitgift* (1822), vol. I, pp. 403–8.
[3] R. G. Usher, *The Rise and Fall of the High Commission* (1913), p. 208.
[4] T. Fuller, *Church History* (1845), century XVII; book X, §§ 18–19, vol. V, pp. 489–90. Ed. J. S. Brewer.
[5] Lambeth Palace, Library. Secker MSS. VI, ff. 463 *seq.* 'Convocation'; probably copied from Bishop Gibson's MSS.

of the suggestion compelled him to 'shoot in the dark', yet he would 'deliver his conceptions'. He thought that the rise in prices had made subsidies comparatively of little use and that a tax upon land was possible, though the sum to be required of the clergy should be fixed by others, and not by themselves. 'If we submit to that which is demanded, the mouth of detraction is stopped, since we do as much as is demanded. In all the King's wants, the clergy should shew themselves free hearted and liberal, because the church is defended in the Kingdom.'[1] Further, Dr Timothy Halton, Provost of the Queen's College, and himself a member of Convocation, held that it was a wise thing to do; since 'the sums then expected from the clergy in proportion to the laity were so large, they could not be raised in the way of subsidies according to the low valuation in the King's Books'.[2] The clergy had already voted in Convocation four subsidies at the rate of 4s. in the pound to be paid within four years; and accordingly in the first parliamentary aid to include them, the act of 16–17 Car. II, c. 1, they were freed from the payment of two of these subsidies. The act furthermore contained a clause providing that 'nothing herein contained shall be drawn into example to the prejudice of the ancient rights belonging unto the Lords Spiritual and Temporal, or Clergy of this realm, or unto either of the Universities, or unto any Colleges, Schools, Almshouses, Hospitals or Cinque Ports'. The right of the clergy to tax themselves, though conceded theoretically in words, had, however, been finally lost.

An unintended consequence of this financial transaction was that sitting Convocations ceased from 1664 to the Revolution twenty-five years later. If Sheldon had made the best of a bad financial bargain, his action had fatally compromised the status and prestige of Convocation. Throughout the rest of the reign of Charles II (with the royal Declaration of Indulgence, the Test Act and the various suggestions of a Comprehension), and during the short rule of James II with the Romanist assault on the established church, the Convocations remained inactive thanks to their being allowed to hold purely formal meetings only. The House of Lords indeed on 19 November 1675 resolved

that his majesty be humbly moved from this house: that he would be pleased to direct the Lord Archbishop of Canterbury and the Lord Archbishop of York that the Convocation of the Clergy may meet frequently;

[1] Tanner MSS. 47, f. 201 (29 October 1664).
[2] Secker MSS. VI, f. 464.

and that writs may issue out for the supplying the places of such members of the Convocation as are dead, or removed; and that when they are met, they do make unto the king's majesty such representations as may be for the safety of the religion established.[1]

This address was presented to the king, who agreed to it, but notwithstanding, Convocation remained in suspense during a vital quarter of a century.

The events of the Revolution therefore came upon a majority of the clergy completely unprepared. The Convention Parliament of 1688, like its predecessor at the Restoration, was unattended by a Convocation; but when it turned itself into a regular Parliament under the authority of the new sovereigns, William and Mary, and particularly when there was brought before it a 'Bill for uniting their majesties' Protestant subjects', the question of the advisability of referring the matter to Convocation was raised. This Comprehension Bill was introduced into the House of Lords on 11 March 1689 and received a third reading on 8 April. A clause petitioning the sovereigns to nominate a commission of thirty divines to revise the Book of Common Prayer, the Canons and the constitution of the ecclesiastical courts, led to a proposal to include laymen in the commission, which was lost since the number of votes on each side was equal. When the Bill was sent to the House of Commons, it was resolved to invite the Lords to concur in a petition to the king to refer the whole question to Convocation. Tradition ascribed the royal decision to abandon the parliamentary Bill to the influence of Burnet and Tillotson. Burnet indeed avowed that he

at that time did imagine that the clergy would have come into such a design with zeal and unanimity; and feared this would be looked on by them as taking the matter out of their hands; and for that reason argued so warmly against this, that it was carried by a small majority to let it fall.[2]

Tillotson likewise reminded the king

of the reproach often cast upon the reformation by the papists, that it was founded chiefly upon parliamentary authority, and that no handle ought for the future to be given for such an objection; that the affairs of the church chiefly belonged to synodical authority, and if they were passed by the members of the Convocation, they would not only be more acceptable to the body of the clergy but would be more religiously observed by the laity. He added that...it would be best, as had been formerly done, for his majesty to authorise by his Letters Patent several of the most

---

[1] *Journals of the House of Lords*, vol. XIII, p. 30.
[2] G. Burnet, *History of My Own Time*, vol. IV, pp. 18–19.

eminent of the clergy to consider of some methods of healing the wounds of the church and establishing a durable peace; that so what they should agree upon, being laid before a Convocation, might first have their sanction, and then that of parliamentary authority.[1]

The king accepted this advice, issuing a commission to ten bishops and twenty of the inferior clergy to prepare matters for the consideration of the Convocation, which he likewise ordered to be summoned. When Convocation met in November 1689, presided over by Bishop Compton of London owing to the suspension of Sancroft for refusal to take the oath to William and Mary, at its third session on 25 November the lower clergy elected as Prolocutor Dr William Jane, dean of Gloucester by a large majority over Dean Tillotson of Canterbury; and this was taken as an indication of their unfavourable attitude towards the proposals of the commission for revision of the Liturgy, of which Tillotson had been a foremost member and from the third meeting of which Jane had withdrawn. Accordingly the projected revision was never laid before Convocation; which, after a difference between the Upper and Lower Houses concerning the form of their reply to the king's message, was prorogued. It may be observed in passing that in the royal licence to this Convocation, the king limited the bishops and clergy to consideration of the heads specified in the accompanying letters of business. Such a restriction was without precedent; for the traditional tenor of the royal licence was first to grant a general power to confer and agree upon such canons as the bishops and clergy should think fit, and then to authorise them specifically to confer on such matters as should be sent to them under the king's sign manual or privy signet. In the 1689 licence the first general clause was omitted; though in practice the omission had no importance since the Convocation never considered any of the specific issues commended to them.

The failure of Convocation to address itself to either of the principal matters mentioned in the royal letters, namely the revision of the Liturgy and that of the Canons and of the ecclesiastical courts, inflicted irreparable damage on the church. With the passing of the Toleration Act and the legal protection and recognition thereby given to orthodox Protestant dissenters, the established church was faced by an entirely novel situation, to which the Canons of 1603 were no longer entirely applicable. The omission to revise them at the

---

[1] T. Birch, *The Life of Archbishop Tillotson* (2nd ed. London, 1753), pp. 165–6, citing Nichols, *Apparatus ad defensionem Ecclesiae Anglicanae*, p. 93.

Restoration was doubly underlined now by the second failure in 1689, with the result that the ecclesiastical canons and courts were alike inadequate to the problems of the post-Revolution era. Moreover, the disappointment caused to the king by the attitude of Convocation in 1689 led to the resumption of the policy which had proved so serviceable from the standpoint of the Crown since 1664, namely, that of the suspension of sitting Convocations. Convocation remained therefore dormant once more, until the clarion call of 'the church in danger' was sounded in the ears of the lower clergy by the publication in 1697 of Francis Atterbury's famous *Letter to a Convocation Man*, which gave the signal for the acrimonious controversy which was to continue throughout the reign of Anne.

'On my road hither', wrote Richard Hurd to William Warburton in 1760, when the dust of this dispute had long settled into oblivion,

> I chanced to pick up Dr Atterbury's book on the English Convocation, which has been my principal amusement ever since. It has given me a higher idea of the capacity, as well as industry, of this writer, than I had entertained before, from what I had seen of his productions. The main question he discusses, whether the Convocation on their legal meeting, have a right to debate and consult together on matters within their sphere, seems unanswerably cleared, and his determination very justly made in their favour. And yet I perceive much more was afterwards written in the controversy.

Warburton concurred in this verdict.

> Your reflection on the writer is as just as all you say on the question. His book had exactly the same effect on me: it raised my idea of his abilities extremely. I was on my guard against everything he said, for I knew he had two of the dullest fellows in the world to combat, Wake and Kennett; and I was aware how much the dexterity of controversy in a genius is of force to annihilate such adversaries. But he goes upon *principles* and all they could possibly oppose are *precedents*; and these are nothing when they oppose the genius of a Constitution.[1]

On the point of dullness the reader may readily agree, and may thereby excuse himself from penetrating into the details of the controversy; for Atterbury himself justified the acerbity of his style with the plea that ''twas to inspirit a dull and dry subject'. But historians generally have judged him the loser in the constitutional issues on which he challenged his adversaries; since matters of this kind must be determined rather by precedents than by abstract

---

[1] *Letters from a Late Eminent Prelate* (2nd ed. 1809), nos. CXLIV–V, pp. 309–10, 314 (to Hurd).

notions. In the first stage of the literary controversy two main points emerged; whether the Convocation, being customarily summoned with each Parliament, ought to sit and do business; and whether in so doing it needed a royal licence to embark on any kind of business other than the making of Canons. The historical researches of both parties established the fact that the lower clergy had an undeniable right to represent their grievances to the bishops and to offer their opinions on any matters conductive to the good of religion and the church; whilst it was for the Upper House to determine what, if any, action should be taken. If such action must take the form of canonical enactment, then a royal licence was necessary; but short of this, both houses had considerable freedom of deliberation and debate. Atterbury's chief point, however, was to secure the revival of sitting Convocations, the disuse of which since 1689 he ascribed to the averseness of archbishops Tillotson and Tenison and of the king, without pondering the significance of the like attitude on the part of Sheldon and Sancroft and of the later Stuart sovereigns.

In 1701 this primary objective was attained; whereupon the controversy changed its principles and character. For Atterbury now contended for so close a parallel between Convocation and Parliament as to place the Lower House of Convocation in the same position of independence in relation to the Upper House as was enjoyed by the House of Commons in respect of the House of Lords. It may well be that the motive of this contention was his realisation that, as the right of the lower clergy to a final negative upon resolutions of the bishops had sprung from the need of their consent to clerical taxation, so the surrender of this right of taxing themselves might result in the loss of the power of veto. Notwithstanding, it was evident that the claim was subversive of the fundamental principles of an episcopal church and the subordination of presbyters to bishops therein. Atterbury's chief opponent in this second phase of controversy was Gibson, whose historical learning gained the field in a series of books and pamphlets, one of which, the *Synodus Anglicana*, remains the standard authority on convocational procedure.

More important than Atterbury's pretentious excursions into ecclesiastical history, however, were the practical expressions of his claim for a parity between the two houses of Convocation, as reflected in the proceedings of a majority of the lower clergy. For they asserted a right of the Lower House to put its Prolocutor in the chair before his election had been confirmed by the archbishop and bishops; a power to adjourn themselves by a vote of their own house and to a shorter day than that to which the archbishop had prorogued the synod, and to hold formal sessions on these intermediate days; an authority to give leave to their members to be absent without reference to the archbishop as President; and a right to appoint committees of their whole house, and to insist on a free conference with the Upper House instead of presenting their answers in writing to documents sent down from the Upper House when so required by the archbishop and bishops; and in summary to assert that entire independence embraced in their self-chosen style of 'the Commons Spiritual'. To this the archbishop and bishops replied that the Convocation was an ecclesiastical synod, formed on the model of ancient synods, and not a replica of Parliament; that its proceedings, both before and since the Reformation, had been agreeable to this model; that the Prolocutor was an officer of the Upper as well as of the Lower House, being liable to be sent for by the Upper House on all occasions and charged with messages to the Lower, and therefore his election must be confirmed by the archbishop; that Convocation had always been prorogued by a schedule signed by the archbishop with the consent of his brethren and sent by the hand of the Registrar to the Prolocutor, who then intimated it to the lower clergy; that the pretence of asking the consent of the Lower House to such prorogation was an innovation, as were the claims to adjourn to a different day from that stated in the schedule and to hold intermediate sessions; and that at the opening of each Convocation absent members were put by the archbishop into a state of contumacy and so continued, until they received his leave to absent themselves. Between these two positions, adopted respectively by a majority of the lower clergy on the one hand and by the Upper House on the other, there might seem to exist only the relation of contradiction; and there could be no doubt that in principle the bishops were in the right. Accordingly the Lower House was divided into an aggressive majority and a dissentient minority.

Between these two extremes, little ear was given to the voice of moderates, like Humphrey Prideaux, archdeacon of Suffolk, who in respect of the claim of the bishops that the President adjourned the whole Convocation, and not merely the Upper House, by the schedule, so far concurred with them, as thinking them in the right. But as to their requiring that the lower house should break up so soon as the schedule came down to them and appoint no committees to sit and act on the intermediate days, he was clearly of opinion that in both these particulars, they were wholly in the wrong; for as the bishops usually break very early to attend the service of the house of lords in parliament, and then send down the schedule of adjournment to the lower house, if on receipt of this schedule the lower house must immediately break up also, what time would they have to despatch the business before them? It seems natural from the reason of the thing that the day of session be allotted for the business of it; and if so, what leisure can there be, unless on intermediate days, for any committee to sit and do the business referred to them?[1]

In 1702 indeed the bishops offered recognition of the allowance of discretion to the Prolocutor, as to the time of his intimating to the Lower House his receipt of the schedule of prorogation, in order to allow the completion of the day's business; and of the meeting of committees between the sessions of the synod for the preparation of business; but in the heated temper of the Lower House, this pacific overture was refused.

The archbishop therefore was left with the alternatives, either of replying to the direct challenge of the lower clergy by declaring them contumacious as a result of their contempt of his authority and by proceeding to ecclesiastical censures against them, or of seeking subterfuges to avoid such a head-on collision. The former course would need the steadfast support of the sovereign through her ministers in order to be effective; but the administration blew hot and cold according to the political circumstances of the day and the progress of the war of the Spanish Succession. Thus in 1706 Tenison secured a letter from the queen expressing her 'resolution to maintain our supremacy, and the due subordination of presbyters to bishops, as fundamental parts of the constitution of the Church of England'; whilst in the following year this admonition was repeated, with the further threat in the event of future illegalities by the Lower House 'to use such means for the punishing offences of this nature, as are warranted by law'.[2] In 1710, however, after the Tory victory in the general election following upon the Sacheverell fiasco, a series of meetings to consider matters of business to be laid before the Convocation of Canterbury was held in the deanery-house of

---

[1] *The Life of Humphrey Prideaux* (1748), p. 103. For an interesting, if somewhat acetic, sketch of Prideaux, see R. W. Ketton-Cremer, *Norfolk Assembly* (London, 1957), pp. 65–91.

[2] E. Cardwell, *Documentary Annals*, vol. II, no. CLXX, pp. 413–14.

Westminster, attended by the archbishop of York, the bishops of Rochester, Bath and Wells, Exeter, Bristol and St David's, certain members of former Lower Houses, namely, Atterbury, Smalridge and Stanhope, together with two statesmen, the earl of Rochester and Robert Harley; from which conclave Tenison was pointedly and deliberately excluded. In such circumstances a consistent policy of firm resistance by the archbishop to the claims of the Lower House could not be pursued, apart from a refusal of the Upper House to consider any matters presented by the lower clergy until the irregularities had ceased—a course of action which would reduce the synod to complete impotence.

Accordingly Tenison strove to ward off trouble by judicious prorogations; taking advantage of the death of the Prolocutor in 1702 to go 'in haste to the Convocation in order to prorogue them without choosing a new Prolocutor', and not allowing the Convocation elected in 1708 to embark on any business. By another expedient he used his right of Option to secure nomination to archdeaconries and thereby to increase the number of supporters of the bishops in the Lower House. So far as was practicable he inclined to prevent business from coming before the synod; though these makeshift devices provoked some of his subordinates to wrath. 'If my lord archbishop resolve to hold frequent sessions' wrote Gibson to Wake in 1707

and to preside in person, or when he is not able, by a commissary, in order to a correspondence with the lower house, and the receiving and considering such papers as they shall think fit from time to time to offer; it seems very convenient that this should be understood before our meeting, that intimation may be given to our friends in the country to come up, to the end we may make a creditable appearance, and that as many as give good reasons why they cannot attend in person, may send their proxies. Hitherto the way has been to tell the members of our side that they may stay at their cures, because no business is intended; while the other side were summoning up the most considerable of their members to carry such measures for perplexing the administration in church and state as they have in their view; and thus far, our superiors have given them the opportunity of having their papers received above. While the archbishop and bishops meet as an house, we shall think ourselves bound to attend; but we, the small gleanings in and about London, cannot but think it a hardship that his grace and the bishops should keep our friends in the country upon an assurance that no business will be done, and then all the winter shall meet in Convocation and hold their sessions, in expectation of what the lower house may offer, with all the formality they could do if business of the highest importance, proposed by the queen or the archbishop, were depending. If his grace will be pleased to know her majesty's thoughts as to the laying of business before them, and, finding she has none, will signify it to the bishops and let them know withal that in consideration of his own infirmities (few winters passing without a long fit of the gout), he proposes to do nothing the next Convocation, but only to send a commissary with power to prorogue; then we shall reckon ourselves discharged from attendance, and our friends may fairly stay in the country. But if the resolution be to hold sessions in form, we think it very unfair that the greatest part of our members should be suffered, or rather encouraged, to stay in the country, while we who are but a handful in comparison are insulted by numbers; not to mention the disadvantage it is to our cause, that when any matter of moment is depending, we have so few eye-and-ear-witnesses to transmit true and fair accounts of what passes into the several dioceses....I think it is plain that, all things considered (his grace's infirmities, the difficulty of getting a commissary to his mind without giving offence to several senior bishops, and the mischief the clergy will probably be attempting) it would be the best way to prorogue from time to time by a commissary; but it is very fit we should know beforehand whether that, or regular sessions are to be the practice.[1]

The truth of this diagnosis was attested by the recollection of a proctor for the diocese of Lincoln, 'who was one, and that a very zealous one, of the first that stood by my lords the bishops when a mighty torrent strove to carry all the other way; the odds were about 50 to 17'.[2] It was confirmed also by the experiences of White Kennett, who found himself the chief antagonist of Atterbury in the stormy proceedings of the Lower House and left several accounts of the conflict.[3] The natural consequence of this strife was to reduce the sessions of Convocation to nullity, since the transaction of business between the two houses became virtually impossible; and to produce a crescendo of tempest which culminated in the Convocation of 1710. In that year Atterbury was elected Prolocutor of the Lower House by a large majority, and the Royal Letters of Business expressed the mingled hope and threat that 'the despatch of such business as properly belonged to them' would 'not be frustrated, nor the ends of such assemblies defeated, by any unseasonable disputes between the two houses of Convocation about unnecessary forms and methods of proceeding'. Insult was added to injury, moreover, by the circumstances that the content of these Letters was made known to Archbishop Tenison only after their compilation; and that in the further royal licence of 23 January 1711 he was

---

[1] Arch. W. Epist. 17, Miscellaneous I, f. 178.
[2] N. Sykes, *William Wake* (1957), vol. I, p. 154.
[3] G. V. Bennett, *White Kennett, Bishop of Peterborough* (1957), c. 3.

not designated 'President of the Convocation of this Province' in accordance with precedent, whilst, without his prior consultation, certain bishops were named of the Quorum, one of whom must necessarily be present before the Upper House could transact business. The former omission was believed to be a deliberate attempt to support the thesis that the archbishop was not President of the whole Convocation by virtue of his office; and the latter infringed his right to commission such bishops as he himself wished, to preside in his absence and thereby to exercise a right of negative on proceedings. A second royal licence on 21 February aggravated the affront by adding to the Quorum two very junior bishops over the heads of their seniors. Furthermore, even a determined protest by a majority of the Upper House, with a threat to do no business until satisfaction was given, could produce only a compromise settlement; by which the queen on the one hand affirmed that she

doth not intend that any person nominated of the quorum in her royal licence...should preside in the place of the archbishop by virtue of such commission, or have a negative during his presence in any matter or thing which the President and the bishops or the greater part of them, shall treat of or agree upon pursuant to the said licence;

and on the other hand the Upper House acquiesced in the omission to designate the archbishop as president of the Convocation.[1]

Not until the elevation of Atterbury to the bench as bishop of Rochester in 1713 did Convocation enter placid waters; and such considerable progress was then made in relation to the reform of excommunication and commutation, to marriage licences and the provision of forms of service for the reception of converts from popery and dissent, that on 8 July 1714 the bishop of London, presiding in the absence of the archbishop,

in the name of the upper house and by their direction did give the thanks of their lordships to the lower house for their great pains and diligence in despatching so many of the heads of business recommended by her majesty to the convocation, that those which were already agreed upon by both houses would not be laid before her majesty and engrossed so as to be subscribed by both houses at present, but would be laid before her as they are, for her inspection and approbation; meanwhile their lordships hoped that at the next meeting of the synod the other heads recommended by her majesty would likewise be so finished that canons might be made thereupon and the subscription of both houses given to all of them together.

[1] Sykes, *William Wake*, vol. I, pp. 125–30.

The adoption of these delaying tactics was to prove unfortunate, for the death of the queen on 1 August led to a period of uncertainty until the Protestant succession in the House of Hanover had been safely accomplished, which was followed shortly by the death of Tenison in December 1715. Notwithstanding, there had been welcome signs, as Wake had remarked in the previous July to the archbishop of Dublin, that 'the two houses are at this time in a perfect good understanding and make it their business to hold well with one another'. Upon Wake's own succession to the primacy, therefore, he was in good hopes of making satisfactory progress, when the episode of Hoadly's Bangorian sermon led to the hasty and ill-conceived intervention of the ministers of state, against the wish of the archbishop, to effect the prorogation of the assembly by a royal writ. For the rest of Wake's archiepiscopate the sessions of Convocation were purely formal; and when the Lower House persisted in its claim to adjourn itself by its own consent, the Upper House in 1728 entered upon its Acts a solemn protest together with a reaffirmation of the principle that the adjournment of both houses was effected by the President's schedule of prorogation; and therewith the theoretical controversy was ended.[1]

With the accession of Potter to the primacy in 1737, however, hopes ran high of a restoration of sitting Convocations. It was well known that the new archbishop favoured this step; and moreover he believed himself to have received assurances that

> though the Convocation had not sat for many years, yet the right of sitting was still preserved entire, together with all the original powers of the archbishop. That further, no absolute prohibition had been given him from above against their sitting, nor any general discouragement to it, but that the royal licence might be easily obtained for that purpose, whenever it should be likely to him and other sincere friends of the Church that the convocation might sit to good effect and unto the real benefit of this Church.[2]

Furthermore Gibson also was very anxious to renew the practice of sitting Convocations, and had proposed certain practical expedients for facilitating the discharge of business without infringing the archbishop's prerogatives as President of the whole Convocation. He suggested that recognition should be accorded of the Lower House's rights

> (1) to enter originally upon the consideration of all such matters as they thought proper; (2) to appoint select committees for particular purposes,

---

[1] *Ibid.* pp. 136–48.   [2] *Ibid.* p. 145.

and for preparing matters to be laid before the house on the day appointed in the upper house for the next meeting of the synod; (3) to lay before the upper house any representations whatsoever they judged proper; and (4) to continue their debates after the upper house had risen and after the schedule of prorogation was brought down to the lower house and put into the hands of the prolocutor, he having a discretionary power to intimate it to the clergy when he saw proper, in case he had received no special direction about the time, which had never happened nor probably ever would; (5) to dissent finally on any matter, so as to hinder its passing into a Synodical Act.

In addition, Gibson was prepared to consider the further concession, by which

at the opening of a convocation the prolocutor appoints nine or ten members of the lower house...to be his assessors; and, considering the frequent interruptions that must happen in their debates, if the prolocutor was to convey to the upper house all resolutions of the lower house (which yet in strictness is his office and his alone) could there be any inconvenience if the upper house should be content to receive any written paper by the hand of one of the assessors, confining all messages by word of mouth to the prolocutor in person and reserving to the upper house their indisputable right of sending for him at pleasure?[1]

With such favourable auspices the experiment of a sitting convocation was tried accordingly in 1741. Unfortunately the Act Books of this Convocation are not extant; and the chief authority for its proceedings consists of accounts published by Archdeacon George Reynolds of Lincoln, a principal actor in the proceedings of the lower house. The Convocation met on 2 December 1741 in St Paul's cathedral for the preliminaries; and on 27 January Reynolds 'moved the lower house to take under consideration the state of the ecclesiastical courts, clandestine marriages, the qualifications of persons to be admitted to holy orders, and the titles and salaries of curates'. The House thereupon resolved unanimously 'that the archdeacon should reduce the particulars of his motion into writing, to be offered to the consideration of the house at the next session'. Accordingly Reynolds drew up seven propositions.

1. That the dilatory proceedings in ecclesiastical courts are a delay of justice, and of great expense and vexation to the subject; 2. That the admission of appeals by the Court of Arches from Interlocutory Decrees of inferior courts in causes of correction, is a great obstruction to the necessary exercise of discipline; 3. That the practice of granting marriage licences to persons unknown, or when one or both of them is but casually

---

[1] N. Sykes, *Edmund Gibson, Bishop of London* (1926), p. 51.

resident in the jurisdiction, without letters testimonial of the Ordinary of the place from whence they come, opens a door for clandestine marriages; 4. That complaints are made of a claim of the Prerogative [or other] Courts of Canterbury to exercise concurrent jurisdiction through the Province in the probate of wills and the granting of marriage licences. And inasmuch as such claim may prove a great discouragement to the officers of inferior courts, whose assistance in the exercise of diocesan jurisdiction is necessary, it is submitted to the consideration of this house, how far an enquiry ought to be made, whether the prerogative [or other] courts claim a right to grant marriage licences to the subjects of other bishops, or to prove wills, when the testator's effects lie within the jurisdiction of one bishop. 5. That the omission of governors and other members of [some] colleges to sign testimonials or therein to certify their belief of the fitness of the person for the order, office or employment to which he desires to be admitted, renders their testimonials less useful and effectual. 6. That the giving fictitious titles introduces a supernumerary clergy into the church and is the occasion of many inconveniences. 7. That much reproach is brought upon the beneficed, and much oppression upon the unbeneficed, clergy by curates accepting too scanty salaries from incumbents.

When these proposals were presented to the Lower House on 5 March, Dr Zachary Pearce, dean of Winchester, moved 'that the propositions prepared by the archdeacon in obedience to the order of the house, should not be received'; and this was agreed. Thereupon Reynolds published the document; and on 20 May when the House next met, Dr Thomas Chapman, chaplain to Archbishop Potter, observed 'that the publication of matters that had passed in this house, pending the synod, was irregular; that there were many orders upon their books for keeping their debates secret; that he had read the archdeacon of Lincoln's pamphlet and was of opinion that it was a libel upon the constitution; and, referring to a passage which he insisted was libellous upon the constitution', proceeded to move 'that the archdeacon should be censured before his propositions were taken under consideration'. Before the House came to a resolution, however, the Pro-Prolocutor intimated that the session was adjourned. Thus, in Reynolds' picturesque if somewhat flamboyant comparison, 'in a synod which sat longer than that of Nicaea, or that which formed the Thirty-Nine Articles, or the Canons, the only proposition made about business was rejected without discussion, and the introducer of it threatened'.[1] The episode, however, marked the end of sitting convocations for more than a century.

[1] G. Reynolds, *An Historical Essay upon the Government of the Church of England* (1743), pp. 205-7, 241-4; also *A Letter to the Reverend Dr Lisle, Prolocutor of the Lower House of Convocation* (1742).

With the untimely end of Potter's experiment, it is convenient to strike a balance of loss and gain in the Convocation controversy. The first and most immediate consequence was the discrediting of synodical assemblies. 'These disputes', as Gibson observed, 'occasioned jealousy and coldness between the bishops and their clergy, accusations against both as unfit to be trusted in a public assembly together, discontinuance and contempt of Convocations, [and] disappointment of the benefits which might have arisen, particularly from many good canons in which they had already made progress.'[1] There can be little regret indeed at the termination of the protracted disputes which had disfigured the history of Convocation, both in the pamphlet warfare without and the acrimonious debates within, during the reign of Anne. But a longer view of the services rendered by Convocation from the summoning of Henry VIII's Reformation Parliament in 1529 to the outbreak of the Civil War in 1640, would correct this narrower perspective and emphasise the many valuable projects set forward by its means. Even during the period of controversy itself many useful schemes had been carried to the verge of completion; and it was unfortunate for the church that they remained without authority. Thus the forms of service for the consecration of churches and churchyards, for the reception of converts from popery and dissent, and for the visitation of prisoners, were equally useful and necessary, yet all remained unauthorised. In addition to this provision of services outside the scope of the Book of Common Prayer, there was an admitted need for revision of some of the Occasional Offices contained within its covers. Dean Prideaux testified that it was 'the opinion of many that there are some defects in our present Liturgy, such as that there are whole Offices wanting in it, as for the receiving of penitents, the preparing of the condemned for their deaths, the consecration of churches etc.; and that some of those Offices which are established, do not in all particulars answer the occasions for which they were appointed, as may be instanced in the Office of the Visitation of the Sick'. Further he desired the authority of Convocation for a *Book of Family Devotions*, drawn up in 1689; and when this hope was frustrated he urged Archbishop Tenison 'to publish it with his own authority, but the archbishop wished to wait until it could obtain the concurrence of Convocation, and then the book was lost by

---

[1] Secker MSS. VI, f. 470.

Bishop Williams of Chichester '.[1] The suspension of sitting Convocations thus placed an absolute barrier to the revision and enrichment of the Book of Common Prayer, and stereotyped its Offices without hope of flexibility. Nor were the resulting ill consequences of a purely negative character; for the vacuum created by the lapse of Convocation was filled by Parliament. Profiting by the dual circumstance of the authorisation by statute of the Prayer Book of 1662 and the express assertion by the House of Commons of its right to debate the alterations made by Convocation, and reinforced by the suspension of sitting Convocations after 1717, the temporal legislature assumed all the functions of ecclesiastical deliberation. The classic expression of this claim was made by Lord Hardwick's celebrated judgment in the case of Middleton v. Crofts in 1737;

> Now the constant uniform practice ever since the Reformation (for there is no occasion to go further back) has been that when any material ordinances or regulations have been made to bind the laity as well as clergy in matters ecclesiastical, they have been either enacted or confirmed by parliament; of *this* proposition the several Acts of Uniformity are so many proofs, for by these the whole doctrine and worship, the very rites and ceremonies of the Church and the literal form of public prayers are prescribed and established.

Here lay the realisation of Peter Heylyn's prophetic fears; and hereby the church was bound fast in the straitjacket of parliamentary control, thanks to the ill-fated Convocation controversy.

A similar fate befell the projects for reform of the Canons and of the ecclesiastical courts. Nothing more was heard of the revision of the Canons of 1603 and 1640; whilst, although considerable progress had been made during the last years of Anne's reign in preparing a scheme for the substitution of sentence of contumacy for that of excommunication for minor offences, and Gibson published in 1717 his Convocation sermon on this theme together with proposals for the preparation of the offices of Official Principal and Vicar-General, the suspension of sitting Convocations which followed shortly, made an end likewise of these projects. The loss to the church thereby was evident. Indeed Archdeacon Reynolds averred in 1743 that

> no instance can be given of the use of one body of Canons in any national Church for 140 years without any Synodical reform, except in this Church; and therefore how perfect soever the system of Canons was in 1603, yet whatever is variable in the state of the church may be presumed to have varied within this period in some degree; so far at least as

---

[1] *Life of Humphrey Prideaux*, pp. 59-61.

that the same rules may be less adequate to the present state of opinions, manners, acts of parliament and decisions of the courts of judicature, than upon their first establishment.[1]

The paralysis of ecclesiastical procedure was felt equally in the judicial as in the legislative sphere. The judicial character and function of Convocation were admitted on all sides in principle, though differences of opinion emerged when theory was translated into practice. By the first Act of Appeals in 1533 the Upper House of Convocation of the appropriate Province had been designated as the final court of appeal in causes touching the king, whose decision 'shall be taken for a final decree, sentence, judgment, definition and determination, and the same matter, so determined, never after to come in question and debate, to be examined in any other court or courts'. In the following year, however, appeals from the archbishops' courts were to be made to the Court of Chancery, and 'upon every such appeal, a commission shall be directed under the great seal to such persons as shall be named by the king's highness ...to hear and definitively determine such appeals'. The Convocation nevertheless retained its judicial function; and one of the principal points emphasised in Atterbury's *Letter to a Convocation Man* of 1697 was the necessity for the exercise of its judicial powers in condemnation of heretical books and their authors. Accordingly in 1701 the lower clergy presented a request to the Upper House for the suppression of John Toland's *Christianity not Mysterious*, from which several specific passages were cited as 'pernicious, dangerous and scandalous positions and destructive of the Christian faith'; to which the bishops replied that

upon our consulting with counsel learned in the law concerning heretical, impious and immoral books, and particularly concerning a book of Toland's sent up to us from the lower house, we do not find how without a licence from the king, which we have not yet received, we can have sufficient authority to censure judicially any such books; but on the contrary we are advised that by so doing both houses of Convocation may incur the penalties of the statute of 25 Henry VIII. (c. 19), [the Second Act of Appeals].[2]

The question was next raised in a more direct manner in 1710 in relation to William Whiston, successor of Newton in the Lucasian chair of mathematics at Cambridge, whose study of the theological

---

[1] G. Reynolds, *An Historical Essay*, p. 232.
[2] E. Cardwell, *Synodalia*, vol. II, pp. 701–7.

tenets of the pre-Nicene fathers, had led him to the conclusion that their doctrine of the Trinity was not Athanasian but 'Eusebian' or Arian. In order to propagate his conclusions he had founded a Society for the Restoration of Primitive Christianity; and in 1710 was deprived of his professorship by the university, and in the following year published *An Historical Preface to Primitive Christianity Revived,...dedicated to the Most Reverend Thomas, Lord Archbishop of Canterbury, President, and to the Right Reverend the Bishops of the same Province, his Grace's Suffragans, and the Reverend the Clergy of the Lower House in Convocation assembled.* It could not be expected that so direct a challenge would be ignored; and on 16 March 1711 the Lower House informed the Upper that

this book contains assertions in our opinion so directly opposite to the fundamental articles of the Christian religion, that out of our duty to God, our zeal for preserving the purity of the catholic faith, and our concern to prevent the scandal that may arise from our silence, we think ourselves obliged to lay it before your lordships, praying your opinion after what manner it may be proper for this synod to proceed in relation to that book.

On the 19th the bishops approved three resolutions; first, that notice should be taken of the book; secondly, 'that it appears as well from modern as from ancient precedents, that the archbishop and bishops in convocation have power to judge in matters of this nature'; and thirdly, that if the archbishop concurred in the two foregoing resolutions, he should be desired 'to give direction for the method of proceeding in this case'. On 11 April, therefore, Tenison communicated to the bishops his formal and considered opinion concerning methods of proceeding. He began by distinguishing two points: 'I. The censure of the book and doctrine. II. The censure of the person.' The former was simple and straightforward. All that was necessary was to cite 'the particular passages wherein he has asserted his pernicious tenets most plainly and expressly'; and then to specify 'the particular places of Scripture, and in the council of Nice, and the Articles of our own church, upon which the charge of heresy may be most clearly grounded'.

Difficulties multiplied, however, in regard to censure of the author. Three methods were mentioned by the primate to his suffragans, 'which you will weigh and consider well, in order to judge how far each of them will be safe and expedient, and how far effectual. The first method is by the court of convocation, in which such a judicature hath been evidently exercised in many instances both before and since the reformation, and which seems the most desirable method in the present case, if the following difficulties do not stand in the way'. First, the archbishop suggested that 'such a court being final, or the last resort, from which no appeal is provided' by the 25 Henry VIII, c. 19 (the second Act of Appeals), 'it may seem doubtful how far a prosecution without an appeal will be consistent with' the royal supremacy as defined in the Act of Uniformity of 1559. Secondly, it was uncertain 'how far it will be consistent with' the Henrician Act of 1534 above-mentioned, 'which in the course of the appeals directed to be thenceforth made, doth not mention Convocation'. An additional difficulty in this method of procedure was 'that there does not appear to have been any exercise of such a judicature for this last hundred years or thereabouts, in which time matters of such nature were usually considered and adjuged in the High Commission Court while that remained; and when the court was suppressed, it was enacted 17 Car. II, c. 2, that no court should be thenceforth erected with like power, jurisdiction or authority, but that all commissions erecting any such court shall be void'. The bishops were therefore enjoined to consider 'how far the revival of this judicial authority in a convocation, empowered to proceed and act by her majesty's commission or licence, may be construed an erecting of a court with like power etc as the High Commission had'. Furthermore, the statute II Car. II, c. 9 (An Act for taking away the Writ *De Haeretico Comburendo*), had provided that 'nothing in this act shall extend or be construed to take away or abridge the jurisdiction of Protestant archbishops or bishops or any other judges of any ecclesiastical courts in cases of atheism, blasphemy, heresy or schism, and other damnable doctrines and opinions, but that they may proceed to punish the same according to his majesty's ecclesiastical laws, by excommunication, deprivation, degradation, and other ecclesiastical censures, not extending to death, in such sort and no other as they might have done before the making of this act'. Consequently Tenison bade the bishops 'to consider whether the provision there made...extends to convocation, or only to the ordinary and established courts of every archbishop and bishop'. Finally, when the Lower House of Convocation had complained in 1689 of several heretical books, the bishop of London acting as President, with the concurrence of his brethren of the Upper House, had replied that they had received legal counsel to the effect that such matters should be dealt with in the appropriate courts and that the Convocation should not concern itself therewith.

The second alternative method of proceeding was 'for the archbishop to hold a Court of Audience, and calling to him his provincial bishops, as assessors there, to examine, proceed and give sentence, as in his Court of Audience; into which he is fully empowered by a special proviso 23 Henry VIII. cap. 9, § 4 (the Bill of Citations)[1] to cite any person out of his diocese, wherein he dwells, in case that the bishop or any immediate judge or ordinary dare not, or will not convene the party to be sued before him; and from which court (as within the statute 25 Henry VIII. cap. 19) a regular appeal lies to the queen's delegates in Chancery'. The third way of proceeding was that 'the bishop, in whose diocese he inhabits, may of his own accord cite him into his court; or the cause may be remitted or specially recommended to him, as his proper ordinary, by the archbishops and bishops in convocation, which we find hath oftentimes been done in cases of the like nature'. The archbishop's conclusion, therefore, was that the two last methods seemed 'to be the most plain and clear in point of legality'; but since the first was 'the most solemn, provided it may be pursued legally', a petition should be presented by the Upper House to the queen, 'that her majesty will be graciously pleased to lay the case before her reverend judges for their opinions thereupon'.

Confronted by such a barrage of difficulties in the way of formal censure of Whiston by Convocation, the bishops on 22 April duly requested Her Majesty

to lay this case before your reverend judges, and others whom your majesty shall in your wisdom think fit, for their opinion, how far the convocation, as the law now stands, may proceed in the examining, censuring and condemning such tenets, as are declared to be heresy by the laws of this realm, together with the authors and maintainers of them.

Unfortunately for the peace of the church and the resolving of episcopal doubts the judges and the attorney and solicitor-general, to whom the issue was submitted, spoke with a divided voice. Eight judges plus the law officers were of opinion

---

[1] 'Provided always that it shall be lawful to every archbishop of this realm to call, cite or summon any person or persons inhabiting or dwelling in any bishop's diocese within his Province for causes of heresy, if the bishop or other ordinary immediate thereunto consent, or if that the same bishop or other immediate ordinary or judge do not his duty in punishment of the same.'

that of common right there lies an appeal from all ecclesiastical courts of England to your majesty, in virtue of your supremacy in ecclesiastical affairs, whether the same be given by express words of parliament or not; and consequently that a prosecution in convocation, not excluding an appeal to your majesty, is not inconsistent with the statute of I. Eliz. cap. I, but reserves the supremacy entire.

This statement, however, was qualified by disabling reservations; in which the signatories, who as at present advised were 'of opinion that such jurisdiction, as the law now stands, may be exercised in the convocation', nevertheless stated, that

this being a matter, which, upon application for a prohibition on behalf of persons who shall be prosecuted, may come in judgment before such of us as have the honour to serve your majesty in places of judicature, we desire to be understood to give our present thoughts, with a reserve of an entire freedom of altering our opinion, in case any records or proceedings, which we are now strangers to, shall be laid before us, or any new considerations, which have not occurred to us, be suggested by the parties or their council to convince us of our mistakes.

The minority of four judges held that,

as the law now stands, the convocation hath not any jurisdiction originally to cite before them any person for heresy, or any other spiritual offence, which according to the laws of the realm may be cited, censured and punished in the respective ecclesiastical courts or jurisdictions of the archbishops, bishops and other ordinaries, who, we conceive, have the proper judicature in those cases, and from whom and whose courts the parties accused may have their appeals, the last resort wherein is lodged in the crown.

They argued that the Henrician statutes took no notice of Convocation, either as to jurisdiction or appeals; and they were also uncertain whether the judiciary power of Convocation as claimed, resided in the whole body or in part of Convocation. Nor could they find any precedents for such a claim, which, if allowed, would invade the ordinary jurisdictions of the archbishops and bishops. Therefore they concluded 'that heretical tenets and opinions may be examined and condemned in convocation authorised by royal licence, without convening the authors or maintainers of them'.

Notwithstanding this division of opinion, the archbishop was exhorted by royal letter, that 'we cannot doubt but the convocation will now be satisfied they may employ the power, which belongs to them, in repressing the impious attempts lately made to subvert the foundation of the Christian faith', since 'according to the opinion of eight of our twelve judges and of our attorney and solicitor general, as the law now stands, a jurisdiction in matters of heresy and condemnation of heretics is proper to be exercised in convocation'. The bishops, however, decided that where lawyers feared to tread, the spiritual assembly should not rush in; and accordingly Convocation prudently contented itself with a censure of Whiston's opinions without touching his person.[1] In face of such confusion of opinion, no other course of action was open to them. Nor was it surprising that Gibson should add the cautious comment in his *Codex*, that 'how far the Convocation of each Province, which had once an undoubted right to convict and punish heretics in a synodical manner, doth still retain or not retain that authority, I shall not presume to say, till the learned judges be clear and final in their opinions, and that point shall have received a judicial determination'.[2] Wake, moreover, was of opinion that 'it is not so much the Convocation that judges, as the Archbishop in Convocation'; so that it was 'the part of the Lower House to discover and accuse, of the bishops to counsel and assist, but of the archbishop to hear and judge'.[3] Burnet avowed further that 'two great doubts still remained, even supposing we had a jurisdiction; whether only of the bishops, or what share the lower house had in this judiciary authority; the other was, by what delegates, in case of an appeal, our sentence was to be examined; were no bishops to be in the court of delegates? or was the sentence of the archbishop and his twenty-one suffragan bishops, with the clergy of the province, to be judged by the archbishop of York and his three suffragan bishops?'[4] Even if Atterbury's favourite theory of a strict parallel between the Commons Spiritual and Temporal were allowed, this would confine the judicial power to the Upper House. But after the bold advice of the queen's administration to Tenison to proceed judicially against Whiston, the issue of the action of Convocation descended to the level of comedy. A copy of the censure agreed by both houses of the opinions expressed in the *Historical Preface* was sent to the queen for her royal assent; but no answer was returned before the prorogation on 12 June. When Convocation reassembled, two bishops were deputed to ask for an answer, but could obtain no other reply than that the document had been diplomatically mislaid. A further copy was sent, to which also no answer was vouchsafed. 'So Whiston's affair sleeps',

---

[1] E. Cardwell, *Synodalia*, vol. II, pp. 753–69.    [2] E. Gibson, *Codex*, vol. I, p. 427.
[3] Sykes, *William Wake*, vol. I, p. 91.
[4] Burnet, *History of My Own Time*, vol. VI, pp. 51–2.

commented Burnet on the inglorious end of the attempt to assert the judicial powers of Convocation in matters of heresy.

Behind the façade of legal contradiction, however, the brute fact was plain that judicially as well as legislatively, Convocation had been rendered ineffective. The Court of High Commission under Elizabeth and the early Stuarts had reduced the Court of Delegates to insignificance. Nor, when the High Commission was abolished in 1640 and its reconstitution prohibited at the Restoration, was any efficient substitute established in its place. James II essayed its revival by his Ecclesiastical Commission, which in turn was abolished at the Revolution of 1688. But the vacuum remained unfilled. Sir Leoline Jenkins indeed proposed the conversion of the Court of Delegates into a permanent body, instead of a changing personnel of commissioners appointed separately on the occasion of each appeal (of which there were thirty-seven cases during Charles II's reign), in order to give continuity to the court, but his suggestion was not carried into effect. Had it been executed, it would have been serviceable in his own time, and, as Canon Kemp has remarked, 'might have avoided the unhappy history of our appeal court in the nineteenth' century.[1] Instead, as Archdeacon Reynolds observed of the ecclesiastical aspect of the Revolution settlement,

if the High Commission was a distasteful remedy, and had fallen either under popular prejudice or the just censure of the nation, still some remedy was needful to supply the exigencies of the ecclesiastical administration.... The Church had then experienced the imperfections of a new form of government for twenty years; new in this respect, that it was left to shift for itself, without the accustomed aids from the Crown, or occasional orders of Synod to the Consistories, or liberty of making a Synodical Representation,...notwithstanding the King's Declaration in 1660 concerning the regulation of religion in many respects, especially as to the abuse of excommunication and absolution. So that episcopal consistories during that period had a charge upon them, far exceeding their abilities in any age, when improved to the utmost pitch they were capable of.[2]

The Church did not lack erudite canonists, for in 1713 Gibson published his *Codex Juris Ecclesiastici Anglicani*, and in 1726 there appeared John Ayliffe's *Parergon Juris Canonici Anglicani*. In the Introductory Discourse to his *Codex*, moreover, Gibson made a vigorous plea for the restoration of that relationship between church

---

[1] E. W. Kemp, *An Introduction to Canon Law in the Church of England* (1967), p. 37.
[2] G. Reynolds, *An Historical Essay*, p. 187.

and state envisaged in the famous preamble to the Henrician Act of Appeals. From this he deduced that

England is governed by two distinct administrations: one spiritual for matters of a spiritual nature, and the other temporal for matters of a temporal nature. And for the same ends, hath it two legislatures, the one consisting of persons spiritual and the other of persons temporal; whose business it is, to frame laws for the government of church and state; and these laws being enacted and confirmed by the Prince, as Sovereign and Supreme Head, become obligatory to the people and rules for the administration of justice in spiritual and temporal matters.[1]

Therefore he desired to assert the mutual obligation of the two authorities to respect each other's franchises. His ideal was the translation into practice of the theory of this preamble that

when any cause of the law divine happened to come in question, or of spiritual learning, then it was declared, interpreted, and showed by that part of the body politic, called the spiritualty, now being usually called the English Church, which always hath been reputed, and also found of that sort, that both for knowledge, integrity and sufficiency of number, it hath been always thought, and is also at this hour, sufficient and meet of itself, without the intermeddling of any exterior person or persons, to declare and determine all such doubts, and to administer all such offices and duties, as to their rooms spiritual doth appertain.

Accordingly he sought a return to the practice of Elizabeth I of forbidding Parliament to concern itself with ecclesiastical matters, which were the proper province of Convocation. Similarly in regard to judicial proceedings, in order to fulfil the principle of the same preamble that 'both their authorities and jurisdictions do conjoin together in the due administration of justice, the one to help the other', he wished the temporal and spiritual courts to be on terms of strict equality under the Crown; so that the usurpations practised by the former to the prejudice of the latter through the issue of prohibitions might be forbidden. At the same time he was anxious for such reforms in the courts Christian as would make them more efficient and expeditious, so that no objection might lie against their jurisdiction on the grounds of abuses, corruption, and extortions. Neither his erudition nor his zeal, however, availed to arrest the decline of the ecclesiastical power.

To the credit account of the Convocation controversy there may be placed indeed the considerable series of learned historical works which it called forth, the very dust of which writings Stubbs

---

[1] Gibson, *Codex*, vol. I, p. xxix.

reckoned as gold. But this was a solitary and light weight to cast into the scales against so many disadvantages as ensued from the termination of sitting Convocations. Gibson, setting down his reflections in 1744 for the benefit of a happier posterity, emphasised 'two very good effects which sitting Convocations had; the first, in training up those of the clergy who were chiefly concerned in the debates there, to a facility and readiness of speaking in the debates of a higher assembly; and the second in turning the minds of the whole body to a much closer attention to the public concerns of the Church than had been observed among the clergy since the disuse of sitting Convocations'.[1] Both parts of this judgment were substantiated by other witnesses. Bishop Thomas Newton remarked the ill-effects of the suppression of Convocation in disabling bishops to take part in debates in the House of Lords, since Convocation had been 'a kind of school of oratory for the clergy'.[2] Hurd was moved by his perusal of Atterbury to put to Warburton 'the question, whether *much real service* can be done religion by these synods, which could not as well be done without them? because if this be so, there are manifest inconveniences to be apprehended from their meeting'. In reply Warburton confessed: 'I believe all you say of the mischiefs they produce; but I think we have avoided one extreme only by falling into another.' It was much that two such divines should agree that 'there is no doubt but the Church has lost very much of her dignity and authority by this disuse of her sitting Convocations; and by this means religion itself may have been considerably disserved'. Warburton indeed went further, being indignant that 'for the sake of screening a writer who was for destroying the very being of a religious society, the Convocation has been kept gagged for about forty years together'.[3] In his *Alliance between Church and State* he contended that

there is reason that propositions for such laws [on ecclesiastical matters] should sometime come from the Church; which we must suppose well skilled (as in her proper business) in forming and digesting such new regulations, before they come before the consideration of the legislature. ...For to have laws framed and modelled solely by the State, and (without previous communication) imposed upon the Church, is making of it the meanest and most abject of all the State's creatures. For every little

---

[1] Sykes, *Edmund Gibson*, p. 50.

[2] 'Life of Dr Thomas Newton' in *Lives of E. Pocock, Z. Pearce, T. Newton and P. Skelton* (1816), vol. II, p. 186.

[3] *Letters from a Late Eminent Prelate*, nos. CXLIV–V (to Hurd), pp. 309–14.

company and corporation hath the honour to be consulted with, before any law is enacted that may affect its constitution.[1]

Warburton with his customary acumen had laid his finger on the sorest point in the contemporary relations of church and state. The result of the suspension of sitting Convocations was to realise in full measure the prediction of Heylyn that 'questionless, some busy members of the House of Commons will thrust themselves into concernements of religion, when they shall find no Convocation sitting to take care thereof'. The principal beneficiary from the demise of Convocation was Parliament, which assumed the function of an ecclesiastical legislature; and this at a time when its proper powers and authority were being notably enhanced, so that Convocation lost any hope of maintaining even a relative degree of independence of its formidable rival. Meanwhile Convocation was hard pressed to preserve even the outward forms of its constitutional procedure. Dr Zachary Pearce was justly praised because

all the while he was Prolocutor, he attended the House in Henry VII's chapel every day to which it stood prorogued; he always gave notice of the day of meeting in the *Daily Advertiser*, and engaged some of his acquaintance among the members who lived in or near Town to be present there; he read the Latin Litany as soon as they were met; and while he waited with them in the chapel till the archbishop's schedule came down for the prorogation of the Convocation, he invited all who were present, with the two actuaries, to dine with him at his house in St Martin's churchyard, which they generally did.[2]

Such observance of the traditional order 'for the forming and perfecting of that poor, harmless creature (of man's invention) called the Convocation', as Edmund Pyle disdainfully recorded,[3] was little more than a preserving of the memories of sitting Convocations in the days of their dispersal. The effect of the surrender of the right of taxing themselves in 1664 and of the suspension of 1717 was to realise even more emphatically Thomas Fuller's description of the Convocation of 1620:

Should we now look into the Convocation, we should find them on Wednesdays and Fridays devoutly at the Litany, otherwise having little employment, as empowered by no commission to alter anything; so that sitting among the tombs of Westminster church they were (as once one of their Prolocutors said) *viva cadavera inter mortuos*, as having no motion or activity allowed unto them.[4]

[1] Warburton, *The Alliance between Church and State* (1736), pt. II, sect. III, p. 84.

[2] 'Life of Zachary Pearce' in *Lives of E. Pocock, Z. Pearce, T. Newton and P. Skelton*, vol. I, 394.    [3] E. Pyle, *Memoirs of a Royal Chaplain* (1905), p. 224.

[4] T. Fuller, *Church History*, Book X, § 27, vol. V, p. 496.

# III

# COMPREHENSION VERSUS TOLERATION

'Though I must confess', wrote Bishop Morley of Winchester to Sheldon on 7 April 1673, in relation to a Bill for the Ease of Protestant Dissenters, which had been debated in the parliamentary session just ended,

I could have been content that the imprudent subscription to the clause of assent and consent together with the declaration against the Covenant (which must cease ten years' hence) might have been taken away now, if it would have divided the Presbyterians from the rest of the Sectaries and united them to the Church by subscribing to whatsoever it is by the Act of Uniformity required of them; yet I never would have consented, nor ever will consent, to that which they call a Comprehension, that is, to their being admitted into the Church or to any employment or preferment in the Church, without an express and exact conformity and subscription to all the Articles and Canons of the Church without any dispensation either in point of judgement or in point of practice, in relation either to the one or to the other.[1]

Despite his stiffness of attitude, Morley had laid his finger skilfully on the essential point of Anglican strategy in relation to those Protestant Dissenters whom the Restoration settlement had excluded from the ministry of the re-established Church. Agreement with the Presbyterians seemed to many possible, and to some churchmen most desirable, whilst the Independents, Baptists and other Sects in such an event might well continue to suffer oppression and persecution. Comprehension v. Indulgence therefore became speedily the *leitmotiv* of ecclesiastical politics during the generation dividing the Restoration from the Revolution. Morley, furthermore, was regarded at first sight as a suitable and even sympathetic negotiator for a *rapprochement* with the Presbyterians. Baxter in 1660 reckoned him 'a moderate, orthodox man', full of 'pacificatory professions'; whilst Burnet confirmed this estimate of him as 'a Calvinist with relation to the Arminian points', who 'was thought a friend to the puritans before the wars'.[2] For this reason Baxter

---

[1] Tanner MSS. 42, f. 7.
[2] M. Sylvester, *Reliquiae Baxterianae* (1696) Lib. I, part II, § 81, p. 218. G. Burnet, *History of My Own Time*, vol. I, p. 304.

had sought 'one hour's discourse with him to know whether concord was really intended', immediately after Parliament had voted for the return of Charles II.

The outcome of the tortuous diplomacy which led to the Act of Uniformity was as profoundly surprising as disappointing to the Presbyterians. 'Some plain and moderate episcopal men', as Baxter believed, 'thought of reconciliation and union with the said Presbyterians; yea, and a reward to the presbyterians for bringing in the king.'[1] The justice of this expectation was undeniable; for without presbyterian support the restoration might not have been achieved, and had they insisted on safeguarding their own position in relation to the ecclesiastical settlement before the actual return of the king or even before the dissolution of the Convention Parliament, they might have ensured success. Instead the revision of the Book of Common Prayer was effected by the Convocations, with little regard to the multifarious points raised by Baxter and his colleagues at the Savoy Conference, and the Act of Uniformity by its stringency made conformity exceedingly difficult for clergy of even moderate Presbyterian opinions. The rigid requirements of this Act in respect both of episcopal ordination and of the form of assent and consent to the Book of Common Prayer were reinforced by the circumstance that the revised Liturgy was difficult to procure by St Bartholomew's day 1662; so that, as Burnet affirmed, 'many that were well affected to the church, but that made a conscience of subscribing to a book that they had not seen, left their benefices on that very account'.[2] Moreover, it was suspected that some bishops were not sorry to see the departure of so many puritan ministers. Bishop Seth Ward described the 'clergy-presbyters' of his diocese of Exeter, together with their brethren of London especially, as 'the enemies of the Church', of whom he desired 'an universal riddance at once'. When some of their number from the city of Exeter and its neighbourhood came to him, and 'did in effect say that they could have given satisfaction to the Act if they had rightly understood it, viz, if they had understood that the assent and consent was to the *use* of things contained in the Liturgy', he added the observation that 'the truth is, the people in many places are glad to be rid of them'.[3]

Notwithstanding, some leading Anglicans and many Presby-

---

[1] M. Sylvester (ed.), *Reliquiae Baxterianae*. I, II, p. 229.
[2] G. Burnet, *History of My Own Time*, vol. I, p. 318.
[3] Tanner MSS. 48, ff. 45, 48. Ward to Sheldon, 20 and 27 September 1662.

terians wished to reopen the door to an agreed compromise which would allow the return of the latter to the national church, and thereby strengthen considerably its position against the inveterate common foe of popery. An additional incentive was given by the personal religious policy of the king, who desired to secure such concessions for papists as could only be purchased at the price of a general toleration of all dissenters from the established church, and this in turn depended upon the number of Protestant dissenters being such as to outweigh the papists. 'It was thought', reported Burnet of the royal stratagem,

a toleration was the only method for setting it a going all the nation over. And nothing could make a toleration for popery pass, but the having great bodies of men put out of the Church and put under severe laws, which should force them to move for a toleration, and should make it reasonable to grant it to them. And it was resolved, that whatever should be granted of that sort should go in so large a manner, that papists should be comprehended within it.[1]

The fact of Charles' preference for Toleration, therefore, made many moderate churchmen incline to Comprehension; and the swing of the pendulum between the two alternatives affords the clue to much of the complex religious history of his reign.

The first shot in the royal campaign was fired so early as 26 December 1662 by a Declaration, in which Charles, alluding to his promises in the Declaration of Breda and to the re-establishment of the Church of England by the Act of Uniformity, announced his intention to try and persuade Parliament to concur in giving legislative sanction for the exercise of his royal dispensing power. On 7 February following however, the Speaker of the Commons replied that the Declaration of Breda was 'not a promise in itself, but only a gracious declaration of your majesty's intentions to do what in you lay, and what a parliament should advise you to do'. Despite this unpromising overture, a Bill was introduced into the House of Lords to enable the king by letters patent or otherwise to dispense with the Act of Uniformity; but it was lost in committee.[2] During the following summer rumour was busy again with the possibility of Comprehension or Indulgence; and when a Member of Parliament asked Baxter's opinion as to which was preferable, he declared 'for

[1] G. Burnet, *History of My Own Time*, vol. I, p. 307.
[2] D. Ogg, *England in the Reign of Charles II* (2 vols., Oxford, 1934), vol. I, pp. 203–4. F. Bate, *The Declaration of Indulgence, 1672* (1908), pp. 36–9.

the conjunction of both', though liking Comprehension better in principle.[1] Instead the dissenters were greeted by the Conventicle and Five Mile Acts, the latter being by way of riposte to a further Bill concerning the royal dispensing power to be exercised in favour of dissenters both Protestant and papist, introduced into the House of Lords in 1665, which failed to secure committal. Comprehension therefore took the field formally in 1667 when a vigorous pamphlet campaign was opened by *A Proposition for the Safety and Happiness of the King and Kingdom both in Church and State and prevention of the Common Enemy, by way of Accommodation and Indulgence in Matters of Religion*, published on 18 June and ascribed to David Jenkins, a member of the judiciary in Wales, who advocated comprehension for the Presbyterians and indulgence for the Independents. Amongst various replies to this kite-flying, one of Sheldon's chaplains, Thomas Tomkyns, issued *The Inconveniences of Toleration*, and a deprived Presbyterian minister, John Corbet, wrote *A Discourse of the Religion of England, asserting that Reformed Christianity settled in its due Latitude is the Stability and Advancement of this Kingdom*.

These effusions were but the preliminary to a more serious venture, in the shape of a Bill of Comprehension, drawn up by Sir Robert Atkins, a Judge of the Common Pleas and Recorder of Bristol, against the meeting of parliament on 10 October. The Bill was short and restricted in scope. It proposed

that all ministers already ordained whether under episcopal ordination or presbyterian in the late times, and any other hereafter episcopally ordained, being above the age of 23 years, of good life and conversation, and able to answer and render to the Ordinary an account of their faith in Latin, who shall within three months next after publication hereof in the presence of the Bishop of the diocese, or Guardian of the Spiritualties, wherein such person now resides, declare their assent, and subscribe to all the Articles of Religion which only concern the confession of the true Christian faith and the doctrine of the Sacraments mentioned in an Act of Parliament made in the 13 Elizabeth [cap 12],

should be capable of preaching and administering the Sacraments and holding any ecclesiastical benefice, including those with cure of souls; provided that the service of the Book of Common Prayer should be read before the sermon either in person by the said minister or by a Deacon. It was further proposed that the use of the

---

[1] M. Sylvester (ed.), *Reliquiae Baxterianae*, I, II, pp. 430, 433-4.

cross in baptism and the wearing of the surplice by the minister should be optional, and that communicants should be allowed to receive the Sacrament in a posture other than kneeling. Colonel John Birch, M.P. for Penrhyn, undertook to introduce the Bill into the House of Commons, but failed in resolution, though he 'intended it, and once faintly offered at it, but, despairing of success, sate down'. Therefore the proposed measure was never printed and remained only in manuscript. Its proposal to solve the thorny problem of ordination by according equal recognition to episcopal and presbyterian orders was hardly likely to commend itself even to moderate Anglicans, any more than its modified form of assent to the Book of Common Prayer and of subscription to the Articles of Religion.[1]

Accordingly a further attempt was made in February 1668, in response to an overture of the previous month to Baxter and Manton by Sir John Barber, physician to the king, to the effect that the Lord Keeper, Sir Orlando Bridgeman, wished to discuss with them comprehension and toleration. A conference ensued between Dr John Wilkins (shortly to become bishop of Chester) and Mr Hezekiah Burton, the Lord Keeper's chaplain, on the episcopalian side, and Baxter, Manton and Bates on the presbyterian. The basis was to be the Declaration of Breda of 1660, promising 'a liberty to tender consciences and that no man shall be disquieted or called in question for differences of opinion in matter of religion, which do not disturb the peace of the kingdom; and that we shall be ready to consent to such an act of parliament as upon mature deliberation shall be offered to us for the full granting that indulgence'. It was now proposed that this 'might be confirmed in parliament and pass into law'; and to this end two projects, for the Comprehension of Presbyterians and an indulgence to the sectaries respectively, were

[1] Details of the Comprehension projects of 1667–8 are to be found in Bodley B. 14, 15 Linc., a manuscript account in the hand of Thomas Barlow (afterwards bishop of Lincoln). Much of his account is printed in *The Theological Works of Herbert Thorndike* (1854), vol. v, pp. 301–8; and from it Dr John Stoughton compiled his record in *A History of Religion in England*, vol. iii: *The Church of the Restoration* (1911). The Bodleian MSS. was traced and identified by the late Reverend J. W. H. Nankivell in his B. Litt. (Oxford) thesis on 'A Survey of the Attempts at Religious Comprehension in the Church of England during the XVIIth Century, with special reference to the period from the Restoration to the Revolution'. I am indebted to the kindness of Mrs M. Nankivell for permission to see and to use this dissertation, which is now in the Hurd Library, Hartlebury Castle; and to Dr P. C. Moore, Hurd Librarian, for sending me a copy for perusal. Matthew Sylvester's *Reliquiae Baxterianae* adds many illustrative details from the Presbyterian side.

framed to give substance to the declaration, the former being drafted by Sir Matthew Hale, Lord Chief Baron. The proposers had received assurances that the king's speech would contain a recommendation to this effect; and on 10 February 1668 accordingly Charles informed Parliament that 'for the settling of a firm peace, as well at home as abroad, one thing more I hold myself obliged to recommend to you at this present: which is, that you would sincerely think of some course to beget a better union and composure in the mind of my Protestant subjects in matters of Religion'. The House of Commons, however, before the reading of the king's speech, had already, 'upon relation of the insolent carriage and Conventicles of Non-conformists and Sectaries in each county, voted that the king should be desired ...to send out a Proclamation to put the laws against the non-conformists in execution'. When Secretary Morrice conveyed to His Majesty this resolution of the House, Charles replied, promising action, but adding that 'I doubt not you will take the second part of my Speech into consideration'. On 4 March the Commons voted that their whole house, headed by the Speaker, should renew their request to the king. A long and rambling debate on the union of Protestant subjects followed, which was adjourned on various occasions, and on 8 April when the question was put 'that his majesty be desired to send for such persons as he should think fit, to make proposals to him, in order to the uniting of his Protestant subjects', it was negatived by 176 votes to 70.[1] Instead the House passed a Bill for suppressing seditious conventicles—to replace the Conventicle Act of 1664 which had expired—which was sent up to the Lords but failed to complete its course there before the royal prorogation. To Bishop Hacket it seemed that 'for affairs of Parliament referring to the Church, the finger of God is immediately in it, that by your Grace's dexterity the House of Commons have passed such a godly vote'.[2]

Notwithstanding the failure of this Comprehension scheme, it is worth while to consider the contents of Hale's Bill both as representing an agreed compromise between the episcopalian and presbyterian divines and as foreshadowing a good deal of later ecclesiastical diplomacy on the same theme. In regard to the vexed question of presbyterian ordinations—since, as Baxter admitted, 'the great stop

---

[1] W. Cobbett, *Parliamentary History*, vol. IV, pp. 404, 413–22; *Journals of the House of Commons*, vol. IX, pp. 44, 60, 65, 77; F. Bate, *Declaration of Indulgence*, pp. 60–2.
[2] Tanner MSS. 45, f. 288 (4 March 1667/8). Hacket to Sheldon.

in our treaty was about reordination, and Dr Wilkins still insisted on this, that their consciences must be accommodated who took them for no ministers who were ordained without bishops'[1]—it was proposed: that ministers who had received presbyterian ordination during the Interregnum should be admitted to the exercise of the ministerial function by episcopal imposition of hands with the formula, 'Take thou a legal authority to preach the Word of God and to administer the Holy Sacraments in any congregation of the Church of England, where thou shall be lawfully appointed thereunto'. In respect of subscriptions and declarations, in addition to the customary oaths of allegiance and supremacy and the declaration against simony, only one further declaration, couched in general terms, was to be required.

I, A.B., do hereby profess and declare that I do approve the doctrine, worship and government established in the Church of England as concerning all things necessary to salvation; and that I will not endeavour myself, or by any other directly or indirectly, to bring in any doctrine contrary to that which is so established; and I do hereby promise that I will continue in the communion of the Church of England, and I will not do anything to disturb the peace thereof.

The 'nocent ceremonies' were to be optional, and the surplice in parish churches likewise, provided that the minister wore a gown as an alternative; whilst various suggestions were put forward for alterations in the Liturgy. Changes in the Canons of 1603 corresponding to those proposed in the Book of Common Prayer were also specified; whilst in addition, reforms were to be made in the Canons relating to pluralism and ecclesiastical courts, and (which was perhaps of particular interest), it was proposed 'that several things may be added to the Canons out of the Constitutions of 1640, as the 9th Constitution about one book of Articles of Visitations, and the 11, 12 and 13 concerning Chancellors, and the 17th concerning vexatious citations'; and 'that instead of excommunication for small offences, some other penalty may be inflicted'. A Bill of Indulgence for the Sectaries, drawn by Dr John Owen, was also drafted, providing that they

may have liberty for the exercise of their religion in public, and at their own charges to build or procure places for public worship either within or near towns; that the names of all such who are to have this liberty be registered together with the congregation to which they belong and the names of their teachers;

[1] M. Sylvester (ed.), *Reliquiae Baxterianae*, I, III, p. 37.

that persons thus indulged shall not be qualified to bear any public office, but should fine for officers of burden and should pay a fee for their indulgence; and that they should be free from all penalties inflicted for non-attendance at the established church, but should be liable for all parish dues and prohibited from preaching against the established religion. Finally a time limit, suggested at three years, was to be attached to this legal toleration.[1]

In face of the rigid Anglicanism of Parliament, however, the dissenters' hopes turned once again to the royal prerogative; but Charles had been compelled to give way to the Commons because he needed supplies. Not until his agreement with Louis XIV by the secret Treaty of Dover in 1670 could he find relief from dependence upon parliamentary aid, and so venture once more to try out the limits of his prerogative in favour of toleration. In March 1672 he issued his famous Declaration of Indulgence, in which, after promising protection for the Church of England as 'the basis, rule and standard of the general and public worship of God', he proceeded to suspend the execution of all penal laws in matters ecclesiastical in relation both to Protestant and popish dissenters, to announce his intention of issuing licences for Protestant ministers and their places of worship to conduct such worship in public, and finally to grant to papists the right of divine worship in their private houses only. The Declaration was indeed a testing of cannon; for its inclusion of papists provoked the determined opposition of leading Anglican prelates on the one hand, whilst on the other hand it contained evident implications of a constitutional character in its assertion of the king's authority by virtue of his ecclesiastical supremacy to override acts of Parliament. Notwithstanding, the Protestant dissenters resolved to avail themselves of the royal indulgence, having concluded it hopeless to expect clemency from Parliament or the bishops. Led by the London ministers, addresses of thanks poured in from all parts of the kingdom, accompanied by a steady stream of applications for licences from March 1672 to February 1673, and the issue, as has been estimated, of 1508 such licences to preachers.[2] Herein lay the portents of serious danger for the Church of England; for if Protestant dissenters were ready to accept indulgence by royal declaration, notwithstanding the inclusion also of papists and in defiance of the authority of Parliament, that Church might find

[1] Bodley Library B. 14, 15, Linc.; H. Thorndike, *Works* (1854), vol. v, pp. 304-5.
[2] F. Bate, *Declaration of Indulgence*, p. 98.

itself unequal to the task of waging battle on two fronts, and the part of prudence might be the ancient maxim of *divide et impera*. In short, comprehension might be preferable to an universal toleration, and the alliance of the Presbyterians become a necessary defence against Recusants and Sectaries.

As yet, however, these issues lay in the future. The immediate question was that of the reaction of Parliament, especially of the Commons, to Charles' policy. In anticipation of the session, Sheldon summoned all the bishops to attend upon this 'more than ordinary occasion', when he had 'great reason to believe that there is a necessity of raising all the force we can make'.[1] On 5 February 1673 the king put a brave face upon his situation, assuring his Parliament that 'I am resolved to stick to my Declaration'; to which the Commons replied by presenting on the 14th a petition, in which they affirmed 'that penal statues in matters ecclesiastical cannot be suspended but by act of parliament', and requested therefore 'that the said laws may have their free course until it shall be otherwise provided for by act of parliament'. To this on the 24th Charles returned a temporising answer, defending his Declaration and promising 'if any bill shall be offered him which shall appear more proper to attain the aforesaid ends and secure the peace of the Church and Kingdom', to 'concur in all ways that shall appear good for the Kingdom'. Such a soft answer, however, could not turn away the wrath of the Commons; who on the 26th replied by a further petition, reaffirming the illegality of the suspending power claimed by the sovereign and pressing for 'a full and satisfactory answer' to their former address. After further fruitless attempts to engage the Lords on his side against the Commons, Charles gave way, and on 7 March cancelled his Declaration; and after still more considerable delaying tactics on 3 February 1675 an Order in Council recalled all licences issued under the Declaration and commanded the suppression of Conventicles. Furthermore Parliament forced upon the king in 1673 acceptance of the Test Act, which required all office-holders, in addition to the oaths of supremacy and allegiance, to make a declaration against Transubstantiation and to receive the Holy Communion according to the usage of the Church of England. This statute was the retort courteous to Charles' avowed purpose in his Declaration to give toleration to his coreligionists, and its enact-

---

[1] Bate, *Declaration of Indulgence*, pp. 106, 110–11, 115–18, 121–3.

ment signalised the unity of Lords and Commons in opposition to any relief to papists.

In other respects also the episode of the Declaration marked a watershed in the religious history of the reign. Notwithstanding the renewal of persecution after the withdrawal of the royal indulgence, Protestant dissent had received such a fillip as to ensure the eventual failure of a policy of repression. The number of licences issued had revealed the latent strength of Nonconformity; Presbyterian ordinations, not held since the Restoration, had been resumed; and a considerable number of dissenting congregations dated their formation and continuous history from 1672. Furthermore the Commons' debates on the royal declaration had given evidence of a new sentiment in favour of toleration. 'Throughout the debate, few ventured to oppose the principle of religious toleration'; and the historian of the Declaration interpreted this 'as indicative of the continued growth of kindlier feelings towards Protestant Dissenters and of the ease with which Conformists and Nonconformists could be brought to combine against a Roman Catholic domination'.[1] Both these portents were to prove of great importance during the reign of James II. Indeed the desire to afford relief to Protestant dissenters was shown forthwith by the Commons' resolution 'that a Bill be brought in for the ease of his Majesty's Protestant subjects that are dissenters in matters of religion from the Church of England'; and by the series of 'heads and resolves agreed...for the subject matter of the said Bill'. These proposals, accepted by the House on 27 February 1673, provided: that ease should be given to Protestant dissenters who subscribed the Articles of doctrine of the Church of England and took the oaths of allegiance and supremacy; that they should be relieved from all pains and penalties for not coming to church; that the clause in the Act of Uniformity for assent and consent should be repealed; that Nonconformists should be freed from all pains and penalties for meeting together for the performance of religious exercises, provided that all such teachers should give notice to the Quarter Sessions of the place of their meeting, and should themselves subscribe the requisite oaths and declarations; that the doors and passages of all places for public worship should be open and free during the times of meeting; and that the Bill should continue in force for one year, and from thence to the end of the

---

[1] Bate, *Declaration of Indulgence*, pp. 109–10.

next session of Parliament. The Bill received a first reading in the Commons on 6 March, and a third reading on the 19th, when it was sent to the House of Lords.[1] There a series of wrecking amendments were inserted, particularly one giving to the king the right 'to issue out proclamations, if he saw cause, either of liberty or restraint'; which in effect revived the suspending powers so lately denied to the sovereign. Accordingly no agreement had been reached between the two houses when the royal prorogation on 29 March took place.[2] The provisions of the Bill, however, were significantly prophetic of 1689.

From the side of the Anglican episcopate also the events of 1672–3 were of great importance. Sheldon's rallying of the maximum episcopal support in this session of Parliament, though directed primarily against the royal favours to papists, had regard to Protestant dissenters as well. The influence of the bench indeed was thrown heavily against the Bill for the ease of Nonconformists; and Sheldon received the congratulations of his brethren upon its defeat. Bishop Morley was 'very glad in the meantime that the aforesaid Bill miscarried, which would have been an establishment of schism by a law, and that would have been much worse than any connivance, nay than any toleration can be by the king's dispensation or declaration only.... Therefore I am very glad that Bill (if it were such an one as I have heard it was) did not pass.' Archbishop Sterne of York likewise hoped 'the Bill for Indulgence is at an end for this time, and that it will never proceed so far again, if it begin anew'.[3] It was one thing, however, to congratulate Parliament on having done nothing to the prejudice of the church, and another to suppose that matters would rest there. If toleration by royal declaration was to be defeated in Parliament, and a legal indulgence carried in the Commons to be wrecked in the Lords, thanks to the efforts of the bishops with the support of the court party, whence might a solution to the problem be expected?

In these conditions Comprehension once more raised its head. Towards the end of 1673 the earl of Orrery approached Baxter 'to draw him up in brief the terms and means which I thought would satisfy the Nonconformists, so far as to unite us all against popery;

---

[1] *Journals of the House of Commons*, vol. IX, pp. 258–71.

[2] *Journals of the House of Lords*, vol. XII, pp. 579–80. There are two MSS. copies of the Bill, with the Lords' amendments, in Tanner MSS. 43, ff. 189, 191; to the former of which is appended an account of the Commons' disagreements with these amendments.

[3] Tanner MSS. 42, ff. 7 and 46, cited in Bate, *Declaration of Indulgence*, p. 127.

professing that he met with many great men that were much for it, and particularly the new Lord Treasurer, Sir Thomas Osborne, and Dr Morley, Bishop of Winchester, who vehemently professed his desires of it'. Despite assurances from other quarters, also 'testifying the said bishop's resolution herein', Baxter was justifiably sceptical about Morley's good intentions; wishing 'them all to tell him... that he had done so much to the contrary and never anything this way since his professions of that sort, that till his real endeavours convinced men, it would not be believed that he was serious'.[1] In view of Morley's express affirmation to Sheldon on 23 September 1672 that 'I shall quickly make it appear that I am no more a Presbyterian than I am a Popish bishop, though I have been said to be both the one and the other, and indeed as much one as the other', and of his further denunciation of Comprehension on 7 April 1673, there was good ground for Baxter's hesitancy.[2] Either Morley's earlier reputation far outlasted his later conduct or his capacity for dissembling outstripped the sincerity required in a successor of the Apostles. In the present case, when Baxter *more suo* had drawn up a comprehensive statement of his terms for union, they were submitted to Morley for his comments, who prefaced his reply with the observation that he had 'no hope of peace or healing' from their author; and in turn Baxter remarked of Morley's strictures that 'he fully made me see that all his professions for abatement and concord were deceitful snares, and that he intended no such thing at all'.[3]

Notwithstanding this unpromising conclusion, 'some great men of the House of Commons drew up a Bill, as tending to our healing, to take off our oaths, subscriptions and declarations, except the oath of supremacy and allegiance and subscriptions to the doctrine of the Church of England according to the 13. Eliz. But showing it to the said bishop of Winchester, he caused them to forbear and broke it'.[4] Instead, Morley introduced into the House of Lords on 13 February 1674 a Bill 'for composing differences in religion and inviting sober and peaceably-minded Dissenters into the service of the Church'. The measure was confined to the repeal of two clauses of the Act of Uniformity: the second which required an 'unfeigned assent and consent to all and everything contained and prescribed in and by... the Book of Common Prayer', and the sixth which ordered a formal

---

[1] M. Sylvester (ed.), *Reliquiae Baxterianae*, I, III, p. 109.

[2] Tanner MSS. 43, f. 33; 42, f. 7.

[3] M. Sylvester (ed.), *Reliquiae Baxterianae*, I, III, pp. 109, 113.    [4] *Ibid.* p. 140.

renunciation of the Solemn League and Covenant.[1] There was nothing in the Bill which went further than Morley's avowal to Sheldon in the previous year 'that the imprudent subscription to the clause of assent and consent together with the declaration against the Covenant (which must cease ten years hence) might have been taken away now'.[2] It offered little to the Presbyterians to induce them to throw in their lot with the Episcopalians and thereby to desert their fellow-dissenting brethren. Even so, after being read a first time on 13 February, a second time on the 19th and sent to a Committee of the whole House for consideration on the 25th, it disappeared with the royal prorogation of Parliament on the 24th.[3] Moreover the policy of Danby, the king's chief minister, was based upon the close alliance of Crown and church; and in October 1674 Charles summoned the bishops to ask their advice; who, after a series of meetings attended amongst others by Sheldon, Morley, Ward, Crewe and Pearson, recommended the suppression both of popery and of conventicles, the latter particularly by the withdrawal of the preachers' licences issued under the Declaration of 1672, which would remove the last protection of their congregations.[4]

In view of this association, it was the more remarkable that the names of Morley and Ward continued to be pressed upon Baxter, despite his scepticism, as 'the two bishops that were for Comprehension and Concord, none so forward as they'. Not until he was informed, however, that Dean Tillotson of Canterbury and Dr Edward Stillingfleet, prebendary of Newington in St Paul's cathedral were anxious to meet himself and other presbyterian divines 'to treat of an Act of Comprehension and Union', did he consent reluctantly to embark on further discussion. Tillotson assured him that Morley and Ward 'had set them on work', and Baxter accordingly met the two doctors privately, and after several meetings an agreement was reached on a draft, which they desired permission to communicate privately to Bishops Ward of Salisbury and Pearson of Chester (Morley, who was reckoned by Baxter as 'likeliest to frustrate', being out of town). Ward, however, thought the project impracticable; and on 11 April 1675 Tillotson informed Baxter that 'several things could not be obtained'. He continued further that 'I am unwilling my name should be used in this matter;

---

[1] *Hist. MSS. Comm. IXth Report*, part II. Appendix, *House of Lords MSS.*; p. 44b.
[2] Tanner MSS. 42, f. 7.     [3] *Lords Journals*, vol. XII, 636, 644.
[4] Bate, *Declaration of Indulgence*, p. 140.

not but that I do most heartily desire an accommodation, and shall always endeavour it. But I am sure it will be a prejudice to me and signify nothing to the effecting of the thing, which as circumstances are, cannot pass in either house without the concurrence of a considerable part of the bishops and the countenance of his majesty, which at present I see little reason to expect.'[1]

When so impeccable a latitudinarian as Tillotson could write in such despairing terms of Comprehension, it was evident that a majority of the leading Anglican prelates had not yet reached a temper of accommodation. Dr Samuel Parker, one of Sheldon's chaplains (and afterward raised to the see of Oxford by James II) stigmatised any *rapprochement* with the Presbyterians as disloyalty to the Church of England.

Therefore they [the Presbyterians] presently entered into a new conspiracy with some treacherous divines in the English Church, men that liked nothing in the Church but its preferments, in all other respects fanatics.... For now they were pleased to call it a Comprehension.... In this gang were one or two bishops, a few presbyters, with two pragmatical lawyers.... The archbishop, than whom no one was more vigilant or ready to find out their treacherous stratagems, heard of all their counsels from day to day; and I myself have heard him publicly and very sharply reproving them, according to his authority, for their audacious presumption, in that a bishop or two and a few presbyters should attempt to repeal the sacred law of the Church without their Metropolitan and a Synod of their Province.... But the archbishop, being of a mild and generous disposition, threatened nothing, but only exhorted them friendly to acquiesce a little till they should obtain, or at least ask, the consent of himself and his brethren, the bishops.... I remember I was present when a certain bishop solemnly promised entirely to quit this design and attempt nothing further; and yet the very same day, when there was a meeting held for carrying on this affair, to my knowledge he went to the meeting and laboured the point as much as he could.[2]

There can be little difficulty in identifying the two blackamoor bishops—John Wilkins and Herbert Croft. Wilkins, who had married Oliver Cromwell's sister, was raised to the see of Chester in 1668 and Croft had been bishop of Hereford since 1662. When the Lord Lieutenant of Ireland, Lord John Berkeley, praised Wilkins as 'a very rational man' to Bishop Hacket, the latter replied 'that I took him to be a shallow man, both in philosophy and divinity.

[1] M. Sylvester (ed.), *Reliquiae Baxterianae*, I, III, pp. 156–7. T. Birch, *Life of Tillotson* (1753), pp. 43–4.
[2] S. Parker, *History of His Own Time in Four Books* (translated from the Latin by T. Newlin (1727)), pp. 36–7.

I marvel what he with his Comprehensive Bills will say to the name-
less good man that hath printed the small piece at Oxford, called
*Toleration Disapproved* from the pens and testimonies of all his dear
brethren.'[1] High-churchmen like Morley were therefore delighted
when Chester was filled in 1672 by the learned patristic scholar and
editor of Ignatius and Cyprian, John Pearson.[2] Croft published in
1675 *The Naked Truth or the True State of the Primitive Church*,
a persuasive plea for comprehension; and upon an earlier occasion
in the House of Lords,

> out of his zeal to unity in the Church, said that to so good an end as that
> was, he should not only be content to part with any of the ceremonies and
> much more to leave them all as indifferent in their use as they were in their
> nature, but even to dispense with belief in some things in the Creed itself,

such being the 'passionate transport of his zeal for peace in the
Church'. This confession brought down upon his head the wrath
of Morley, who replied that

> I was so far from being of his opinion that all the ceremonies ought to be
> left indifferent in the use of them, to bring in any of our dissenting
> brethren, that I had rather give my vote to the altering or abolishing of
> them all than to the leaving of anyone of them arbitrary or indifferent as
> to the using or not using of it. For this...would be evidently to set up
> and establish a schism by law, and consequently an everlasting bar to
> peace by keeping the partition wall both in doctrine and practice betwixt
> us, and would be made the shibboleth for the godly party (as they call
> themselves) to be known by, and thereby to divide the laity as well as the
> clergy from one another, and consequently make a perpetual faction in the
> state as well as a schism in the church.[3]

To bridge the gulf dividing these standpoints there was need both
of new men and new measures in church and state. The first of these
came with the promotion in 1678 of Sancroft, dean of St Paul's, to
the archbishopric of Canterbury in succession to Sheldon. For
although Sancroft was suspect to Burnet, as one who 'had put on a
monastic strictness' and whose promotion pleased the high-church
party, yet he was of different calibre from his predecessor, and during
his primacy was to show himself a warm friend of members of the
foreign Reformed churches in England and a cordial advocate of
comprehension at home. Events likewise conspired to enforce the
moral of the ecclesiastical situation, as the Exclusion controversy and

---

[1] Tanner MSS. 44, f. 196 (Hacket to Sheldon, 23 April 1670). *S.T.C.* I, no. 4047,
lists this pamphlet as from the pen of William Assheton.
[2] *Ibid.* 43, f. 33.        [3] *Ibid.* 42, f. 7.

the popish plot emphasised the growing crisis. In 1680 indeed the House of Commons revived the idea of comprehension, resolving on 3 November to bring in a 'Bill for the better uniting of His Majesty's Protestant Subjects', and referring the matter to a committee which on the 18th agreed on the heads to be embodied in the 'Bill for Uniting His Majesty's Protestant Subjects to the Church of England'. The measure proposed to recognise and accept presbyterian orders conferred during the Interregnum, to accept subscription only to the doctrinal articles of the Thirty-Nine Articles, to allow the nocent ceremonies to be optional and the use of the gown instead of the surplice in parish churches, and to omit the oath of canonical obedience and that against the Solemn League and Covenant. But although the Bill received a first reading on 16 December and a second on the 21st, it disappeared with the royal prorogation on 18 January 1681, as did a parallel measure in the House of Lords; and when the Commons resumed consideration of the matter at Oxford on 26 March 1681, once again prorogation put an end to its progress.[1]

The accession of James II, however, and the policy he pursued in religious affairs soon brought comprehension to the fore again. With the Declarations of Indulgence of 1687 and 1688, Sancroft realised the perilous position of the Church of England, openly attacked by the papists with the support of the Crown, yet threatened by the possibility of the willingness of dissenters to accept toleration at the hands even of James II, if nothing could be secured from the church and Parliament. Moreover the Roman Catholic assault narrowed the differences between Anglican and Presbyterian, and suggested the serious consideration of Comprehension as a matter alike of policy and of practical urgency. Accordingly in their Petition to James II refusing to read his Declaration of Indulgence, the bishops specifically exculpated themselves

from any want of due tenderness to Dissenters, in relation to whom they are willing to come to such a temper, as shall be thought fit, when that matter shall be considered and settled in parliament and convocation;

whilst Sancroft in his *Articles to all the Bishops within his Metropolitan Jurisdiction* further enjoined the clergy to

have a very tender regard to our brethren, the Protestant Dissenters,...
and that they warmly and most affectionately exhort them to join with us
in daily fervent prayer to the God of peace, for an universal blessed union

---

[1] *Commons Journals*, vol. IX, pp. 645, 681, 687, 711; *Lords Journals*, vol. II, pp. 694, 711–12, 714.

of all reformed churches, both at home and abroad, against our common enemies; that all they, who do confess the holy name of our dear Lord and do agree in the truth of his holy word, may also meet in one holy communion, and live in perfect unity and godly love.[1]

Nor did the primate stop short at pious professions. Rather he took practical steps to set on foot concrete projects for comprehension. As Wake testified in his speech in the House of Lords in 1710 at the impeachment of Sacheverell, who had aspersed comprehension as a 'popular engine...to pull down the Church',

the person who first concerted this supposed design against our Church, was the late Most Reverend Dr Sancroft, then Archbishop of Canterbury. The time was towards the end of that unhappy reign;...when we were in the height of our labours, defending the Church of England against the assaults of Popery and thought of nothing else, that wise prelate, foreseeing some such revolution as soon after was happily brought about, began to consider how utterly unprepared they had been at the restoration of King Charles II to settle many things to the advantage of the Church; and what a happy opportunity had been lost for want of such a previous care, as he was therefore desirous should now be taken, for the better and more perfect establishment of it. It was visible to all the nation, that the more moderate Dissenters were generally so well satisfied with that stand which our divines had made against popery, and the many unanswerable treatises they had published in confutation of it, as to express an unusual readiness to come in to us. And it was therefore thought worth the while, when they were deliberating about those other matters, to consider at the same time, what might be done to gain them without doing any prejudice to ourselves. The scheme was laid out, and the several parts of it were committed, not only with the approbation, but by the direction of that great prelate, to such of our divines as were thought the most proper to be entrusted with it. His Grace took one part to himself....The design was in short this: to improve, and, if possible, to enforce our discipline; to review and enlarge our Liturgy, by correcting of some things, by adding of others; and, if it should be thought advisable by authority, when this matter came to be legally considered, first in Convocation, then in Parliament, by leaving some few ceremonies, confessed to be indifferent in their natures, as indifferent in their usage, so as not to be necessarily observed by those who made a scruple of them, till they should be able to overcome either their weaknesses or prejudices, and be willing to comply with them.

In support of his argument Wake appealed to the statement in the petition of the bishops relating to the dissenters, which 'manifestly referred to what was then known to several, if not all, the subscribers, to have been at that very time under deliberation'.[2]

---

[1] E. Cardwell, *Documentary Annals*, vol. II, clxiv–v, pp. 368, 375–6.

[2] *The Bishop of Lincoln's and Bishop of Norwich's Speeches in the House of Lords at the opening of the Second Article of the Impeachment of Dr Sacheverell* (1710), pp. 4–5.

Brother George Every has shown convincingly that in 1688 Comprehension was a high-church policy.[1] Such was the conversion wrought in the leaders of this party by the actions of James II. Perhaps the most conclusive of contemporary evidences of the changed ecclesiastical atmosphere since the unqualified denunciation of Comprehension by Morley (who had died in 1684), may be gathered from the testimony of John Kettlewell, himself a Non-juror.

Concerning this matter, there are different accounts given, according as the parties relating the same are differently interested. Truth, which is generally in the midst, seems to be so here. As the Church of England never pretended to infallibility, there could not be wanting a pretence for such a review at this time. And as even that Church which asserts herself infallible, is not thereby so tied down against all alteration, as to reject a reformation of discipline or even new Orders and Constitutions for the use of certain of its members, this pretence was much stronger.[2]

With Sancroft as principal author of the scheme and Kettlewell bestowing his blessing in principle, the prospect seemed bright for the fulfilment of the hopes of Prideaux that

all our Offices might have been rendered so complete, perfect and un-exceptionable, that not only many of the Dissenters amongst us, but also foreign Churches of the Protestant Communion, might have been per-suaded to introduce them into their public religious assemblies, and unite in the same form of worship as well as in the same faith with us.[3]

Meanwhile, as Kettlewell's account related,

there were several consults at Lambeth upon this subject, and certain articles were drawn up for the better securing and strengthening of the Protestant Interest and Religion and for making the Church of England the head of that Interest; which were communicated to some of the chiefs among the Protestant Dissenters for their approbation.

It was, therefore, a tragic stroke of ill-fortune which deprived the church of the leadership of Sancroft and others of his episcopal brethren, owing to their conscientious inability to take the oaths to the new sovereigns, at the moment when the realisation of their project seemed within sight. But although the primate would take no step which implied recognition of William and Mary, he did not withdraw his support for Comprehension. When Clarendon and

---

[1] G. Every, *The High Church Party, 1688–1718* (1956), ch. 2.
[2] *A Complete Collection of the Works of John Kettlewell, with his Life* (ed. G. Hickes and R. Nelson, 1719), vol. I, p. 53.
[3] *Life of Prideaux*, p. 61.

Thomas Tenison dined with him at Lambeth on 3 January 1689, they introduced the question

of the approaching Convention and whether he would not think of preparing something against that time on behalf of the Dissenters. Dr Tenison added, it would be expected something would be offered in pursuance of the petition which the seven bishops had presented to the king, for which they had been put into the Tower. The archbishop said he knew well what was in the petition, and he believed every bishop in England intended to make it good, when there was an opportunity of debating these matters in Convocation; but until then, or without a commission from the king, it was highly penal to enter upon church matters. But however he would have it in his mind, and would be willing to discourse to the bishops or other clergy thereupon, if they came to him.

The conversation ended with a further assurance by Sancroft 'that when there was a Convocation, those matters would be considered of; and in the meantime he knew not what to say, but that he would think of what had been offered by us'.[1] On 14 January there was a meeting at the deanery of St Paul's attended by Bishop Lloyd of St Asaph, Deans Stillingfleet of St Paul's, Tillotson of Canterbury, Sharp of Norwich, Simon Patrick of Peterborough, and Dr Tenison,

to consult about such concessions as might bring in Dissenters to our communion. For which the bishop of St Asaph told us he had the archbishop of Canterbury's leave. We agreed that a bill should be prepared to be offered by the bishops, and we drew up the matter of it in ten or eleven heads.[2]

Further conferences between the earl of Nottingham and sundry bishops led to the introduction of a Comprehension Bill into the House of Lords on 11 March. That the measure still enjoyed the cordial support of high-churchmen was admitted by Burnet in the first draft of his *History*, where he observed of the accompanying Bill for Toleration that 'this act was both penned and first offered in the house of lords by Nottingham, who, notwithstanding his zeal for the church had been always both for toleration and comprehension'. Further,

at the same time that the Toleration was proposed to both houses, the bishops who resolved to adhere to King James' interest, moved before they left the house of Lords that heads of a comprehension might likewise be considered for taking in the presbyterians.[3]

---

[1] *Diary and Correspondence of Henry, Earl of Clarendon* (1828), vol. II, p. 240, cited in S. Patrick, *Works*, vol. IX, p. 516; and in G. Every, *High Church Party, 1688–1718*, pp. 27–8.    [2] S. Patrick, Autobiography, in *Works*, (1858), vol. IX, p. 516.

[3] H. C. Foxcroft, *A Supplement to Burnet's History*, p. 317; cf. Burnet, *History of My Own Time*, vol. IV, p. 10.

Indeed during the committee stage several bishops, including some Non-jurors,—particularly White of Peterborough and Turner of Ely—spoke 'very earnestly' in behalf of Comprehension.[1] In principle therefore it was still a high-church project.

The full import of the withdrawal of Sancroft and his Non-juring brethren from all participation in the ecclesiastical measures of the Revolution settlement became evident, however, in the proceedings of the Royal Commission appointed to prepare a Comprehension scheme for the consideration of Convocation and Parliament. Not only did their absence deprive the commission of its natural and authoritative leadership, but it also encouraged several of the members in turn to dissociate themselves from the business. The personnel of the commission embraced the archbishop of York, the bishops of London, Winchester, St Asaph, Rochester, Carlisle, Exeter, Salisbury, Bangor and Chester, together with twenty of the inferior clergy, including the deans of St Paul's, Peterborough, Canterbury, Norwich, Winchester and Christ Church, the Master of Trinity College, Cambridge and the regius professors of Divinity in both universities. The first meeting was attended probably by twenty-four divines; but amongst the absentees were Archbishop Lamplugh of York, and Bishops Trelawny of Exeter and Smith of Carlisle, who never attended any session. Further secessions followed shortly; when Sprat of Rochester at the second meeting expressed doubts concerning the legality of the commission and whether obedience to it did not run the risk of a *praemunire*, to which Dr Jane, dean of Gloucester and regius professor at Oxford, assented; and at the third meeting Sprat absented himself, whilst Bishop Mews of Winchester, Deans Aldrich of Christ Church and Jane went out so soon as the commissioners began to discuss the 'nocent ceremonies'. The leadership fell to Bishop Compton of London and Dean Tillotson; and thanks to their resolution and perseverance a report was drawn up. Brother Every has given his opinion that 'the final choice of divines for commissioners is a credit to the honest desire of the government to give fair representation not only to all kinds of clergy, but to all parties in the Church of England', supporting this by a careful analysis of their personnel; and he has further stated that 'we may doubt if the recommendations of the commission differed on any point of importance from those which would have been made if the Higher Churchmen had pulled

[1] G. Every, *The High Church Party*, p. 35.

their weight'.[1] The fatal weakness, however, lay in the absence of
Sancroft, and to a lesser degree of Lamplugh of York. The latter
indeed was important solely *officii virtute*; but Sancroft's defection
together with that of his fellow Non-juring bishops inflicted a mortal
wound on the commission and its proceedings. It was the heaviest
blow to befall the church that, when presented with a second chance
to revise its Liturgy and Canons and to repair the omissions of the
Restoration, the indispensable leadership and authority were lacking.
From this standpoint the Non-juring secession was a disaster difficult to exaggerate and overestimate.

Since the detailed proposals of the commission did not reach the
stage of debate in Convocation, consideration of their character
must remain an academic exercise. It may be observed, however,
that conditional reordination was proposed as the solution of the
problem of presbyterian orders; the nocent ceremonies and the
wearing of the surplice were to be dispensed with in cases of conscientious scruple, and clerical subscriptions and declarations were
to be reduced in number and simplified in content; and further, the
commissioners embarked on a thoroughgoing revision of the Book
of Common Prayer. Brother Every has argued 'that the commission
would have been better advised if, instead of discussing liturgical
reform in detail, they had contented themselves with trying to put
the concessions contained in the Comprehension Bill into an acceptable form', thereby embodying the minimal changes to be offered
in order to induce moderate Presbyterians to return to the church.
His contention that 'liturgical revision offered a serious prospect of
a schism about liturgies, instead of about the succession to Canterbury and five other sees, [since] liturgical conservatism would be a
powerful weapon in the hands of the Non-Jurors', carried the concurrence of Burnet, looking back upon the events of 1689.

There was a very happy direction of the providence of God observed in
this matter. The Jacobite clergy, who were then under suspension, were
designing to make a schism in the church, whensoever they should be
turned out and their places should be filled up by others. They saw it
would not be easy to make a separation upon a private account; they therefore wished to be furnished with more specious pretences; and, if we had
made alterations in the Rubrics and other parts of the Common Prayer,
they would have pretended that they still stuck to the ancient Church of
England, in opposition to those who were altering it and setting up new
models; and, as I do firmly believe that there is a wise Providence that

[1] G. Every, *The High Church Party*, pp. 43, 46–7.

watches upon human affairs and directs them, chiefly those that relate to religion; so I have with great pleasure observed this in many instances relating to the Revolution. And upon this occasion, I could not but see that the Jacobites among us, who wished and hoped that we should have made those alterations, which they reckoned would have been of great advantage for serving their ends, were the instruments of raising such a clamour against them, as prevented their being made. For by all the judgments we could afterwards make, if we had carried a majority in the Convocation for alterations, they would have done us more hurt than good.[1]

Against this standpoint, however, must be set the loss of the last opportunity for revising the Prayer Book and Canons, thanks to the desuetude of sitting Convocations resulting from the fiasco of 1689. Certainly the defection of Sancroft and his Non-juring brethren had put an end to hopes of Comprehension, For, although consideration of the subject might be revived more than half a century later in amicable discussions between Doddridge and Chandler from the Dissenters' side and archbishops Herring and Secker and bishop Sherlock on the Anglican side, nothing was done even to try the experiment once more. Herring was by nature pusillanimous and timorous; and whilst regarding Comprehension as 'a very good thing', which he 'wished with all his heart', and even believing 'this was a proper time to make the attempt', he took no steps to carry the matter further. Secker likewise though heartily 'wishing that such things as we think indifferent and you cannot be brought to think lawful, were altered or left free in such a manner that we might all unite', and having 'no reason to believe that any one of the bishops wishes otherwise,...and some wish it strongly,...nor perhaps were the body of the clergy ever so well disposed to it as now', concluded by saying that 'still I see not the least prospect of it'.[2] Comprehension indeed faded out of the realm of practical politics with the Non-juror schism and the consequent inaction of Convocation in 1689.

Attention must be turned therefore to the other measure introduced into the convention parliament, simultaneously with that of comprehension, namely the Toleration Bill. This Bill 'for exempting their Majesties' Protestant Subjects dissenting from the Church of

---

[1] G. Every, *High Church Party*, p. 56; G. Burnet, *History of My Own Time*, vol. IV, pp. 58–9.

[2] N. Sykes, 'Ecumenical Movements in Great Britain in the XVIIth and XVIIIth Centuries', in R. Rouse and S. C. Neill, *A History of the Ecumenical Movement* (London, 1954), pp. 162–4.

England from the penalties of certain Laws' was sponsored likewise by Nottingham; and had a surprisingly swift passage into law. Introduced into the House of Lords on 11 March, it reached the Commons on 18 April and received the royal assent on 24 May. 'The bill of toleration passed easily'; as Burnet noted, 'there was now an universal inclination to pass the act; but it could not be expected that the nation would be in the same good disposition towards them at another time.... It seemed to be suitable, both to the spirit of the Christian religion and to the interest of the nation'.[1] But Macaulay observed significantly that the Comprehension Bill 'was indeed a neater specimen of legislative workmanship than the Toleration Bill'.[2] Nor did the contents of the Indulgence belie its chilling title, from which indeed Sacheverell at his impeachment was to deduce 'that upon diligent enquiry he had not been able to inform himself, that a toleration hath been granted by law'.[3] If its superscription was negative, its provisions were niggardly. It granted freedom of public worship and legal protection to the persons and property of those taking part therein, to orthodox, that is Trinitarian, Protestant dissenters; whose places of meeting must be registered either in the ecclesiastical courts or with the justices of the peace; whose assemblies for divine service must be held with open doors; and whose ministers had subscribed the doctrinal articles of the Thirty-Nine Articles of Religion and taken the oath of allegiance and the declaration against Transubstantiation. Special provision was made for Baptists not to subscribe Article 27 concerning infant baptism, and for Quakers to substitute an affirmation for the oath and to profess their belief in the doctrine of the Trinity and the divine inspiration of the Scriptures; whilst a specific clause excluded from the benefits of the Act both papists and anti-Trinitarians. A proposal to attach a time limit of seven years to the measure failed to obtain a majority in the Commons; for though 'some proposed that the act should be only temporary, as a necessary restraint upon the Dissenters, that they might demean themselves so as to merit the continuance of it, when the term of years now offered should end, this was rejected'.[4] It may be conjectured that the speedy passing of the Toleration Bill into law and the lack of

---

[1] G. Burnet, *History of My Own Time*, vol. IV, pp. 16–17, 21.
[2] T. B. Macaulay, *History of England* (ed. C. H. Firth, 1913), vol. III, p. 1394.
[3] *The Tryal of Dr Henry Sacheverell* (Dublin 1710), p. 9.
[4] G. Burnet, *History of My Own Time*, vol. IV, p. 16.

careful scrutiny of its detailed drafting were due to the greater importance attached by contemporaries to the Comprehension measure. If this latter Bill had ben enacted, the number of dissenters to whom the indulgence applied, would have been comparatively small, and their existence would have constituted no serious threat to an established church embracing both Presbyterians and Episcopalians. Indeed as Macaulay further observed, 'the Church was but too well able to hold her own against all the sects in the kingdom; and if those sects were to be thinned by a large desertion and the Church strengthened by a large reinforcement, it was plain that all chance of obtaining any relaxation of the Test Act would be at an end; and it was but too probable that the Toleration Act might not long remain unrepealed'.[1]

With the failure of Comprehension, however, and the consequent coalescence of the numerous and important body of Presbyterians with the other Protestant dissenters outside the established church, the Toleration Act assumed a new and growing significance. The leaders of the Church of England had now to adapt themselves to the legal recognition of organised dissent; and their disquiet increased as the strength of this element in the religious and ecclesiastical life of the nation became evident. During the first year after the passing of the Toleration Act 796 temporary and 143 permanent places of dissenting worship were registered, exclusive of the Quakers; whilst during the decade 1691–1700 the numbers rose to 1247 temporary and thirty-two permanent, and during the following decade to 1710 there were registered 1216 temporary and forty-one permanent meeting-houses.[2] The very magnitude of these figures inspired alarm amongst Episcopalians; whilst the indirect effects of the indulgence were seen in such reports as that of Wake at Lincoln in 1715 that 'if any persons be admonished to come to the Holy Communion, or threatened for that or any other neglect, they presently cry they will go to the meetings to avoid discipline'; from which he concluded that 'the canons should be revised and fitted better to the toleration, if that must be continued'.[3]

There lay the rub. *Must* the Toleration be continued? The fact that the issue could be canvassed, indicated a growing apprehension

[1] T. B. Macaulay, *History of England*, vol. III, p. 1399.
[2] E. D. Bebb, *Nonconformity and Social and Economic Life, 1660–1800* (1935), appendix I, p. 17.
[3] N. Sykes, *William Wake*, vol. I, pp. 199–200.

amongst the episcopate of the consequences of the indulgence. Most particularly criticism was directed against the dissenting academies and against the custom of occasional conformity. Thanks on the one hand to the ejection of so many ministers in 1662 and on the other hand to the virtual exclusion of dissenters from the universities of Oxford and Cambridge by the requirement of subscription to the Thirty-Nine Articles, in the former at matriculation and in the latter on graduation, the dissenting academies came into existence to provide both a theological training for ministers and a higher education for the sons of dissenting parents intending to enter the learned professions. Their history has been written too often to need recapitulation;[1] and it may suffice to mention that, whereas in 1689 they numbered about a score, after the passing of the Toleration Act they multiplied rapidly, and from being individual and private ventures became a kind of joint-stock enterprise by the establishment in 1689 of the Presbyterian Fund, followed in 1695 by the Congregational Fund and in 1705 by the Lady Hewley Fund to provide bursaries for candidates for the dissenting ministry. Accordingly the academies became the object of hostile attention on the part of Episcopalians. That of Richard Frankland, a graduate of Christ's College, Cambridge, set up at Rathmell in 1670 (and enjoying the distinction of being the first academy in the north of England), had suffered many migrations, before returning to its original home in 1689. By 1695 it mustered eighty students, and during the years from 1690–6 the Presbyterian Fund alone supported twenty-six students there. As early as September 1690 Frankland was cited by some clergymen of the rural deanery of Craven to appear in the archiepiscopal court at York for 'contempt of the law and jurisdiction of the court in teaching youth at Rathmell without licence of the Ordinary'. On 24 October he was excommunicated, and on 8 February 1691 his excommunication was formally published in Giggleswick church. The intervention of powerful friends at the court of William and Mary, notably Lord Wharton and Sir Thomas Rokesby, secured a royal order for his absolution from the sentence of excommunication and for the publication of this order likewise in the parish church at Giggleswick. After a short time, however, Frankland was again presented in 1692; and Archbishop Sharp of York, prudently

---

[1] H. McLachlan, *English Education under the Test Acts* (Manchester, 1931); Irene Parker, *Dissenting Academies in England* (Cambridge, 1914); O. M. Griffiths *Religion and Learning* (Cambridge, 1935).

reporting the case to the Justices of the Peace at Wakefield, confirmed that Frankland had not sought his archiepiscopal licence. At the same time Sharp conferred with Tillotson on the delicate matter of appropriate action; and the latter advised him to assure Frankland that, whilst 'you would never do anything to infringe the act of toleration, but did not think his case came within it', nevertheless 'his instructing of young men in so public a manner in university learning, is contrary to his oath to do, if he have taken a degree in either of our universities,...so that your grace does not in this matter consider him at all as a Dissenter'. It was a diplomatic, if perhaps somewhat unworthy, *ruse de guerre* to invoke the Stamford Oath of 1334, by which graduates bound themselves not to lecture *tamquam in universitate* outside Oxford and Cambridge, in order to avoid the appearance of violating the Toleration Act. The matter was settled amicably in two interviews between Sharp and Frankland, at Skipton and Bishopthorpe respectively; in which the archbishop 'began at first to be somewhat hot', but finally 'did much yield to and comply with what I said to him'; and on the second occasion, though Frankland declined an invitation to dinner, yet 'I must view his library, take a pipe of tobacco with him and drink some of his wine bottles'.[1] At any rate Sharp twice quashed further indictments against Frankland in 1695 and 1697. A similar case was that of Dr Joshua Oldfield, a graduate both of Lincoln College, Oxford, and of Christ's College, Cambridge, and a friend of Locke and Newton, who was cited in October 1697 before the court of the bishop of Lichfield and Coventry, appealed therefrom to the court of King's Bench; and after considerable delay secured a prohibition to prevent the ecclesiastical court from further proceedings in the matter, together with an intimation of the displeasure of William III at such prosecutions.

It was evident indeed that the education of dissenting ministers involved the perpetuation of dissenting congregations; and that without such a provision dissent would be greatly diminished, if not altogether extinguished. When therefore the rule of the Dutch and Calvinist William III gave place to that of the wholly English and Anglican Anne, another face of things was quickly seen. In 1702 the Lower House of Canterbury Convocation included in their representation to the Upper House a complaint, 'that the suffering

[1] T. Birch, *Life of Tillotson*, pp. 269–72; *Diary and Correspondence of Ralph Thoresby* (ed. J. Hunter 1832), vol. III, pp. 172–8.

of persons to instruct youth as tutors or schoolmasters, without such licence from the ordinary as is required by the act of uniformity and the 77th canon, hath given great occasion to several ignorant and disaffected persons to erect seminaries, wherein not only academical learning is pretended to be taught, to the prejudice of the two universities; but also, as we are informed and persuaded, such principles are also instilled into youth, as tend to perpetuate the schism we now labour under and to subvert the established constitution'. Accordingly the lower clergy concluded by emphasising 'how the numbers of unlicensed schools and seminaries are multiplied, and the danger arising from their daily increase', and by stating 'their duty at this time most earnestly to beseech your lordships that you would please to use your authority and interest for the suppressing such seminaries'.[1] In the debate in the House of Lords on 'the church in danger' in 1705, Sharp affirmed that 'he apprehended danger from the increase of dissenters, and particularly from the many academies set up by them; and moved that the judges ought to be consulted what laws were in force against such seminaries and by what means they might be suppressed'.[2]

It was not surprising that sentiments discreetly uttered in the House of Lords or conveyed in messages between the two houses of convocation in Henry VII's chapel and the Jerusalem chamber of Westminster Abbey respectively, should be proclaimed from the housetops in less restrained quarters. In the dedication to Queen Anne of the second volume of Clarendon's *History of the Great Rebellion*, published in 1702, it was asked: 'What can be the meaning of the several seminaries and, as it were, universities, set up in divers parts of the kingdom, by more than ordinary industry, contrary to law, supported by large contributions, where youth is bred up in principles directly contrary to monarchical and episcopal government?' Again, in the following year, in the preface to the third volume, the dissenting academies were referred to as institutions 'where the fiercest doctrines against monarchical and episcopal government are taught and propagated, and where they bear an implacable hatred to your majesty's title, name, and family'.[3] Not to be outdone, Sacheverell at his impeachment openly avowed that in his offending sermon he 'had in his eye some abuses' of the Toleration Act, 'by the dis-

---

[1] E. Cardwell, *Synodalia*, vol. II, pp. 712–13, 718.
[2] T. Sharp, *Life of John Sharp, Archbishop of York* (1828), vol. I, pp. 363–4.
[3] Clarendon, *History*, vol. II, pt I, p. vi; vol. III, pt I, p. xvii.

senters themselves; who...erect seminaries for educating youth in principles opposite to the doctrine, discipline and worship of our church; whereas that act was intended for the ease of those whose minds through the unhappy prejudices of education, were already estranged from the Church; not, as he humbly conceived, to indulge men in the most effective methods to propagate and perpetuate their schism'.[1]

The veiled menace in this statement became overt by the introduction into the House of Commons in 1714 of a Bill 'to prevent the growth of schism, and for the further security of the Churches of England and Ireland', usually known as the Schism Act. It required all schoolmasters and teachers to hold an episcopal licence, which could be granted only after production of a certificate of the applicant's having received the Sacrament according to the Church of England within a year before; and if any such applicant should afterwards resort to any conventicle, he should be disqualified from keeping or teaching in any school. In all schools the Catechism of the Book of Common Prayer must be taught; but exemptions were provided for tutors in noble families, members of the foreign Reformed churches teaching only the children of aliens, and all who teach 'reading, writing, arithmetic or any part of mathematical learning only, so far as such mathematical learning relates to navigation or any mechanical art' and is given in the English tongue. The dissenters were not slow to recognise that this measure laid the axe to the root of the tree of their entire education; and accordingly exerted their utmost efforts to petition members of parliament to vote for its rejection. When it was carried in the House of Commons by 237 votes to 167, Edmund Calamy 'sat up all night, the very night before the bill came into the house of lords', to draw up a series of 'Queries humbly proposed to my lords the bishops upon the bill now depending in the house of peers, to prevent (as is pleaded) the growth of schism'. The London dissenters met on three several days to discuss what could be done to protect their interests; and resolved to appeal to Harley, who was, together with St John, an alumnus of the Dissenting Academy at Sheriffhales—but without avail. In the Lords, however, the bill was carried by the narrow margin of 79 votes to 72, and five bishops, Wake of Lincoln, Moore of Ely, Evans of Bangor, Tyler of Llandaff and Fleetwood of St Asaph, signed a formal protest against its passing. Even at this late stage in

[1] *The Tryal of Dr Henry Sacheverell*, pp. 234–5.

its progress, some leading London citizens were so alarmed as to determine to petition the queen for the exercise of her veto; but Calamy divulged their intention to Sunderland, who immediately summoned the would-be petitioners to the Painted Chamber of the House of Lords, and there in the names of Townshend and himself begged them to desist. 'What was proposed', he said,

was the falsest step that could be taken; the queen was most heartily engaged in this bill from the beginning; and therefore now, at last, to address her to put a negative on it, was perfectly ridiculous; our moving for a negative from the throne to a bill that had passed the two houses, was a stabbing the whiggish cause to the heart, and would expose us to such reflections as we could never be able to bear or wipe off. By such a step, we should do the whig lords the greatest mischief, and discourage others from ever appearing or acting as our friends.[1]

The deputation was dutifully persuaded, and providence intervened to save the dissenting interest; for the day on which the act was to come into operation was that of the queen's death, and so it remained a dead letter.

The second vulnerable joint in the dissenters' armour was their exclusion by the Test and Corporation Acts from office under the Crown and in Corporations, save by the expedient of occasional communion with the Church of England. Of the origins and character of occasional conformity as a purely religious practice without any political reference, the statements of Calamy and other dissenters to Burnet in 1702 left no room for doubt.

We told his lordship, that the communicating with the Church of England was no new practice among the Dissenters, nor of a late date, but had been used by some of the most eminent of our ministers ever since 1662, with a design to show their charity towards that Church, notwithstanding they apprehended themselves bound in conscience ordinarily to separate from it; and that it had been also practised by a number of the most understanding people among them, before the so doing was necessary to qualify for a place. We reminded him that Mr Baxter and Dr Bates had done it all along.[2]

It seems probable that the adoption of the reception of the Sacrament according to the Church of England as a test for public service, was based upon knowledge of the existing practice of leading Presbyterians, which was accepted thereby as a means of differentiating

---

[1] Edmund Calamy, *An Historical Account of My Own Life*, ed. J. T. Rutt (1829), vol. II, pp. 282–7.
[2] *Ibid.* vol. I, p. 473.

between them and the sectaries whose principles were irrevocably opposed to the national church. For, as John Howe argued,

though to that former sort of communion, there hath for many years bypast been superadded the accidental consideration of a place or office attainable hereby, no man can allow himself to think, that what he before counted lawful is by this supervening consideration become unlawful.[1]

Nevertheless, shortly after the accession of Anne, a sermon at Oxford by the redoubtable Sacheverell summoned the defenders of the church to battle on this issue; and an Occasional Conformity Bill made its appearance in the House of Commons in November 1702. It provided that all officers or freemen in corporations (not only those 'having employment relating to or concerning the government' of corporations, but also inferior officers), who attended a conventicle after having qualified for office by receiving the Sacrament in the Church of England, should be disabled from all such employment, fined £100 plus £5 for each day of their continuance in such employment, and be incapacitated from further employment until they had conformed to the established church for a whole year. The Bill, having passed by large majorities, was sent to the Lords on 2 December; where a series of wrecking amendments were inserted; and finally the Lords rejected the measure by a single vote and even approved the innovation of publishing an account of their proceedings. Despite this initial setback, the Bill reappeared in the autumn of 1703, though with a reduction of the pecuniary penalty to £50, and a raising of the number of persons allowed to gather with a family for dissenting worship without constituting a conventicle from five to twelve. The Commons gave it a third reading on 7 December by 223 votes to 140; but in the Lords it was rejected on 14 December at the second reading by twelve votes. A further attempt in the following year to tack the measure to a money Bill likewise failed; after which, thanks to the exigencies of the war of the Spanish Succession, occasional conformity slumbered till 1711, when a third Bill had an easy passage through the House of Commons, followed by an equally rapid and uncontroversial transit through the Lords as a result of a bargain between Nottingham and the Whigs. Calamy indeed was convinced as regards the dissenters that the Whigs 'made a sacrifice of them by agreement, thinking a time might come to relieve them afterwards without any hazard'; and

[1] R. F. Horton, *John Howe*, p. 83; *Diary and Correspondence of Ralph Thoresby*, vol. III, p. 320.

he added the comment: 'whether they were not herein overreached and outwitted, and whether the damage they did in this way to the common interest, did not overbalance the good they thereby did the nation, posterity must and will be judges'. In any event when the dissenters approached their friends in both Houses of Parliament on the matter, they received cold comfort. 'The agreement was made', they were told; 'and there was no going back; it was the only way to prevent the Peace; and we should be relieved in some other way; these were the most favourable answers we could obtain from such as we thought we might have expected the most from.'[1]

The Occasional Conformity Act of 1711, professing its objective as 'An Act for preserving the Protestant Religion by better securing the Church of England as by law established, and for confirming the toleration granted to Protestant Dissenters', provided: that all office-holders under the Crown and in Corporations who received the Sacrament according to the order of the Church of England and sub-sequently attended a conventicle, should be fined £40 and be rendered incapable 'to bear any office or employment whatsoever'; and that in order to requalify for office, the offender must conform to the established church for one year without attending a conventicle, and receive the holy communion three times in that year. At the same time the statute declared that the Toleration Act 'shall be, and is hereby ratified and confirmed, and that the same act shall at all times be inviolably observed'. It was natural that the dissenters should not so interpret a measure which offered them the harsh alternatives of religious apostasy or exclusion from public life. Two London aldermen, Sir Thomas Abney and Sir John Frazer, conferred with several provincial mayors and justices of the peace as to which alternative they should adopt. Their so-called political friends (despite their recent betrayal of the dissenting interest) advised compliance with the law; and they were seconded by the Resident of the Elector of Brunswick, who emphasised the importance attached by the House of Hanover to 'their continuance in their posts and stations'. The Whig politicians added—for what they were worth—'strong assurances of earnest endeavours of relief to this and other hardships, whenever the Protestant Succession should come to take place'. Thus the dissenters were induced to retain their offices and to accept 'that restrained way of worship the law allowed', to wit, the addition of ten persons to a family for private dissenting

---

[1] E. Calamy, *Historical Account of My Own Life*, vol. II, pp. 243–4.

worship.[1] In this condition, for example, Isaac Watts lived and preached for the next seven years in the household of Sir Thomas Abney. But there could be no doubt of the severe assault carried against the strength of the dissenting interest by the Occasional Conformity and Schism Acts.

From the side of the Church of England also the episode was of considerable significance. Not only had 1688 proved a decisive watershed in its internal history, thanks to the Non-juring schism, but the quarter of a century which followed saw a further dividing of the forces within its communion which had accepted the Revolution settlement in the state. The failure of comprehension and the enactment of toleration produced a deep division between those churchmen who regarded the Toleration Act as of permanent duration and as allowing by implication the continuance of the dissenting academies and of occasional conformity, and those who repudiated these implications as contrary to the intentions of the statute and were even doubtful whether it could be regarded as of more than temporary validity unless its minimal concessions were accepted as maximal. The more liberal view was taken by Simon Patrick and Burnet; the former of whom regarded the Occasional Conformity Bill

as making a manifest breach upon the act of indulgence, which had made great peace, quiet and love among us. For it struck at the very best of the Nonconformists, who, looking upon us as good Christians that had nothing sinful in our worship, thought they ought upon occasion to communicate with us; but imagining they had something better in their way of worship, could not leave it, but adhere to their dissenting ministers. This I took not to be an argument of their hypocrisy, as many called it, but of their conscientious sincerity; and therefore they ought to be tolerated in this practice, which might in time bring them over to us, as I know it had done some worthy persons.[2]

Similarly Burnet held that

this bill put the dissenters in a worse condition than they were in before: so it was a breach made upon the toleration, which ought not to be done, since they had not deserved it by any ill-behaviour of theirs, by which it could be pretended that they had forfeited any of the benefits designed by that act.[3]

This interpretation of the Occasional Conformity and Schism Acts as 'such a breaking in upon the toleration as would undermine it', was hotly challenged by the rigorists, who maintained that the

[1] *Ibid.* pp. 245–6.      [2] Patrick, *Works*, vol. IX, p. 553.
[3] G. Burnet, *History of My Own Time*, vol. V, pp. 105–6.

Toleration Act conceded liberty of public worship under certain specified conditions, no less and no more, and that everything not mentioned in its clauses was *ultra vires*. This standpoint was argued by the defenders of Sacheverell at his impeachment; and was epitomised almost a generation later in retrospect by Archdeacon Reynolds, who contended that 'in short the Toleration Act, which was of the nature of a compact between Conformists and Nonconformists, had been kept only by the former', alleging as evidence that the latter 'proceeded to set up schools and academies for the education of youth, without subjecting their masters on account of their schools to any oaths, tests, examinations or public regulations of any kind'. In this connection he asked, 'what civilised commonwealth ever left at large the education of youth? Not the ancient cities of Greece and Rome, nor the Gothic kings of the ninth century, nor the Protestant states and princes of Germany, nor the discipline of Calvin, much less the Synod of Dort or the Reformed Church of Scotland'.[1] The extent of this difference of opinion was revealed by the episcopal votes on the Occasional Conformity Bill in the House of Lords on 14 December 1703, when nine prelates were for the measure (six in person and three by proxy) and fourteen against (eleven in person and three by proxy). Even more significant was the division amongst those divines who in 1689 had been united in support of both comprehension and toleration, Compton, Sharp, Burnet, Tenison and Patrick; of whom the two first-named voted for the Occasional Conformity Bill and the rest against. The political and ecclesiastical events of the quarter of a century between 1689 and 1714 had resulted in a noteworthy parting of the ways, as Compton and Sharp gravitated steadily towards a high-church Tory position, whilst Tenison, Burnet and Patrick as clearly moved in a Whig and latitudinarian direction. Perhaps the most illuminating evidence of this change may be seen in the several references to Sharp by Burnet at various stages in their relationship. In the first draft of his *History of My Own Time* the author observed in relation to William III's nominations of Tillotson to Canterbury and Sharp to York, that 'these two sees were...filled with two of the greatest prelates, the best preachers, and the wisest and worthiest men that perhaps ever sat in them'.[2] In the second version this eulogy was modified in respect of Sharp, to read: 'So these two sees were filled

---

[1] G. Reynolds, *Historical Essay*, pp. 203–4.
[2] H. C. Foxcroft, *Supplement to Burnet's History*, p. 359.

with the two best preachers that had sat in them in our time; only Sharp did not know the world so well, and was not so steady as Tillotson was.'[1] Finally in Burnet's *Autobiography* all trace of merit in Sharp was expunged: 'Sharp by a great error of Tillotson's was made archbishop of York. He has proved an ill instrument and has set himself at the head of the party, but has suffered much by it in the opinion of many who looked on him before as a man of integrity and simplicity, but few do now retain that opinion, as with regret I confess I do not. I have observed too much art and design in him to be able to think of him as I wish I could do.'[2]

Even more unfortunate was the continuance of this division amongst the episcopate when, the Protestant Succession in the House of Hanover having been safely accomplished, the Whig politicians were expected to redeem their promises to relieve the dissenters of the disabilities inflicted on them by the Occasional Conformity and Schism Acts. For when the question of repeal was first mooted in March 1717, it met with the chilling reply that no fewer than eighteen bishops would oppose the measure on the ground that the Occasional Conformity Act had been 'so lately and unanimously agreed to'. Especially important was the fact that the new primate, Wake, could describe the dissenters as 'those who make us so ill a requital for the toleration that has been so kindly indulged to them and so inviolably been preserved on our part'. In face of this opposition, soundings were resumed in the following autumn concerning the possibility of other means of relief; and a company of bishops, headed by Gibson and including Hough and Talbot (both of whom had voted against the Occasional Conformity Bill in 1703), met to consider whether the sacramental test in so far as it concerned office-holders in corporations might be dispensed with altogether, or that there might be substituted for the actual reception of the Sacrament a declaratory test only. No progress being possible along this line owing to the inflexible resistance of Wake, the Stanhope-Sunderland administration resolved in December 1718 to introduce a comprehensive Bill 'for strengthening the Protestant Interest in these kingdoms', which embraced both sets of earlier proposals. So bold a measure, which, in addition to repealing the two obnoxious acts of Anne's reign, circumvented the Test and Corporation Acts without a frontal repeal, stood no chance

---

[1] G. Burnet, *History of My Own Time*, vol. IV, p. 131.
[2] H. C. Foxcroft, *Supplement to Burnet's History*, p. 504.

of passing in face of episcopal hostility. It received a second reading in the Lords on 19 December by 86 votes to 68; but in committee the clauses relating to the sacramental test were deleted, and the Bill emerged finally as repealing simply the Occasional Conformity and Schism Acts. Once again, however, the bench was deeply divided, eleven episcopal votes being given in its favour and fifteen against; but both archbishops together with the bishops of London, Durham and Winchester had opposed the repeal.

Thus the battle for toleration had been won (though only to a limited degree) after a quarter of a century's fluctuation of fortunes since 1689, whilst the two opposing forces of the Church of England and the dissenters had reached an uneasy armistice and had acquiesced for the time being in an unstable equilibrium. It was evident that the dissenters would not accept as a permanent settlement a measure which left the Test and Corporation Acts unrepealed. Nor could the expedient of annual Indemnity Acts prove satisfactory; first because they were not annual, and also because their terms afforded only an uncertain and unreliable protection. The Indemnity Act of 1714 indeed was not repeated until 1727; and even thereafter there were no similar acts in the years 1730, 1734, 1744, 1749, 1750, 1753 and 1757. It was therefore to be expected that a campaign for the repeal of the Test and Corporation Acts would be opened in due season. Its comparative delay was due partly to the dependence of the dissenters upon the favour of the Whig administration, a dependence symbolised and strengthened by their acceptance of the *Regium Donum*, a bounty 'for the use and behalf of the poor widows of Dissenting ministers', and partly to the divisions within their own ranks resulting from the Salters Hall controversy and its repercussions. Not until 1727 did the ministers of the Three Denominations in London, Presbyterian, Independent and Baptist, constitute themselves into a 'General Body' to watch their several interests; and not until 1732 was the decisive action taken of calling in lay reinforcements to 'consult what steps are fit to be taken in relation to the repeal of the Corporation and Test acts the next ensuing session of Parliament'. Henceforth the dissenting deputies undertook the organisation of the campaign. To a considerable degree this manifestation of an aggressive spirit united the bench in opposition to the proposed repeal. Gibson, who had stoutly supported the repeal of the Occasional Conformity and Schism Acts, as determinedly refused to consider any measure of further relief.

He came out at once with a pamphlet whose title indicated sufficiently both its contents and objective, *The Dispute adjusted about the proper time of applying for a Repeal of the Test and Corporation Acts by showing that no time is proper*. Even Hoadly was employed by Walpole to persuade the Deputies that the present time was inopportune. In 1734, however, after their valuable support of the administration in the recent, critical general election, they pressed their demand; and Walpole though conveying the ministerial counsel against an attempt, promised to leave them freedom of action to do as they wished. On 12 March 1736 Mr Plumer, M.P. for Hertfordshire, moved for leave to bring in a Bill for repealing the Test and Corporation Acts, but was defeated by 251 votes to 123. In 1739 in reply to a further approach, Walpole again averred that 'the time has not yet arrived'; and when the attempt was renewed in March of that year, once again it met with a reverse by 188 votes to 89.[1] Nearly a century was to elapse before success crowned the dissenters' efforts, thanks in large measure to the decline of so many Presbyterian congregations into Unitarianism, with the consequent weakening of orthodox dissent.

The established church therefore maintained somewhat precariously its privileged position against the dissenters, owing chiefly to their internal divisions and to the *vis inertiae* characteristic of the religious no less than the political life of the age. Meantime the paradoxical genius of Warburton erected a specious defence of the existing situation of compromise and stalemate by the ingenious argument of *The Alliance between Church and State: or, The Necessity and Equity of an Established Religion and a Test Law, demonstrated from the essence of Civil Society, upon the fundamental principles of the Law of Nature and Nations*. Warburton argued on the one hand that 'by the Law of Nature every man has a right of worshipping God according to his own conscience', and on the other hand that an established religion plus an attendant test-law were likewise based 'on the great and unerring maxims of the Law of Nature and of Nations'. The reconciliation of these maxims was effected upon the ground of 'civil utility', as 'the great principle whereby we erect an established religion and a test-law'; and since 'we have proved, and it cannot be too often repeated, that public

---

[1] B. L. Manning, *The Protestant Dissenting Deputies* (ed. O. Greenwood, 1952), part I, c. 3; N. C. Hunt, *Sir Robert Walpole, Samuel Holden and the Dissenting Deputies* (1957).

utility and truth do coincide', therefore 'to provide for that utility, truth must be provided for'. Thus the Church of England came to rest in a situation of makeshift compromise, far different from the exclusive position designed by Sheldon and Morley; and solaced itself with Warburton's audacious apologia for this unstable platform as constituting a pattern of alliance between church and state 'formed solely from the contemplation of Nature and the unvariable Reason of Things'.

# IV

## GODLY UNION AND CONCORD

'This ransacking of Records', commented Burnet in his *Vindication of the Orders of the Church of England*, 'though it adds much to the lustre and beauty of the Church, yet is not a thing incumbent on everybody to look into, nor indeed possible for any to be satisfied about.'[1] If the student of English church history is tempted oft-times to echo wearily this despairing conclusion, he must nevertheless cherish a lively gratitude for the patristic studies of its seventeenth-century divines, who not only contributed signally to the lustre and beauty of the Church Catholic, but also earned for their own branch the proud designation *clerus Anglicanus stupor mundi*. For their century was at once an age of polemical divinity and of oecumenical temper. Indeed the two aspects of its history were rather complementary than contradictory. On the one hand the exigencies of controversy, themselves a legacy from the epoch of the Reformation, led to an extensive and intensive exploration of that Christian antiquity to which romanist and reformer alike made their appeal; whilst on the other hand the results of the investigation inspired a desire for, and pointed the way towards, reconciliation and reunion. The reformers of the sixteenth-century had claimed to restore the primitive constitution of the church and had invoked the testimony of the first five centuries of its history in support of their contention. In reply their romanist adversaries had insisted with equal vigour that the verdict of antiquity was in their favour and had stigmatised the Protestants as innovators. Unfortunately for themselves, the reformers had been unable to agree in their interpretation of that primitive tradition to which they had recourse, and in the sphere of ecclesiastical polity in particular the division was not only of episcopacy versus papacy but also of presbyter against bishop. Hence the historical evidences for the origins of episcopacy and papacy alike were the subject of controversial study and polemical argument.

From this controversy the Church of England could not stand aloof. Rather it was drawn ineluctably into a conflict on two fronts.

[1] G. Burnet, *Vindication of the Orders of the Church of England* (1677), p. 104.

For its own self-chosen position in *via media* betwixt Rome and Geneva required it to conduct a continuous campaign in defence of its continuity and orthodoxy against Rome, no less than in behalf of its episcopacy and liturgy against Presbyterianism. Nor was this ecclesiastical warfare a matter of merely academic exercise. During the Interregnum the Anglican clergy who followed the Stuart house into exile had been assailed by many taunts and temptations to apostasy. Anglicanism appeared in sober truth *prope interitum*. At home in England the Church was proscribed and dissolved. Abroad the faithful were but as Zoar, a very little city, and, what was worse, living in a hostile environment. 'I do not remember in ecclesiastical history', commented Richard Watson with bitterness, 'to have read of any number of orthodox Christians chased out of their own country, at a loss for a safe communion in some one or other elsewhere; that [was] our special difficulty or misfortune.'[1] To hold out against persecution at home and pressure abroad seemed too much for so small a company. It was a singularly fortunate circumstance, therefore, that the exiles numbered such able controversialists as Cosin and Bramhall; from whose pens proceeded some of the most effective and important works of Anglican apologetic; as, for example, Cosin's *Validity of the Ordination of Priests in the Church of England*, and Bramhall's *The Consecration of Protestant Bishops Vindicated* on the one side; and the former's *Regni Angliae Religio Catholica* and the latter's *A Just Vindication of the Church of England from the Unjust Aspersion of Criminal Schism* on the other side. To these works of controversial divinity the study of patristic antiquity made an especial and important contribution.

The seventeenth century inherited from its predecessor in this respect a situation of peculiar confusion and deficiency. For the appeal of the reformers to the pattern and exemplar of the primitive church had been gravely handicapped by the state of contemporary historical studies relating to the early Christian centuries. From our vantage point of four centuries' progress indeed, their position seems bizarre. Not only were the pseudonymous works ascribed to Dionysius the Aeropagite generally believed to be authentic and himself an actual disciple of St Paul, but a similar attitude prevailed in regard to the corpus of writings ascribed to Clement of Rome, including the *Apostolic Canons* and *Constitutions* and the *Clementine Recognitions*, which were confidently cited as evidence for the Roman

[1] Cited in Bosher, *Restoration Settlement*, p. 52.

primacy during the early centuries. The avidity with which new discoveries were welcomed, was illustrated by the *Commonitorium* of Vincent of Lerins; which, having been almost entirely unknown during the Middle Ages (since none of the great scholastics cited it), and being extant only in two manuscripts of either the tenth or eleventh centuries and a third of the thirteenth century, was first published in 1528 in the *Antidotum* of Johannes Sichardus. Its vogue thereafter was such that during the remainder of the sixteenth century it enjoyed thirty-five editions and twenty-two translations, followed by twenty-three editions and twelve translations in the seventeenth century, and by twelve editions and twelve translations in the eighteenth century.

It fell to the fortunate lot of the seventeenth century to fill up some of the gaps in patristic knowledge; and therein happily, Anglican scholars played a leading part. Dr F. L. Cross has claimed for the first half of this century the distinction of witnessing 'the most ambitious contribution to Patristic scholarship to which Oxford has given birth';[1] and his eulogy is continued in respect of the post-Restoration period by Burnet's statement that 'learning was then high at Oxford.... They read the Fathers much there' (with perhaps an implied contrast to Cambridge where, thanks to the influence of the men of latitude, 'they read Episcopius much').[2] It is impossible indeed to draw any hard and fast line between the earlier and later halves of the century in the history of patristic study. Ironically the one indubitably authentic work of Clement of Rome, his First Epistle, would appear to have been completely unknown to the Middle Ages, and was first published at Oxford in 1633 by Patrick Young (who, after the fashion of his times Latinised his name as Patricius Junius), from a manuscript in the Codex Alexandrinus brought to England in 1628 as a present from the Patriarch Cyril Lucar to Charles I; and a second edition followed in 1637. It was a testimony of the oecumenical character of historical scholarship that an Anglican divine should thus have brought to light a document which was to be described centuries later by Batiffol as *l'épiphanie de la primauté Romaine*.[3]

A more complex and controversial problem was that of the Epistles of Ignatius of Antioch. During the Middle Ages the seven Ignatian

---

[1] F. L. Cross, 'Patristic Study at Oxford', in *Proceedings of the Oxford Society of Historical Theology* (1948–9), p. 7.
[2] G. Burnet, *History of My Own Time*, vol. I, pp. 332, 324.
[3] P. Batiffol, *L'Église naissante et le Catholicisme* (5th ed. Paris, 1922), p. 146.

Epistles known to Eusebius had suffered interpolation and addition; and furthermore Ignatius was largely represented to medieval scholars by four apocryphal letters bearing his name, two of which were addressed by him to St John and one to the Virgin Mary together with her reply. They were in Latin and their contents indicated a provenance not earlier than the seventh century. 'At the first streak of intellectual dawn', as Lightfoot observed, 'this Ignatian spectre vanished into its kindred darkness';[1] and its place was taken in western Europe by twelve Epistles known as the Long Recension. In 1498 Lefèvre d'Étaples published his *Gloriosi Christi martyris Ignatii Epistolae Undecim*, embracing the seven Eusebian letters, plus one to the Tarsians, one to the Philippians, one to the Antiochenes and one to Hero of Antioch; and the Greek text of these Epistles, plus a Letter to Mary of Cassobola was published by Valentinus Paceus in 1557. At first this Long Recension was generally accepted as authentic. Confessional interests also played their part in the discussion.

Theological and ecclesiastical prejudice entered largely into the views of the combatants. These Epistles contained certain passages which favoured, or seemed to favour the Roman supremacy. Protestant controversialists were offended at these. Again the writer appears throughout as a staunch advocate of episcopacy. To reformers like Calvin who had adopted presbyterianism on principle, this was an unpardonable crime. It is a noteworthy circumstance that Romanist writers for the most part maintained the authenticity and integrity of the twelve Epistles of the Long Recension. One noble exception is the Jesuit Petavius, who remarking on the quotations in early writers, recognised distinctly the fact that these epistles were interpolated. On the other hand Protestant writers as a rule did not deny a genuine nucleus, though they ruthlessly excised everything which conflicted with their theological and ecclesiastical prepossessions.... While continental opinion was thus vague and divided, Anglican writers seem generally, though not universally, to have accepted the twelve Epistles without hesitation. This was the case for instance with Whitgift and Hooker and Andrews.... In England, as on the continent, the question can hardly be said to have been considered on its own merits. Episcopacy was the burning question of the day; and the sides of combatants in the Ignatian controversy were already predetermined for them by their attitude towards this question. Every allowance should be made for their following their prepossessions, where the evidence seemed so evenly balanced. On the one hand external testimony was strongly in favour of the genuineness of certain Ignatian letters; on the other hand the only Ignatian letters known were burdened with difficulties.[2]

[1] J. B. Lightfoot, *The Apostolic Fathers* (1889), part II, vol. I, p. 237.
[2] *Ibid.* pp. 238–40.

In this situation it was the glory of an Anglican scholar to make a definitive advance towards a solution of the problem; for 'to the critical genius of Ussher belongs the honour of restoring the true Ignatius'.[1] His discovery was the outcome of protracted patristic study, extending over eighteen years, of which at the outset he wrote to his uncle Richard Stanihurst of the English college at Louvain, that 'the principal part of my study at this time is employed in perusing the writings of the Fathers and observing out of them the doctrine of the ancient Church; wherein I find it very necessary that the reader should be thoroughly informed touching his authors, what time they lived and what works truly and what falsely attributed to them; either of which being mistaken, must of course bring great confusion in this kind of study'.[2] Now he was to introduce order into confusion. Having observed that the quotations from Ignatius in three medieval English writers, Robert Grosseteste, John Tyssington and William Wodeford agreed exactly with the citations in Eusebius and Theodoret, but differed from the current text of the Long Recension, he set to work to discover MSS corresponding to these citations. Two such Latin MSS rewarded his search, from which he reconstructed the Greek text by removing those interpolations and additions of the Long Recension which did not occur in his newly discovered MSS. In 1644 there appeared his *Polycarpi et Ignatii Epistolae*, which Lightfoot described as combining 'marvellous erudition' with 'the highest critical genius'; but which unfortunately rejected the Epistle to Polycarp as spurious.[3] Two years later Isaac Voss published at Amsterdam the Greek text of the Ignatian Epistles from a manuscript in the Medicean Library at Florence, though the Epistle to the Romans was missing. For his services to scholarship in his *Epistolae Genuinae Scti Ignatii martyris* Voss was invited to England by John Pearson, and from 1673 to his death in 1689 enjoyed a prebend of Windsor, receiving also from the University of Oxford the honorary degree of D.C.L.

But if the editions of Ussher and Voss had settled the critical question of the authenticity of the seven Ignatian Epistles mentioned by Eusebius, their determination of the issue did not find favour in all learned circles.

To one school of contemporary theologians the discovery of Ussher and Voss was a grave disappointment. The French Protestant divines had

---

[1] *Ibid.* p. 243.  [2] J. Ussher, *Works* (ed. C. R. Elrington, 1847–64), vol. xv, letter i, p. 3.
[3] J. B. Lightfoot, *Apostolic Fathers*, part ii, vol. i, p. 243.

attacked the integrity of the Ignatian letters mainly on account of their testimony to the early spread of episcopacy; but they had for the most part expressed themselves in favour of a genuine though indeterminate nucleus overlaid with spurious matter. To these critics the Vossian letters gave no relief. Though the sacerdotal language had disappeared, the testimony to the existence and authority of the episcopate was as strong and precise here as in the letters of the Long Recension. It was too much to expect that under these circumstances the Vossian letters should receive an impartial hearing.[1]

Saumaise in 1645 published his *Adparatus ad Libros de Primatu Papae* in which he argued that the Ignatian letters had been written under the Antonine emperors, whilst David Blondel's *Apologia pro Sententia Hieronymi de Episcopis et Presbyteris* in 1646 assigned them to a date after the death of Clement of Alexandria, about the beginning of the third century. Both writers concurred in rejecting Ignatian authorship altogether. Similar dismay overtook the English puritans, with whom corporately and with John Owen particularly Henry Hammond took issue in his *Answer to the Animadversions on the Dissertations touching Ignatius' Epistles* in 1654; but, as Lightfoot commented, 'the weapons of these English Puritans were taken from the French armoury and their writings do not need any further notice'.[2] The weightiest assault came from Jean Daillé who published in 1666 *De Scriptis, quae sub nominibus Dionysii Areopagitae et Ignatii Antiocheni circumferuntur libri duo*; in which he undertook to prove that though the shorter and longer Epistles were the work of different hands, neither were written by Ignatius. He dated them near the time of Constantine, argued that Eusebius had been deceived concerning their authorship, that the Epistle of Polycarp had suffered interpolation in respect of its references to them, and that the works of Origen containing two sentences from the Epistles to the Ephesians and Romans were of doubtful genuineness. At the same time he amassed the objections raised against the Long Recension on the ground of anachronisms and mingled them with criticism of the Short Recension. In the opinion of Lightfoot, Daillé's work lacked the judicial and discriminating qualities of scholarly criticism.

The spirit of Daillé's work is the reverse of this. It is characterised throughout by deliberate confusion. Though at the outset he states the facts with regard to the different recensions of the Ignatian letters, as

---

[1] J. B. Lightfoot, *Apostolic Fathers*, part II, vol. I, p. 330.
[2] *Ibid.* p. 331.

brought to light by Ussher's discovery, yet he proceeds at once to treat the whole body of Ignatian literature as if it were the product of one author.... Thus for the most part he expends his strength in slaying the slain, for Ussher had already dealt the death-blow to these spurious and interpolated letters. For the rest, his arguments and positions are such as few sane critics, even among the most determined opponents of the Ignatian Epistles, would venture to adopt in the present day.... The literary ability of this work is undeniable; but it has contributed nothing, or next to nothing, of permanent value to the solution of the Ignatian question. Its true claim to our gratitude is of a wholly different kind. If Daillé had not attacked the Ignatian letters, Pearson would not have stepped forward as their champion.[1]

The publication in 1672 of John Pearson's *Vindiciae Epistolarum S. Ignatii*, in addition to bringing the contribution of Cambridge to patristic studies, gave a final quietus to Daillé's arguments. In Lightfoot's judgment

it was incomparably the most valuable contribution to the subject which had hitherto appeared, with the single exception of Ussher's work.... On the whole, compared with Daillé's attack, Pearson's reply was as light to darkness. In England at all events his work seemed to be accepted as closing the controversy.[2]

Divided into two parts of approximately equal length, it examined the internal and external evidence in turn, pursuing each point with a wealth of detailed scholarship. Incidentally in two valuable chapters, Pearson assembled all the evidence for the primitive episcopal regimen of the Church. In his *Address to the Reader*, added whilst his work was in the press, he welcomed the newly-published *Patrum qui temporibus Apostolicis floruerunt Opera* by J. B. Cotlerius, and paid tribute to the scholarly achievement of other Gallican divines, Sirmond, Petavius, De Marca, Launnoy, Valesius and Huet, in whose works he saluted the truly eirenical and oecumenical spirit which should inspire the study of church history.

There remained yet another of the Fathers, Cyprian of Carthage, for whom English churchmen of the seventeenth century had a particular penchant, because his exposition of episcopacy seemed to concur with that of their own church. In 1520 Erasmus had published an edition of his works; and the early Reformers had used Cyprian's Letters and the Textus Receptus of the *De Ecclesiae Unitate* as weapons against Rome. In 1563, however, Manutius first published the Primacy Text, which by its express testimony to the

---

[1] *Ibid.* pp. 331–3.        [2] *Ibid.* pp. 333–4.

Petrine and Roman primacy furnished an invaluable reinforcement to the papal armoury. On the other side, the famous Letter (LXXV) from Firmilian of Caesarea to Cyprian, which contained so strong a castigation of Pope Stephen, was first published in 1564 by Morel, and did something to redress the balance. The ensuing controversy concerning the genuineness of the Primacy Text was of the utmost interest to English churchmen; and in 1682 there appeared from the hand of John Fell, bishop of Oxford and dean of Christ Church, *Sancti Caecilii Cypriani Opera*, to which were prefaced *Annales Cyprianici* by John Pearson, now bishop of Chester. This edition, as Dr F. L. Cross has observed,

was a work of actuality in an age in which many English churchmen could find no higher title for their revered and martyred archbishop than 'Cyprianus Anglicus'. For two centuries it held a permanent place among Latin patristic texts, but it is only fair to add that the most original work in it was not Fell's own but the supplementary *Dissertations* contributed by Pearson.[1]

With regard to the Primacy Text, Fell remarked justly that all editors of Cyprian before Manutius knew nothing *de Cathedra una, Petri primatu, Cathedra Petri super quam fundata est Ecclesia*; and that Manutius relied upon one Vatican manuscript, on the strength of which *quicquid interpolatum est, pro genuino habebitur*. Fell allowed indeed that Pamelius in his edition of 1568 had discovered a further manuscript in the abbey of Cambron, and he was prepared to accept the existence of yet another in Bavaria; but he contended that these were an insignificant handful compared with the manuscripts containing the Textus Receptus. Moreover they were so much at variance with each other as to move him to apply to them the words of the First Evangelist, 'they sought false witness... but found none, yea though many false witnesses came, they found it not'. Fell relied much upon the *eruditissimus Rigaltius*, who had published an edition of Cyprian in 1648 in which he had rejected the Primacy Text, and had alleged the 'absurdity' of Cardinal Hosius's version which interpolated the words *Hic Primatus Petro datur*, adding the comment *Male meriti sunt de Sanctissimo Cypriano qui sapientissimum episcopum faciunt auctorem istius paralogismi*. Fell added his own observation that it would be equally absurd to assert that the powers of Peter

---

[1] F. L. Cross, 'Patristic Study at Oxford', in *Proceedings of the Oxford Society of Historical Theology* (1948–9), pp. 9–10.

had descended to his successors in the see of Rome, and yet to deny that those of the rest of the Apostles had remained with their successors, the bishops of the church.[1] He therefore rejected the Primacy Text and maintained the Anglican tradition concerning the Cyprianic theory of the episcopate: *episcopatus unus est, cuius a singulis in solidum pars tenetur.*

In the preface to his edition of the Ignatian Epistles, Pearson had expressed the hope that a clearer light might shine upon the dogmas of the church, and thereby the controversies of the schools, freed from the patronage of imposters and from the fictitious cloak of antiquity, might the more justly and tranquilly be determined; and that the minds of men might turn with due reverence to follow the primitive church, distinguished by its proper simplicity and no longer depicted (or rather deformed) in false colours.[2] Following upon his tribute to the scholars of the Gallican Church, the juxtaposition was significant. Anglican divines recognised a comity with their brethren across the narrow seas, who also represented a *via media* within the Roman Church; and both companies of scholars were united in study of the primitive church. Indeed the latter half of the seventeenth century marked a notable change in the character and temper of ecclesiastical discussion. Hitherto controversy between Protestants and papists had been characterised by the multiplicity of the questions debated and by the purely dogmatic nature of their treatment. Now attention was concentrated on fewer and more essential points, and appeal was directed to the evidence of antiquity rather than to the sole authority of the Bible. More particularly in discussion of the nature of the church was the testimony of the early centuries of its history of decisive importance. In this latter question the position of the Church of England was crucial.

Les Anglais, cette nation conservatrice dont Bossuet se plaisait à reconnaître le respect pour l'antiquité, n'avaient pas attendu la menace du libertinage croissant pour mêler, sinon substituer tout à fait, la méthode historique à la considération, naguère prédominante, des textes sacrés....

---

[1] *S. Cypriani Opera* (ed. John Fell, Oxford, 1682), pp. 106–7: Notes (e.g. Exiguus omnino iste sit numerus si cum illis conferatur qui veterem tuentur lectionem).

[2] Pearson, *op. cit.* Address to the Reader: Unde spes aliquando fore, ut dogmatibus ecclesiasticis major lux affulgeat, controversiae in scholis agitatae, pudendo impostorum patrocinio nudatae, et ficta Antiquitatis larva spoliatae, aequius tandem et sedatius terminentur, animique hominum ea, qua par est, reverentia Primitivam Ecclesiam sua simplicitate conspicuam, nec alienis coloribus depictam, aut potius deformatam, prosequantur (Library of Anglo-Catholic Theology, vol. I, p. 19).

Les controversistes anglicans...se travaillent à revendiquer pour leur Église le bénéfice d'une tradition perpétuelle et d'une succession ininterrompue.[1]

Practical events furthermore had conspired to reinforce the urgency of ecclesiastical reunion; for the Thirty Years War had resulted in a religious stalemate in the Empire at the cost of widespread devastation, whilst the Civil War in England had emphasised the evils of religious dissension. From the standpoint of both Protestant and papist therefore ecclesiastical reunion was part of the *Zeitgeist* of the latter half of the seventeenth century; and this led to the enunciation of certain fundamentals of belief, upon which agreement was already present and from which further advances might be made.

La théorie des points fondamentaux, base ordinaire de tous les projets formés pour remédier aux divisions intestines de la Réforme, pouvait évidemment s'appliquer indirectement à la situation respective de la Réforme au Catholicisme.[2]

Accordingly the Spanish Franciscan, Christopher Rajas de Spinola, titular bishop of Tina in Croatia and afterwards bishop of Neustadt, entered into discussions with Gerhard Walter Molanus, titular abbot of Lokkum, concerning reunion between Rome and the Lutherans of the electorate of Hanover; whilst Leibniz in his *Systema Theologicum* in 1683–4 made such extensive concessions from the Protestant side on such matters as the Real Presence in the Eucharist, its sacrificial character, and the papal headship of the church, as to earn for his treatise the not unmerited characterisation of 'the closest approach that Protestantism has ever made to Rome'. Moreover Bossuet engaged in a long correspondence with Leibniz; and several years earlier in 1671 in his own *Exposition de la Doctrine de l'Église catholique sur les matières de Controverse*, the bishop of Meaux had espoused (at least in part) the principle of agreement in fundamentals.

On peut dire que, sur les points fondamentaux, catholiques et protestants à cette epoque professaient la même foi. Bossuet, cherchant un terrain d'entente avec ses adversaires, avait choisi celui-là.[3]

Into this movement for ecclesiastical unity a natural affinity of scholarship and temper drew together Anglican and Gallican church-

---

[1] A. Rébelliau, *Bossuet, Historien du Protestantisme* (1891), p. 50.
[2] *Ibid.* p. 28.
[3] F. Cabrol, 'Bossuet, ses Relations avec Angleterre', in *Revue d'Histoire Ecclésiastique*, vol. XXVII (1931), pp. 535–71.

men. Both schools were wedded to patristic study and to the historical method of approach, in an age when these were the dominant standards of reference and comparison. Burnet, for example, contrasted the Italian concern with the study of canon law and the Spanish devotion to scholasticism with the patristic learning of the Gallicans.

> The French have now for above an age been set on a more solid and generous pursuit of true learning. They have laboured in the publishing of the Fathers' works with great diligence and more sincerity than could be expected in any other part of that Church;...so that the state of the former ages of the Church is better understood than in any other nation of that Communion. Nor has the secular clergy, or laity, only laboured with great faithfulness in those enquiries, such as Albaspine, De Marca, Godeau, Launnoy, Huetius, Valesius and Balusius; but even that Order which is not so much admired over the world for great scrupulosity of conscience, has produced there several great men that are never to be named but with honour, such as Fronto Ducaeus and Petavius, but above all Sirmondus through whose writings there runs such a tincture of candour and probity, that in matters of fact, Protestants are generally more inclined to acquiesce in his authority than those of his own persuasion are.[1]

The compliment was returned with interest by Mabillon's inclusion of the works of Bull, Pearson, Ussher and Hammond in his list of books suitable for monastic libraries. Furthermore, the Benedictines of St Maur, as Dr Owen Chadwick has remarked, were typical of

> the age when for the first time since the Reformation we can discern an international amity of scholarship, which leaps over the walls of religious prejudices as well as the barriers of national antipathies....It is an epoch. ...With Mabillon, Montfaucon, Ruinart, Tillemont, we seem to have passed beyond all consciousness, even remote consciousness, of the possible theological or controversial effects of their researches.[2]

A further example may be seen in the testimony of Abbé Louis Dufour de Longuerue to the high value which he set upon the works of Bishop William Lloyd and of Ussher, and in his appreciative observation concerning Hammond: 'je l'estime fort'.[3] Bull indeed enjoyed a particular pre-eminence. Even the great Bossuet cited his *Defensio Fidei Nicenae* in the *Histoire des Variations*, and referred his opponent, Jurieu, 'to Bull, that learned English Protestant, the

---

[1] G. Burnet, *The Letter Writ by the Last Assembly General of the Clergy of France to the Protestants* (1683), Preface, p. [6].

[2] W. O. Chadwick, *From Bossuet to Newman* (1957), pp. 60–1.

[3] E. de Budé, *Lettres Inédites addressées à J. A. Turrettini*, 3 vols. (1887), vol. II, pp. 247, 255, 262.

treatise where he hath so well defended the Fathers who lived before the Council of Nice'. When Robert Nelson sent to the bishop of Meaux the further work of Bull, *Judicium Ecclesiae Catholicae*, the volume, reaching Bossuet during a general assembly of the clergy of France at St Germain, evoked a formal letter of thanks in the name of all the said clergy.

Quant à l'ouvrage du Docteur Bullus...il est admirable et la matière qu'il traite ne pouvait être expliquée plus savamment et plus à fond. C'est ce que je vous supplie de vouloir bien lui faire savoir, et en même temps les sincères congratulations de tout le clergé de France assemblé en cette ville, pour le service qu'il rend à l'Église catholique, en défendant si bien le jugement qu'elle a porté sur la necessité de croire la divinité du Fils de Dieu.[1]

'I read the letter', commented Burnet, 'and so I can deliver it for a certain truth, how uncommon soever it may seem to be.'[2]

The Anglicans discerned, furthermore, signs of the stirring of a desire for reform among Gallican churchmen as a result of their study of the primitive church, and therewith entertained hopes even of the emergence of a national Church of France. Burnet testified that the learning of the Gallican divines was not

that for which they are chiefly to be esteemed. It must also be acknowledged that from the study of the Ancient Fathers many of them seem to have derived a great measure of their spirit, which has engaged divers of them to set forward as great a reformation as the constitution of their church can admit of. They have endeavoured not only to discover the corruptions in morality and casuistical divinity, and many other abuses in the government of the church, but also have infused in their clergy a greater reverence for the Scriptures, a deeper sense of the Pastoral Care, and a higher value for Holy Orders than had appeared among them for divers ages before. Some of their bishops have set their clergy great examples; and a disposition of reforming men's lives and of restoring the government of the church according to the primitive rules, hath been such that even those who are better reformed, both as to their doctrine and worship, must yet acknowledge that there are many things among them highly imitable and by which they are a great reproach to others, who have not studied to copy after these patterns they have set them.[3]

Contemporaneously the Gallican church had been involved in acute disputes with the papacy, concerning both the *Regale* and Jansenism, which might open a door to schism. Accordingly Burnet

---

[1] R. Nelson, *Life of Bull*, pp. 293–5, 344–5, 383–7.
[2] G. Burnet, *History of My Own Time*, vol. v, p. 185.
[3] G. Burnet, *The Letter Writ by the last Assembly General of the Clergy of France to the Protestants*, Preface [p. 7].

himself when visiting France in the year after the famous Declaration of Gallican Liberties was received with signal honours. The Prince of Condé

had read my *History of the Reformation* that was then translated into French, and seemed pleased with it. So were many of the great lawyers: in particular Harlay, then attorney-general and now first president of the court of the parliament of Paris. The contests with Rome were then very high; for the assembly of the clergy had passed some articles very derogatory to the papal authority; so many fancied that matter might go to a rupture; and Harlay said very publicly, that if that should happen, I had laid before them a good plan to copy from.

Amongst the Sorbonne doctors, Burnet formed particularly favourable impressions of Faur and Picques; the former of whom he reckoned

the best read in ecclesiastical history of any man I saw among them; and I never knew any of that Church that understood the Scriptures so well as Picques did. They declared themselves for abolishing the papal authority, and for reducing the pope to the old primacy again.

Together with some others also, Burnet noted, they

wished for a regular reformation; but their notion of unity of the church kept them still in a communion that they seemed very uneasy in; and they said very freely, they wondered how any one that was out of their communion, should desire to come back into it.[1]

At this same time another English divine, William Wake, residing in the French capital as chaplain to Lord Preston, was making catholic acquaintance and forming the same conclusions as Burnet. When talking to Dr Picques and to the Father-Sacristan of the Grande Chartreuse, he soon discovered that

neither the good Father nor Dr Picques were much concerned for the follies of their church, which in many things they disliked as much as we do. Dr Picques before I left Paris, gave me broad hints that he should not be averse to end his days in England; and had he lived a little longer, he had come over hither with the Abbé Longuerue to see their friends here. That was the pretence; but I believe the true intention would have been to see what provision they might have expected to have been made for them if they should resolve to leave France altogether and settle here. I had several other opportunities of observing their uneasiness in many of the practices of the Roman Church.[2]

When therefore Bossuet delivered the opening sermon at the General Assembly of the French clergy in 1681 on the Unity of the

---

[1] G. Burnet, *History of My Own Time*, vol. II, pp. 386–7.
[2] Wake, 'Autobiography', ff. 16v–17.

Church, there was urgent need to combat these dangerous separatist tendencies.

Bossuet s'est efforcé de retenir certains de ses collègues qui n'hésitaient pas à pousser Louis XIV dans la voie du schisme. Son discours sur *L'Unité de l'Église* n'est pas seulement un chef d'œuvre oratoire, c'est un acte qui eut une influence considérable et contribue à maintenir l'union entre l'Église de France et la papauté.[1]

At the same time the Bishop of Meaux was an ardent advocate of ecclesiastical union. 'La réunion restera sa grande œuvre, à laquelle il apporte tous ses talents, tous ses énergies.'[2] In particular his *Exposition de la doctrine de l'Église catholique* of 1671 was a most persuasive invitation to Protestants to return to the bosom of the Roman Church, embodying the quintessence of the new temper in ecclesiastical discussion.

Jamais cette volonté de simplifier la dispute ne se montra plus franchement et ne s'avança plus loin que dans *l'Exposition* de Bossuet. Jamais on ne s'était aussi rigoureusement astreint à ne traiter que les seules matières qui avaient été, autrefois, de réelles causes de rupture, les seuls points capitaux auxquels les esprits modérés s'arrêtaient encore aujourd'hui.[3]

The earliest version of this apologia seemed indeed to Wake as if it 'would perhaps have been one of the fairest advances towards an union that ever the Church of Rome yet offered'; and three-quarters of a century later Gibbon, whose temporary conversion to Rome was effected in part by it, described the author as having 'the tone of candour and simplicity, and the ten-horned monster is transformed at his magic touch into the milk-white hind who must be loved as soon as she is seen'.[4] In his reply, *An Exposition of the Doctrine of the Church of England*, Wake in turn presented eirenic propositions on behalf of his own church in relation to such disputed issues as tradition, the authority of the church and the papacy. In regard to tradition he affirmed that 'we receive with the same veneration whatsoever comes from the Apostles whether by scripture or tradition, provided that we can be assured that it comes from them. And if it can be made to appear that any tradition which the Written Word contains not, has been received by all churches and in all ages, we are ready to embrace it as coming from the apostles.' For the

---

[1] F. Cabrol, 'Bossuet, ses Relations avec Angleterre', *R.H.E.* vol. XXVII (1931), p. 539.
[2] A. G. Martimort, *Le Gallicanisme de Bossuet* (1953), p. 279.
[3] A. Rébelliau, *Bossuet, Historien du Protestantisme*, p. 77.
[4] E. Gibbon, *Memoirs of my Life and Writings* (ed. G. B. Hill, 1900), p. 70.

universal church also, Wake professed a profound reverence and a belief in its indefectibility; and he avowed further that 'whensoever a General Council shall be freely and lawfully assembled, to determine the differences of the Catholic Church, none shall be more ready both to assist in and submit to it'. Similarly in respect of the pope, he declared of the Church of England that 'we shall be content to yield to him whatsoever authority the ancient Councils of the Primitive Church have acknowledged and the holy Fathers have always taught the faithful to give him'.[1]

Despite so apparently promising an overture, nothing resulted from Bossuet's desire to persuade Anglicans to return to the unity of the Roman Church. From his standpoint he was handicapped by ignorance of the English tongue, by the fact that his correspondents in Great Britain were either Roman Catholic clerics or converted laymen, notably James Drummond, duke of Perth, Lord Lovat, and the duke of Richmond, and by the difficulties of his own circumstances in France. There he was striving on the one hand to retain the Gallican church within the unity of the papal obedience, and on the other hand to set such limits to the exercise of papal powers in France as would satisfy Louis XIV and his counsellors, earning for himself thereby the bitter hostility of the Ultramontanes. Against his inclination he was compelled by royal command to draft the *Cleri Gallicani de ecclesiastica potestate Declaratio* of 1682 and to compose a *Defensio Declarationis Gallicanae*; whilst at the same time he insisted that Protestants must accept both the decrees of the Council of Trent and the papal *plenitudo potestatis* as defined by the 1682 Declaration. 'La base de toute rentrée des Protestans sera toujours l'ensemble des définitions du Concile de Trente et de la profession de foi de Pie IV.'[2] Further (in Bossuet's own words),

notre profession de foi nous oblige à reconnaître l'Église romaine comme la mère et la maîtresse de toutes les Églises, et à rendre une veritable obéissance au Souverain Pontife, successeur de S. Pierre et vicaire de Jésus-Christ....Il est question de reconnaître un chef établi de Dieu; ce que ceux-là feront volontiers, qui aiment la concorde des frères et l'unanimité écclesiastique.[3]

Along these lines no progress was possible; and when Bossuet concluded his letter of thanks for Bull's *Judicium Ecclesiae Catholicae* with the expression of surprise

---

[1] N. Sykes, *William Wake*, vol. I, pp. 28–30.
[2] A. G. Martimort, *Le Gallicanisme de Bossuet*, p. 280.      [3] *Ibid.* p. 284.

qu'un si grand homme qui parle si bien de l'Église, du Salut que l'on ne trouve qu'en son unité et de l'assistance infaillible du Saint Esprit dans le Concile de Nicée, ce qui induit la même grâce pour tous les autres assemblés dans la même Église, puisse demeurer un seul moment sans la reconnaître,

he received no reply from Bull to his request for 'un mot de réponse qui m'explique le sentiment d'un si grave auteur' on the question as to which was the Catholic Church.[1] Instead, in 1705, after Bossuet's death, Bull published his *Corruptions of the Church of Rome*. The truth of the matter was that whilst Bossuet leaned upon the Fathers of the African Church, particularly Cyprian, for his defence of the Gallican Liberties and his determination to place limits to the papal power,[2] his attitude to Anglicans and Protestants reflected the spirit of the Primacy Text of the *De Ecclesiae Unitate* rather than of the Textus Receptus.

Moreover, changes of far-reaching importance were coming over the political and ecclesiastical landscape both in France and England. In 1685 Louis XIV revoked the Edict of Nantes, and to the persuasions of Bossuet was added henceforth the pressure of the dragonnades to effect the conversion of the Huguenots. Two years later Bossuet published his *Histoire des Variations des Églises Protestantes*, which sounded a far different note from the *Exposition* of 1671. In the *Histoire*—'qui reste aujourd'hui encore le livre le plus solide contre le protestantisme'[3]—Bossuet launched his most powerful polemic against all dissidents from the unity of the Roman church. Of its fifteen books, Book VII was devoted to the reformation in England under Henry VIII and Edward VI, Book X to its continuance under Elizabeth, whilst part of Book XI dealt with Wyclif; and further attention was directed to the Church of England in his subsequent *Avertissements* and in his *Défense de l'Histoire*. Contemporaneously with these events, the reign of James II in England witnessed an aggressive Romanist campaign against the Church of England, supported by all the resources of royal authority and thundering forth menaces rather than invitations to brotherly unity and concord. Moreover, when this threat was overthrown by the Revolution of 1688 and the accession of William and Mary, there

[1] Nelson, *Life of Bull*, pp. 386-7.
[2] 'Son image de l'Église, il est allé la puiser chez les Pères Africains. Voilà ses grands maîtres, ceux à qui il doit tout.' Martimort, *Le Gallicanisme de Bossuet*, p. 552. Neither Bossuet's sermon nor the *Declaratio* cited the Primacy Text, but the Textus Receptus.
[3] F. Cabrol, *art. cit.* in *Revue d'Histoire Ecclésiastique*, vol. XXVII, p. 555.

followed shortly a quarter of a century's war between Louis XIV and the Grand Alliance; and the stress of hostilities, then as in modern days, interrupted the intercourse of scholars and their interchange of learned books and speculations. In 1694 Abbé Longuerue wrote to Professor J. A. Turrettini of Geneva that

s'il plaisait à Dieu de nous renvoyer la paix et faire cesser cette malheureuse guerre, je crois que les savants de ce-pays là [England] ne dedaigneraient pas de rétablir le commerce avec nous; car, monsieur, soyez persuadé qu'on ne peut rien faire de bon dans les sciences que lorsque les savants se communiquent mutuellement leurs connaissances, et que la république des lettres ne peut pas se passer du commerce non plus qu'une république politique.

Six years later he again deplored the ill-effects of the protracted war, in relation to the price of books.

Je crois que les impressions des libraires Anglais sont arrestées par la cherté du papier, qui ne diminuera point, puisque le bon papier vient de France et continuera à payer 25% et d'autres droits qui iront à 40%. Il me parait par tout ce que j'ai appris d'Angleterre depuis un an, que la barbarie va s'y établir autant et plus d'ailleurs. Il n'y a aucun libraire en ce pays-là, qui ose entreprendre à ses frais l'impression d'un livre in 12°, s'il est en Latin.[1]

When the Peace of Utrecht, the death of Louis XIV and the safe accomplishment of the Protestant Succession in Great Britain made possible a resumption of learned correspondence between Anglican and Gallican churchmen, a majority of the personnel of the former generation had died. On this side of the channel, however, Wake became archbishop of Canterbury in 1716, whilst the leading doctor of the Sorbonne, Ellies Du Pin, was of a more radical temper than his predecessor, Picques. Indeed Du Pin had earlier fallen under the formal censure of the authorities both in Paris and Rome, and had earned the resolute hostility of Bossuet. On the one hand his *De antiqua Ecclesiae disciplina Dissertationes Historicae* of 1686 had been condemned at Rome, and on the other hand in 1692 an arrêt of the parlement of Paris, at the instigation of Bossuet, had suppressed his *Nouvelle Bibliothèque des auteurs écclesiastiques*, the continuation of which had therefore to appear under varying titles (such as the *Histoire des Controverses et des matières Ecclesiastiques* and *Histoire de l'Église et des auteurs écclesiastiques du XVème siècle*). Bossuet indeed in his *Mémoire de ce qui est à corriger dans la Nouvelle Bibliothèque des auteurs écclesiastiques de M. Du Pin* had discovered no fewer than

---

[1] E. de Budé, *Lettres Inédites addressées à J. A. Turrettini*, vol. II, pp. 235, 266.

eighteen such points. Amongst them were the author's complete silence concerning Purgatory, which, he alleged, was not definitely mentioned by the Fathers of the first three centuries, together with his inclusion amongst matters of ecclesiastical discipline, variable in their nature, of such practices as prayers and oblations for the dead, masses in memory of the departed and invocation of saints; his exclusion of the Apocrypha from the Canonical Books of the Old Testament; his depreciatory attitude towards the veneration of saints and relics, and particularly the adoration of the cross ('il assert formellement qu'elle était rejetée aux trois premiers siècles et il donne gain de cause aux protestants contre les Du Perron et les Bellarmin'); his denial that the Lenten fast was of apostolic institution; his equivocal belief concerning the Eucharist ('il est certain qu'il n'a pas su ce qu'il fallait dire pour bien établir dans les trois premiers siècles la foi de la présence réelle'); and above all his minimising interpretation of the Roman primacy:

notre auteur n'attribue autre chose au Pape sinon que l'Église romaine fondée par les apôtres S. Pierre et S. Paul, soit considérée comme la première; et son évêque comme le premier entre tous les évêques, sans attribuer au pape aucune jurisdiction sur eux, ni dire le moindre mot de l'institution divine de sa primauté; au contraire il met cet article au rang de la discipline, qu'il dit lui-même être variable.

Moreover Protestants were delighted to use this evidence.

Jurieu a objecté M. Du Pin aux catholiques; et on verra les hérétiques tirer bien d'autres avantages de ces livres, s'il n'y a quelque chose qui le note.[1]

To one of his correspondents, M. Gerbais, Bossuet observed of Du Pin that

j'ai souvent trouvé qu'il allait bien vite et qu'il était bien hardi....J'ai trouvé deux choses constantes; l'une, qu'il favorisait les hérétiques et qu'il affaiblissait la tradition,...et qu'il tranchait sur les Saints Pères avec une témérité que les catholiques n'avaient pas coutume de se permettre.[2]

In 1703, again thanks to the intervention of the bishop of Meaux, Du Pin was deprived of his professorship of philosophy at the Collège de France, and exiled by *lettres de cachet*. With the exacerbation of the controversy concerning Jansenism by the papal bull of 1705 *Vineam Domini Sabaoth*, and in 1713 by the constitution of

---

[1] J. B. Bossuet, *Œuvres*, vol. x (1836), pp. 505 *seq.*
[2] Ch. Urbain et E. Levesque, *Correspondance de Bossuet* (1912), vol. v, Letters nos. 712, 715, 729, pp. 73, 81, 114.

Clement XI, *Unigenitus Dei Filius*, it was only to be expected that, when the regency of Philip, duke of Orleans, after the death of Louis XIV restored Cardinal de Noailles to favour and recalled the academic exiles, Du Pin should adopt a much more favourable attitude towards the Church of England than Bossuet had done.

In 1717 accordingly Du Pin intimated to Wake, through the agency of William Beauvoir, chaplain to the British ambassador in Paris, 'his desire of an union between the Church of England and that of France', and in order thereto, 'to beg the favour of a correspondence'. Although Dr Piers Girardin played a not unimportant part in the ensuing discussion, and the Sorbonne also seconded the efforts towards union, Du Pin was the leading theologian on the Gallican side; and in order fully and properly to understand the Anglican position, he studied a French translation of the Book of Common Prayer, the Ordinal and the Articles of Religion. The outcome of this careful investigation was his own *Commonitorium*, or 'essay about union', which was by far the most important single document evoked by the correspondence. Unlike Bossuet, Du Pin did not think himself bound to the literal text of the decrees of the Council of Trent. Thus he professed his opinion that it was not necessary 'to enter into the question whether the five Sacraments recognised by the Roman Church'—in addition to the Dominical Sacraments of Baptism and the Eucharist—'were instituted immediately by Christ; it is sufficient that they should be recognised as Sacraments'; again, he expressed a readiness to abandon the word 'transubstantiation' in regard to the doctrine of the Real Presence, if the Anglican church would accept 'transmutation' in its stead; and in respect of the Eucharistic sacrifice he affirmed of his fellow-churchmen that

we acknowledge as one and perfect the sacrifice of the cross by which Christ fulfilled and abolished all sacrifices; nor do we call the oblation of the host an unbloody sacrifice in any other sense than because in it there is a memorial of this sacrifice, and the offering of it is continued by the several members of the church who offer together with the priest.

On the vexed question of the relationship of Scripture to Tradition, he defined the latter as a source

which does not set forth new articles of faith, but confirms and illustrates those things which are contained in the sacred writings, and defends them with new securities against those who think otherwise; so that new things are not affirmed, but old things from time to time newly expressed;

and he gave as a penetrating example the use by the Council of Nicaea of the word *consubstantialis*. To the Anglican XIXth Article defining the Church, he wished only to add 'under legitimate pastors', because 'the Church is established on the bishops, priests, ministers and faithful laity, and is governed by its pastors'. Likewise he averred that no Roman Catholic would affirm the contrary of the statement in Article XX that 'it is not lawful for the Church to ordain anything that is contrary to God's Word Written'; but he insisted that, though some ecclesiastical Councils had erred, those Councils to which the church had given recognition as General Councils had not erred in matters of faith. With regard to Purgatory he affirmed the need for a purging from sin of the faithful departed before they could enjoy the Beatific Vision, but held that nothing was required *de fide* concerning purgatorial fire. Furthermore, he was willing (with the formal support of the Sorbonne) to allow that the veneration of relics and images and the adoration of the cross, together with invocation of saints, were optional usages.

The most important and far-reaching of Du Pin's concessions, however, related to the authority of the papacy. Claiming that his standpoint and that of the Sorbonne represented the traditional Gallican position, by no means a thing of yesterday but stretching back to the middle ages, he declared that

with respect to the jurisdiction of the pope in regard to our kingdom, it is confined within such narrow limits that it cannot do anything to our hurt; for he can do nothing in regard to temporal matters, and in regard to spiritual matters, he is confined within the rules of the ancient canons. He cannot do anything in those things which belong to the government of a bishop in his diocese, nor perform ordinations, nor decree anything relating to discipline, nor excommunicate anyone, nor take anything else upon himself. We acknowledge his primacy, that is that he holds the first place amongst bishops, as the whole of antiquity and the Greeks also (though separated from the Roman Church) confess. But this primacy does not give him a superior order amongst bishops; he is still their fellow-bishop, though first among bishops.

Du Pin accepted the statement of the Anglican Article XXXVII that 'the Bishop of Rome hath no jurisdiction in this realm of England' as being true not only of temporal, but also 'of immediate spiritual jurisdiction'. He affirmed only that the pope

by virtue of his primacy has this right, to watch that the right faith is everywhere kept and the canons observed, and as often as they are violated to act in accordance with canon law to repair the evil. This is the sole jurisdiction which we ascribe to the Roman pontiff. The other things which belong to him by human ordinance, are not necessary, and each Church ought to enjoy its own liberties, rights and customs, which ought to continue unshaken and which cannot be infringed by the Roman pontiffs.

These were the precise sentiments which Bossuet had so vehemently repudiated in 1692; and even bolder was the conclusion drawn from them that an union of the Gallican and Anglican churches

may indeed be effected or at least set forward without consulting the Roman pontiff. When the union is made, he shall be informed of it, and humbly requested to give his consent. If he consents, the affair will then be finished; but if he refuses, the union will nevertheless be valid; and if he resorts to threats, then an appeal will be made to a General Council.

It was little surprising that Wake should reply that

the honour which you ascribe to the Roman pontiff I consider to differ little from that which our wiser theologians voluntarily have conceded; so that on this point it would not seem difficult for both sides to agree in the same conclusion, or at least to accept mutually a difference of no importance.[1]

Despite Du Pin's liberal concessions, however, it was evident that nothing could eventuate from the correspondence in the way of formal negotiation, unless the temporal authorities in both France and England were prepared to carry through an union by *force majeure*, which in France would evoke strong ecclesiastical protests from Rome; and in neither country did circumstances make this practicable.

There remained, however another topic of controversy, that of the validity of Anglican Orders, which inevitably demanded examination in any discussion of union. Consideration of the theological issues concerning the Anglican Ordinal and Book of Common Prayer had entered upon a new phase with the publication in 1655 by the Oratorian Jean Morin of his *Commentarius de Sacris Ecclesiae Ordinationibus secundum Antiquos et Recentiores Latinos, Graecos, Syrios et Babylonicos*. The author had been summoned to Rome in 1639 by Cardinal Barberini to attend meetings of a commission to consider Greek ordinations; and his first task had been to establish the historical fact that Rome had always recognised Greek ordinations as valid, and in the light of this recognition to examine their Rites

[1] N. Sykes, *William Wake*, vol. I, pp. 279–82, 304–10.

together with those of other Oriental churches. Being recalled to Paris by Richelieu, he continued his investigations into early Latin Rites, seeking for ancient manuscripts in France and Italy. It seemed to him unsafe to base a decision in such important matters on the opinions of scholastic theologians, whom he found to have been unacquainted with Greek Rites, even ignorant of the language in which they were written,[1] and who had judged the issues entirely from the evidence of contemporary Latin Rites. From his own extensive researches two facts emerged with unmistakable clarity; first, that the scholastics had been mistaken in supposing the matter and form of Ordination to reside in ceremonies which were of comparatively late addition to the Rites; and secondly, that all the early evidence both of East and West established imposition of hands with appropriate prayer to be the sole essentials of valid ordination.[2]

The second part of the treatise set forth the evidence of eastern and western ordinals, and a third section developed the author's conclusions therefrom. The most important part was *Exercitatio VII: De Presbyteratus Materia et Forma*, in which, starting from the accepted premises that sacrifice was an essential part of priesthood and that priesthood was the basis of Christianity, Morin examined the four opinions maintained in the Roman church concerning the matter and form of valid ordination. The first held that the tradition of the instruments with the accompanying formula constituted this matter and form; the second, that this together with imposition of hands jointly was necessary; the third, that each of these two parts conveyed a separate authority; so that the delivery of the chalice and paten conferred power to consecrate the Eucharist and offer the Eucharistic sacrifice, whilst the imposition of hands gave authority to hear confessions and to absolve; and therefore 'priore traditione

---

[1] Morinus, *Commentarius*, Praefatio: 'Mihi non satis tutum videbatur ex solis Doctorum Scholasticorum dictatis de re tanti momenti pronuntiare. Experiebar enim eos nulla Graecorum morum scientia tinctos, nulla linguae Graecae cognitione aspersos, numquam illis in mentem venisse ut inquirerent quae, quot, qualesve essent Graecae ordinationes.'

[2] Morinus, *op. cit.* Praefatio: 'Suspicabar multas ceremonias lapsu temporis Ritualibus additas fuisse, quibus Scholastici plerique, praeteritis antiquis, materias et formas Sacramentales assignarunt....Ubique enim in Sacris Diaconatus, Presbyteratus et Episcopatus Ordinationibus, Latinis, Graecis, Syriis, Aegyptiis, antiquis, hodernis, mediis, conspicies manuum impositionem et orationem unicuique gradui convenientem. In antiquissimis vero omnibus, praeter haec duo, nihil aliud occurret quod cum aliqua probabilitatis specie rationem materiae et formae induere possit. Orientales primi novos ritus antiquis materiis et formulis addiderunt....Addiderunt et Latini longe plures, sed multo serius, et paulatim, longoque annorum decursu' (2nd ed. Amsterdam, 1695) [p. 3].

potestatem dari in corpus Christi verum, posteriore in corpus Christi mysticum'; and finally, the fourth placed the essentials in the conjunction of imposition of hands with the anointing of the priest. Morin, however, advanced the novel conclusion that a fifth opinion only was justified, which regarded the imposition of hands as the sole matter of ordination to the priesthood. 'Postrema opinio, ea est quae materiam Sacerdotii constituit solam manuum impositionem. Hanc solam omnis Ecclesia, Latina, Graeca, Barbara semper agnovit. Hanc solam commemorant omnes antiqui Rituales, Latini, Graeci; omnes antiqui et recentiores Patres, Graeci, Latini.'[1] There remained, however, the determination as to which of the three impositions of hands in the Roman Ordinal constituted the essential matter; in which connection he observed that the formula spoken at the third laying-on of hands ('Accipe Spiritum Sanctum; quorum remiseritis peccata, remittuntur eis: et quorum retinueritis, retenta sunt') was unknown for the first twelve hundred years of the church, being a recent addition to the Latin Rite of not more than four centuries' history. Similarly he noted that the contemporary formula used at the delivery of the instruments ('Accipe potestatem offerre sacrificia Deo, Missasque celebrare tam pro vivis quam pro defunctis') was absent from the early Latin and Greek Ordinals— 'profundum et mirum est de hisce rebus apud eos silentium'; and he conjectured that it had made its appearance not more than seven hundred years ago, when it was first used at the consecration of a bishop and thence passed into the ordination of priests.[2] Thus the tradition of the instruments with the accompanying power to offer sacrifices and to celebrate Masses could not be the essential form and matter of priestly ordination. Nor could the imposition of the

---

[1] 'Prima et vulgatissima Doctorum numero et autoritate celebris, docet Sacerdotii materiam esse traditionem Calicis cum vino et aqua et Patenae cum pane, atque in traditione ejusmodi instrumentorum characterem imprimi et sacerdotium creari. Secunda eorum est, qui hanc materiam censent esse tantum partialem, et ei jungi volunt manuum impositionem, ut ex utraque constituatur materia integra.... Tertia opinio idem tradit quod praecedens sed insuper addit, ita separatas duas istas materias partiales, ut materia prius tradita nullo casu effectum posterioris suppleri possit. Aiunt autem prioris materiae sive traditionis instrumentorum proprium effectum esse, sacrificandi et Eucharistiae consecrandae potestatem, posterioris vero seu manuum impositionis effectum, Confessiones audiendi et absolvendi a peccatis auctoritatem, sive priore traditione potestatem dari in corpus Christi verum, posteriore in corpus Christi mysticum.... Quarta opinio manuum impositioni conjungit in unitatem materiae unctionem Presbytero in Ordinatione factum.' Morinus, *op. cit.* Pars III, Exercitatio VII, Cap. I, §§ II–IV, VI, VII, pp. 102–3.

[2] *Op. cit.* p. 105. Pars III, Exercitatio VII, Cap. I, §§ XII, XVI, XVII; Cap. II, §§ I, II.

Gospels upon the head of the bishop-elect at his consecration be the matter of episcopal consecration, which must consist likewise in the imposition of hands with an invocation of the Holy Spirit, which itself need not be imperative but could be precative in its terms.[1]

Although Morin modestly claimed to have put forward only evidences and not decisions—'exercitationes videlicet nos scribere non decisiones'—and dutifully submitted his work to the apostolic see, the result of his investigation was revolutionary. It disposed of the definition of Pope Eugenius IV in the Bull *Exultate Deo* of 1439 that the matter of ordination to the priesthood is the tradition of the instruments and the form is the power to offer sacrifice.[2] In so doing it had disallowed incidentally one of the principal Roman Catholic criticisms of the Anglican Ordinal on the ground of its omission of both the delivery of the chalice and paten and of the accompanying formula. Burnet therefore in his *Vindication of the Ordinations of the Church of England* in 1677 gladly availed himself of this evidence. Thanks, however, to the impartial character of historical study, the Anglican formula at the imposition of hands in the ordination of a priest ('Receive the Holy Ghost; whosesoever sins ye forgive they are forgiven unto them and whosesoever sins ye retain, they are retained') had been shown by Morin to be an even later addition to the Latin Rite than the porrection of the instruments. Burnet accordingly embraced the negative parts of Morin's evidence, as to the absence from early Ordinals of all mention of the power to offer sacrifice and the delivery of the sacred vessels; and proceeded constructively to argue that 'if our Form be the same in which Christ ordained his Apostles, we may be very well satisfied that it is good and sufficient'. In support of his contention he cited further Canon 4, De Sacramento Ordinis, of Session XXIII of the Council of Trent, which anathematised any who affirmed that 'per sacram ordinationem non dari Spiritum sanctum, ac proinde frustra episcopos dicere: Accipe Spiritum sanctum'. In company with Morin, he rejected the interpretation of some Roman Catholic divines, by which it was maintained that the tradition of the instruments gave power to offer sacrifice and to consecrate the Eucharist, whilst the final imposition of hands with the words 'Receive the Holy Ghost'

---

[1] Morinus, *Commentarius*, Pars III, Exercitatio II, Cap. I, § II.

[2] 'Sextum sacramentum est ordinis, cuius materia est illud, per cuius traditionem confertur ordo, sicut presbyteratus traditur per calicis cum vino et patenae cum pane porrectionem;...Forma sacerdotii talis est; "Accipe potestatem offerendi sacrificium in ecclesia pro vivis et mortuis in nomine Patris et Filii et Spiritus Sancti."'

conferred only authority to bind and to loose; and he repudiated also the parallel exegesis that Christ had constituted his apostles to be priests at the Last Supper. *Per contra* he held that the Anglican formula embraced comprehensively all aspects of the priestly office, and that the subsequent injunction, 'Be thou a faithful Dispenser of the Word of God and of his holy Sacraments', conferred all necessary power to celebrate the Eucharist. Dr Humphrey Prideaux in 1687 in his *Validity of the Orders of the Church of England* leaned with equal weight upon the authority of Morin, following his evidence and conclusions even more thoroughly and with greater detail than Burnet. The researches of the French Oratorian indeed had permanently affected the debates concerning the essentials of valid ordination to the priesthood and consecration to the episcopate.

The question of Anglican Orders was arousing considerable interest and discussion at this time both in Italy and France. During his visit to Rome in the pontificate of Innocent XI in 1685, Burnet reported that

Cardinal Howard and the Cardinal D'Éstrees treated me with great freedom. The latter talked much with me concerning the Orders of our Church, to know whether they had been brought down to us by men truly ordained or not; for, he said, they apprehended things would be much more easily brought about, if our Orders could be esteemed valid, though given in heresy and schism. I told him I was glad they were possessed of any opinion that made the reconciliation more difficult; but as for the matter of fact, nothing was more certain than that the ordinations in the beginning of Queen Elizabeth's reign were canonical and regular. He seemed to be persuaded of the truth of this, but lamented that it was impossible to bring the Romans to think so.[1]

In France, Bossuet in a letter of 12 August 1685 to Mabillon expressed a view of Anglican Orders which the editors of his correspondence characterised as 'plutôt favorable à la validité des ordinations Anglaises', though not quite certain, and reserving the decision to the Apostolic See.

Pour l'affaire de l'Angleterre, outre la difficulté des premiers évêques, auteurs du schisme, il y en a encore une grande au temps de Cromwell, où on prétend que la succession de l'ordination a été interrompue. Les Anglais soutiennent que non, et, pour la succession dans le commencement du schisme, ils soutiennent qu'il n'y a aucune difficulté; et il semble qu'ils aient raison en cela. Cela dépend du fait et le Saint Siège ne manquera pas d'agir en cette affaire avec sa circonspection ordinaire.[2]

---

[1] G. Burnet, *History of My Own Time*, vol. III, p. 78.
[2] Ch. Urbain et E. Levesque, *Correspondance de Bossuet*, vol. III, Letter no. 339; and footnote 4; pp. 114–15.

Abbot Cabrol concluded that

à examiner les choses de près, cette lettre n'a rien de bien compromettant. Bossuet est visiblement favorable à la validité des ordinations anglicanes, mais il paraît plutôt s'en rapporter au temoignage des anglicans qu'exprimer une conviction bien personnelle, et du reste il s'en remet sur ce point... au jugement du Pape.[1]

Notwithstanding, when this letter was published amongst the *pièces justificatives* of Le Courayer's *Dissertation sur la Validité des Ordinations des Anglais* in 1723, it caused a sensation and its authenticity was challenged by Le Quien. In his *Défense de la Dissertation* published in 1726 therefore, Le Courayer carried the matter a stage further by citing a letter from M. Caldagues, Precentor of Montferrand, in which the writer affirmed:

J'aurai l'honneur de vous dire que M. Bossuet parlait plus affirmativement sur la validité des ordinations anglicanes en 1699 qu'en 1685. Car je me souviens très distinctement qu'ayant eu l'honneur d'aller chez lui cette année-là avec feu M. Marcel, curé de St Jacques-du-Haut-Pas, et la conversation étant tombée sur l'Église anglicane, ce grand prélat nous dit en poussant un grand soupir, que, si Dieu faisait la grâce aux Anglais de renoncer à leurs erreurs et à leur schisme, leur clergé n'aurait besoin que d'être reconcilié à l'Église et rehabilité; et il ajouta qu'il s'était expliqué de cette manière devant le roi.[2]

Bossuet and Du Pin were agreed therefore at least on this point. For the latter in commenting on Article XXXVI observed that

I should be unwilling for the ordinations either of English bishops, priests or deacons to be pronounced invalid; though perhaps some may be so; but there is nothing to prevent the Gallican Church from approving them, just as the Council of Nicaea ratified the ordinations (be it said without offence) of the Meletians and Novatians. If therefore an union is achieved, all the bishops, priests, deacons and beneficed ministers of the English communion shall be continued in their orders, functions, ministries and benefices, either of right or by concession of the Church.

Accordingly Le Courayer dealt fully with the theological issues concerning the sufficiency of the form and matter of the Anglican Ordinal and the related questions of the doctrine of priesthood and sacrifice in the Book of Common Prayer and Ordinal; and here he leaned heavily on Morin for proof of his contention that the Ordinal, containing imposition of hands with appropriate prayer, had the essentials of valid ordination.

---

[1] F. Cabrol, *art. cit.* in *Revue d'Histoire Écclésiastique*, vol. xxvii (1931), p. 563.

[2] *Correspondance de Bossuet*, vol. iii, pp. 114–15, n. 4.

À commencer par ce qui regarde la matière, la chose n'est pas d'une longue discussion après le sçavant ouvrage du P. Morin sur le Sacrement d'Ordre. Car sur les preuves qu'il en a rapportées, tout ce qu'il y a de habiles théologiens conviennent avec lui, qui l'imposition des mains est la seule matière essentielle de ce Sacrement.

Again,

On ne puisse regarder que comme probable le sentiment de ceux qui font de la seule imposition des mains et de la prière qui l'accompagne, la matière et la forme de l'Ordination; cependant ce sentiment devient demontré et certain, quand il s'agit de décider par le nombre et la qualité des preuves. Si vous en demandez la raison, le sçavant P. Morin la fournit en deux mots, dans ces paroles: Ea enim ad substantiam Sacramenti non pertinent, quae Graeci nunquam usurparunt, nec multis saeculis Latini.[1]

Le Courayer further drew considerably upon the works of Martène and Mabillon in support of his position, which followed the traditional line of Anglican apologetic to the effect that the prayer in the Ordinal at the imposition of hands upon the candidate for priesthood together with the form of words at the delivery of the Bible, read in their context in the whole service, constituted a sufficient doctrine of priesthood and sacrifice, if the Eucharistic sacrifice be regarded as representative and commemorative.

A further example of Morin's influence in his demonstration that the imperative form 'Receive the Holy Ghost' was a late addition to the Latin Rites, may probably be traced in a proposal which the royal commissioners appointed in 1689 to revise the Liturgy intended to recommend to the Convocation:

whether it be not more suitable unto the general rule the Church of England has gone upon of conforming herself to the Primitive Church, to put these words in some such form as this: 'Pour down, O Father of Lights, the Holy Ghost on this thy servant for the office and work of a Priest in the Church of God, now committed unto him by the imposition of our hands; that whose sins he does forgive, they may be forgiven, and whose sins he doth retain, they may be retained; and that he may be a faithful Dispenser of God's holy Word and Sacraments to the edification of his Church and the glory of his holy Name.[2]

The seventeenth-century Anglican divines, however, did not confine the relevance of their patristic studies to the endeavour towards

---

[1] P. F. Le Courayer, *Dissertation sur la Validité des Ordinations des Anglais*, vol. I, c. VI, pp. 103–4; vol. II, c. XII, p. 7.

[2] Secker MSS. 12 (Lambeth Palace Library).

a rapprochement with Gallican churchmen. True to the Janus-like character of their church, they sought closer relations also with the foreign Reformed churches. Here, as with domestic dissenters, the question of episcopacy versus presbyterianism was the predominant issue, and in its determination the Epistles of Ignatius played a vital part. Lightfoot pointed out their influence on Bishop Joseph Hall's *Episcopacy by Divine Right Asserted* in 1639 and Jeremy Taylor's *Of the Sacred Order and Offices of Episcopacy* in 1642, though both works were published before Ussher's demonstration of the authenticity of the Short Recension.[1] Moreover the age was one in which learned studies effected conversions, and divines deliberated long over the disputed interpretations of patristic evidence. Simon Patrick related how at the outset of his public ministry,

I knew no better than to go to a Classis of Presbyters, who then sat, and was examined by them and afterward received the imposition of their hands. This afterwards troubled me very much, when not long after I met with Dr Hammond upon Ignatius' Epistles and Mr Thorndike's Primitive Government of the Church; whereby I was fully convinced of the necessity of episcopal ordination. This made me enquire after a bishop to whom I might resort; and hearing that Bishop Hall lived not far from Norwich, of which he was bishop, thither I went with two other Fellows of our College and a gentleman (Mr Gore with whom I had contracted a great friendship) as a companion and witness of what we did. There we were received with great kindness by that reverend old bishop, who examined us and gave us many good exhortations; and then ordained us in his parlour at Higham about one mile from Norwich, April 5th, 1654.[2]

A generation later Edmund Calamy the younger hesitated considerably between episcopacy and presbyterianism.

I had it now particularly under consideration whether I should determine for conformity or nonconformity. I thought Oxford no unfit place to pursue this matter in....I was entertained from day to day with what tended to give any man the best opinion of the church by law established. ...I read several of the Fathers, and, among the rest, Ignatius' six Epistles of Bishop Ussher's Latin and Isaac Vossius' Florentine Greek editions....I read also Bishop Pearson in defence of these Epistles, as well as Monsieur Daillé and Larroque in opposition to them....However I must own that with all the eyes I had, I could not discover any more in those that go under the name of Ignatius' Epistles, than a pastoral episcopacy.

---

[1] J. B. Lightfoot, *Apostolic Fathers*, pt. II, vol. I, pp. 240–1.
[2] S. Patrick, 'Autobiography', *Works*, vol. IX, pp. 423–4; Hall ordained Patrick as deacon and priest on the same day.

Chief amongst the factors which drove Calamy to embrace Non-conformity was this distinction between what he called 'pastoral episcopacy' and the Anglican 'diocesan episcopacy'.

No one thing is more evident as to the primitive times, than that a bishopric and a parish were the same thing....Even afterwards their dioceses were but small....I could not tell how to conceive that their bishoprics could be like ours in England.[1]

At a still later date Secker during his early studies 'read the Apostolical Fathers, Eusebius' Ecclesiastical History, Whiston's Primitive Christianity, and many other chiefly theological books'; whereby he was 'pretty well satisfied of the lawfulness of conforming to the Church of England as a layman', though not yet sufficiently persuaded to accept ministerial ordination.[2]

The chief concern of Anglican divines, however, was with the foreign Reformed churches and their lack of episcopacy. The Act of Uniformity of 1662, reflecting the firmer emphasis upon episcopacy which resulted from these patristic studies, had closed the gaps through which, in the earlier half of the seventeenth century, foreign ministers had been admitted to Anglican benefices, both with and without cure of souls, upon the credit solely of their presbyterian ordination. Henceforth the unvarying requirement of episcopal ordination for ministering in the Church of England meant that foreign presbyters would need to be re-ordained, a circumstance which caused both umbrage and misunderstanding amongst the continental Reformed churches. In reply to their puzzled inquiries, Anglican apologists argued that, whilst presbyterian orders could be regarded as valid when given in churches which, through ineluctable historical necessity, had lost episcopacy, it was the duty of individual ministers of such churches residing in England to take advantage of the opportunity of securing episcopal ordination, and of their churches to consider the wisdom of restoring episcopacy and thereby recovering the fullness of the traditional ministry of the church. The practical issues involved became more urgent when the aggressive wars of Louis XIV abroad and his persecution of Huguenots at home brought a steadily increasing stream of refugees to Great Britain. It has been estimated that during the decades preceding and following the revocation of the Edict of Nantes, a gross total of 80,000 French refugees were granted asylum; and that during the

---

[1] E. Calamy, *An Historical Account of My Own Life*, vol. I, pp. 224–7.
[2] Secker, *Memoirs* (Lambeth Palace Library), f. 7.

last quinquennium of the reign of Charles II, before the revocation, 1154 received denization in England.[1] Sancroft, who showed great friendship to members of the foreign Reformed churches, was anxious to ensure their conformity to the Church of England, by admitting their ministers to Anglican Orders and providing for their performance of divine worship according to a French translation of the Book of Common Prayer. During the same year in which Louvois began the use of the dragonnades in Poitou, Sancroft on 27 February 1681/2 addressed to the rector of Boughton-Malherb in Kent a letter of commendation in behalf of the Marquis de Venours, a French nobleman who with his household had left his native land, and had leased from the earl of Chesterfield a house in that parish;

intending to settle himself there, together with a little colony of his fellow-countrymen, who are not only professors of the Protestant religion, but confessors and sufferers for the same, and all desirous to serve God and to perform the public offices of our most holy religion according to the use of the Church of England (to the government and discipline whereof they do also entirely submit themselves). I do therefore require you and the rest of the inhabitants of your parish and your neighbours, both ministers and others, to receive and assist them as occasion shall be offered, with all the expressions and instances of Christian charity and brotherly kindness due to afflicted strangers of the same faith and communion with us. And because they understand not the English language and are therefore permitted to perform divine offices in the French tongue, (as they are, and have been for several years, performed in the French Church at the Savoy), I have therefore appointed, and do hereby appoint, Mr Jacques Rondeau, a Presbyter of the Church of England, to officiate and preach to them in your parish church of Bocton-Malherb; and do hereby require you to give them to that purpose free access into and use of the same, at such hours and times of the day as may not hinder your ordinary public assemblies in the same.[2]

Moreover Sancroft graciously granted to Rondeau, together with two others of his fellow countrymen, Andrew Lortie and Elias Brevet, a faculty to receive both the Orders of Deacon and Priest at the same time and *extra tempora* from the bishop of London, for 'good testimony of his conversation and abilities for undertaking the Office of Ministry according to the Discipline of the Protestant or Reformed Churches of France'; and subsequently in 1683 licensed him in similar terms to officiate and preach to the French Protestants

---

[1] Ch. Weiss: *Histoire des Réfugiés Protestants de France depuis la Révocation de l'Édit de Nantes* (1853), vol. I, book III, c. I, p. 268.

[2] Tanner MSS. 36, f. 239. Lambeth Act Books, IV, f. 180.

at Hollingbourne and Broomfield in Kent.[1] From such individual acts it was but a short step to the injunction to all the bishops of the province of Canterbury in 1687, to require their clergy likewise to exhort the Protestant dissenters 'to join with us in daily fervent prayer to the God of peace for an universal union of all reformed churches, both at home and abroad, against our common enemies'.

The most important and far-reaching achievement of Sancroft in this field, however, was his co-operation with Compton in securing the grant by Charles II of royal bursaries for the education at Oxford of intending ministers of the *Unitas Fratrum*, by which means Adam Samuel Hartmann brought to England in 1680 from Lissa in Poland two of his pupils, one of whom, Daniel Ernst Jablonski, was to bear lifelong impressions of his residence here.[2] For although he came with great prejudices against the Church of England (regarding it with horror and thinking its churches to be avoided as much as those of the papists), he soon became one of its warmest admirers and imitators. At Christ Church he was particularly influenced by Fell, and therein especially by the latter's edition of Cyprian, a devotion which bore fruit many years later when Jablonski, now a bishop of the Moravian Church and court-preacher at Berlin, employed the several days of a jolting journey in an unsprung carriage in reading afresh the works of the African bishop. In addition to the influence of Fell, Jablonski was much indebted to the friendships which he formed with Sancroft himself, Compton, Wake and William Beveridge; thanks to which he became an ardent advocate of episcopacy and of the Book of Common Prayer. Few more romantic examples of the casting of one's bread upon the waters in order to find it after many days can be cited than the circumstance, recorded by Secker,[3] that Bishop Thomas of Lincoln in the debate in the House of Lords in 1748 on a Bill requiring episcopal clergy in Scotland to have Letters of Orders granted by some English or Irish bishop, affirmed that he knew of two cases of Scottish clergymen who had applied for, and received, ordination to the presbyterate at the hands of Jablonski himself, having journeyed for that purpose to Prussia. Secker likewise testified to

---

[1] Lambeth Act Books, IV, ff. 179, 307.

[2] For Jablonski, see Ernst Benz, *Bischofsamt und Apostolische Sukzession im Deutschen Protestantismus* (1953); N. Sykes, *Daniel Ernst Jablonski and the Church of England* (London, 1950); Hermann Dalton, *Daniel Ernst Jablonski* (1903); N. Sykes, *William Wake*, vol. II, pp. 60–81.

[3] Secker MSS. 1351 (Lambeth Palace Library).

his own knowledge of similar instances in respect of Danish and Swedish bishops.

But the returns of gratitude made by Jablonski for his education at Oxford were not confined to such isolated acts. Rather he devoted the greater part of his long life to an endeavour to unite the Lutheran and Reformed churches within the dominions of the Prussian king, by the restoration of an episcopate in the apostolic succession and by the introduction of a German translation of the Book of Common Prayer. Nor was this project the sum of his ambition; for he dreamed of the further union of such a Prussian episcopal church with the Church of England, thereby laying the foundation for a wider unity of all Protestant churches. His first endeavours in 1701, when he hoped to turn to profit the occasion of the coronation of the Elector Frederick III as King Frederick I of Prussia by introducing episcopacy, were unhappily frustrated. Notwithstanding his own consecration to the episcopate of the *Unitas Fratrum* in 1699, and the cordial support of Leibniz, who wished also to have the Reformed Court-Preacher at Berlin, Ursinus, consecrated as archbishop by Jablonski and two other bishops possessing a valid (though perhaps irregular) apostolic succession, political opposition was too powerful to allow of success; and the anointing of King Frederick was performed by Ursinus and the Lutheran Court-Preacher at Königsberg, von Sanden, with the mere title of bishops but without consecration. Jablonski turned therefore to the second item in his programme, that of introducing into the royal chapel a German version of the Book of Common Prayer, in order to prepare the way for further progress when the times were propitious.

Such a condition seemed to be realised in 1710 when the change of administration in England brought Archbishop Sharp to the fore as ecclesiastical adviser of the queen's ministers, seconded by Bishop Robinson of Bristol, whose experience of a quarter of a century's residence as chaplain and envoy at Stockholm had given him an unusual acquaintance with the ecclesiastical affairs of northern Europe. Indeed the possibility of using the liturgy, polity and confessional standards of the Church of England as a providential means of creating an episcopal church in Prussia aroused the warm interest of English high-churchmen. Sharp responded enthusiastically to the overture made by Jablonski. Dr George Smalridge was equally zealous in commending to the archbishop an 'affair which may tend so much to the glory of God and the good of his Church', and in which moreover 'the honour of your own church and the edification of foreign churches seem to be so much interested'; whilst the Lower House of Canterbury Convocation informed the Upper House of their gratification at

the present endeavours of several Reformed Churches to accommodate themselves to our liturgy and constitution, mentioned in the late form of address sent down by your lordships. They are very desirous of knowing your lordships' opinion, in what manner it may be proper for this convocation, with her majesty's leave and encouragement, to express their great satisfaction to find them in such good dispositions, and their readiness to maintain and cherish such a fraternal correspondence with them, as may strengthen the interest of the reformed religion against the common enemy.

Smalridge indeed believed that a crucial moment in the relationship of the Church of England with the foreign Reformed churches was at hand; in which

we should still be importunate with them to receive episcopacy; and if, after being called upon and shewn that the reception of it is practicable, they will still obstinately refuse to embrace it, we shall not be obliged to entertain the same charitable opinion of them which we and those who have gone before us have hitherto done.

Despite the zeal of churchmen both in England and abroad, political obstacles repeatedly prevented the success of Jablonski's schemes, alike in negotiation with Sharp and the Tory administration of Anne and later with Wake and the Whig ministers of George I.

Simultaneously other foreign Protestant churches, recognising the Church of England as the head and cornerstone of the Protestant interest, were increasingly appreciative both of its polity and of its liturgy. Several continental divines received election as Corresponding Members of S.P.C.K.; whilst at Neuchâtel Jean Frédéric Ostervald introduced in 1702 his *Catechisme ou Instruction dans la Religion Chréstienne* and in 1713 his *Liturgie de Neuchâtel*, which showed marked tendencies to deviate from the standards of Calvin and to approximate to those of the Book of Common Prayer. At Geneva, Jean Alphonse Turrettini maintained an oecumenical correspondence with scholars of other lands, including Tillotson, Burnet and Wake in England. The way was well prepared therefore for Wake's efforts towards Protestant union; in which the influence of contemporary patristic studies was abundantly illustrated by his ubiquitous emphasis on the apostolic origins of episcopacy and the necessity for its restoration in the foreign Reformed churches. In his letter of 1 March 1717 to the Antistes of Zurich he gave characteristic expression to this conviction.

We wish, indeed, we fervently desire, that the ancient and (so far as we can gather from the sacred record) Apostolic government of the Church, that is the episcopal, as it prevails amongst ourselves, had been everywhere retained. We pray our common Lord that in his own time he will restore this order to all the Reformed churches; and having restored it, will preserve it until the end of the world. We are confident that this indeed will be granted to them in due time by our most merciful Saviour.[1]

Unfortunately his endeavours towards unity were defeated by internal controversies amongst the Swiss churches concerning subscription to the *Formula Consensus*, which sought to impose a rigidly Calvinistic interpretation of their confessional standards; and his pleas for the taking of episcopacy into their ecclesiastical system met with nothing beyond polite compliments and praise for the Anglican polity. It is indeed a sobering exercise for English churchmen to reflect that a twentieth-century Rector of Neuchâtel University in his inaugural address extolling the *Grandeur d'Ostervald*, whilst recognising that his hero 'à l'heure où les pourparlers d'union avec les Anglicans semblaient avoir des chances d'aboutir, était disposé à se rallier à la notion anglicane de l'épiscopat', nevertheless equated Wake's emphatic insistence on episcopacy with the rigid Calvinistic doctrine of reprobation as illiberal obstacles to Ostervald's enlightened efforts for reunion.

Désireux personellement d'y travailler sur le terrain du Christianisme pratique, Ostervald ne pouvait empêcher ni les Anglicans d'estimer indispensable l'organisation épiscopale, ni les Calvinistes d'insister sur le dogme centrale du Calvinisme.[2]

The solitary practical outcome of Anglican correspondence with foreign churches therefore was the recognition by Act of Parliament of the *Unitas Fratrum* as 'an ancient Protestant Episcopal Church' in 1749. A younger generation than that of Jablonski had established a community at Herrnhut in Saxony on the property of Count Zinzendorf, to whom Jablonski addressed several letters in 1729 emphasising the urgent necessity of preserving the episcopal succession amongst the Moravian Brethren. Accordingly Jablonski himself consecrated to the episcopate David Nitschmann, a member of the Hernnhut settlement, in 1735, and two years later he and

---

[1] N. Sykes, *William Wake*, vol. II, p. 4.

[2] M. Neeser, *Grandeur d'Ostervald* (1938), pp. 18, 28 (Inaugural Address, 28 October 1937).

Nitschmann consecrated Zinzendorf to the same order and office. During the early part of 1737 Zinzendorf visited London to seek permission for the Moravian brethren to settle in the English colonies in North America, especially Georgia, and was favourably received by Archbishop Potter. The latter indeed followed the precedent of his predecessor, Archbishop Wake, in recognising the *Unitas* as 'an apostolic and episcopal church, whose doctrines contained nothing whatever militating against the Thirty-Nine Articles of the Church of England'. When, however, the visit of Zinzendorf resulted in the planting of an outpost of Moravianism in London itself, Bishop Gibson took umbrage and adopted an attitude of hostility towards the Fetter Lane Society. In 1742, therefore, this Society applied for a licence under the Toleration Act to conduct their worship as 'Moravian Brethren formerly of the English Communion'; a step which was sharply reprobated by Zinzendorf, who paid a further visit to London in 1747 to secure an act of Parliament recognising the *Unitas* as an episcopal church. Once again he obtained the cordial support of Potter, in face of the antipathy of Gibson; and in 1749 the desired statutory recognition was granted, despite the initial opposition of Gibson's successor in the see of London, Thomas Sherlock, but with the approval of Archbishop Herring of Canterbury and Bishop Maddox of Worcester.[1]

Notwithstanding the scanty harvest of so much earnest effort towards union, the results of Anglican patristic study and scholarship were of great importance. An impressive apology for episcopacy had been constructed, friendly correspondence had been initiated with eminent Gallican divines, and the foreign Reformed churches had been brought to recognise the value of the Anglican *via media* with its firm hold upon the historic episcopate. In all these respects the seeds had been sown of a tree whose leaves are for the healing of the churches. Posterity, still awaiting the fulfilment of their hopes, may nevertheless be grateful for the endeavours of seventeenth-century churchmen in 'keeping up a correspondence and thereby laying a foundation for an union, which may meet with more encouragement hereafter, and which without such a preparatory, would possibly never be brought about or attempted'.

[1] D. Benham, *Memoirs of James Hutton* (London, 1856); D. Cranz, *The Ancient and Modern History of The Brethren: translated by B. La Trobe* (London, 1780); N. Sykes, *Edmund Gibson*, pp. 322–32; A. G. Spangenberg, *Life of Count Zinzendorf* (London, 1838); *Report of the Committee appointed by the Archbishop of Canterbury to consider the Orders of the 'Unitas Fratrum'* (Cambridge, 1907).

# V

# TRUE RELIGION AND SOUND LEARNING

'Is it possible', asked Burnet in respect of Bossuet's *Histoire des Variations*,

that he is so ignorant either of Antiquity or of the age of the Schoolmen, as not to know how long they were before they settled on almost all the notions of Divinity? Father Petau can inform him how dark the Fathers of the first three centuries were even in their ideas of the Trinity; and it were easy to shew that even after the definition of the Council of Nice, it was long before they settled on the same notion of the Unity of the Divine Essence with that which has been received now for many ages in the Church.[1]

The comment was a shrewd home-thrust at Bossuet, who had contended that Protestants alone were innovators, whilst the dogmas of the Roman church were unvarying and immutable. But, whilst cogent as an *argumentum ad hominem*, it had disquieting potentialities when deployed in a wider context. For if the testimony of the ante-Nicene Fathers on such a vital issue as the relationship of the three Persons of the Trinity was uncertain and even of doubtful orthodoxy, what became of the Anglican appeal in matters of belief to 'that which is agreeable to the doctrine of the Old or New Testament and that which the catholic fathers and ancient bishops have gathered out of that doctrine'? The exaltation of the sole authority of the Bible, epitomised in Chillingworth's famous dictum, 'The Bible, I say, the Bible only is the religion of Protestants', had encountered admitted difficulties in respect of the Trinitarian definitions of the *Quicunque Vult*. Now, however, the doctrines of the Fathers of the pre-Nicene period were likewise suspect and called into question. Moreover, this suggestion came from a member of the Society of Jesus. Heterodox opinions concerning the Trinity had been current indeed in many quarters since Faustus Socinus; and Arian sentiments had found expression in more recent Protestant divines. Episcopius, although maintaining against Socinus the pre-existence

---

[1] G. Burnet, *A Letter to Mr Thevenot, containing a Censure of Mr le Grand's History of King Henry VIII's Divorce; to which is added a Censure of M. de Meaux's History of the Variations of the Protestant Churches* (1689), pp. 37–8.

of the Son not only before his birth of the Virgin Mary, but also before the creation of the world, had nevertheless spoken with much disrespect of the Nicene creed as 'precipitately framed by the bishops out of fury and unblest party spirit'; and his editor, Curcellaeus likewise had used expressions in his preface which were open to suspicion. But if heresies might be half-expected from such sources, it was a very different matter when a learned Jesuit lent the weight of his erudition to depreciation of the ante-Nicene Fathers.

This was the head and front of Petau's offending. The independence of judgment which had led him to admit the presence of interpolations in the Long Recension of the Ignatian Epistles—'a noble exception', as Lightfoot averred, to the generality of Roman Catholic scholars—caused him to give equal affront and discomfiture to his fellow-churchmen by his admissions concerning the Trinitarian doctrines of the early Fathers in his *De Theologicis Dogmatibus*. Naturally Jurieu made much play with Petau against Bossuet; and, which was worse, Christopher Sandius in his *Enucleatae Historiae Ecclesiasticae* turned Petau's admissions to the service of Socinianism. It was a sense of the wounds thus inflicted on orthodoxy in the house of its friends which moved Bull, whilst acknowledging Petau as 'a great man fully furnished with learning of every kind', to write the *Defensio Fidei Nicenae* in refutation of his conclusion 'that almost all the bishops and fathers before the council of Nice held precisely the same opinions as Arius'. Indeed, Bull commented, 'Unlucky Arius! that Petavius was not yet born, to become the patron and advocate of his cause in the conflict at Nicaea'. So surprising and subversive were these opinions of Petau as to lead Bull to entertain the suspicion that, apart from 'that bold and restless temper which is his wont in criticising and commenting on the holy fathers', he had written with the purpose of exalting papal prerogatives, on the one hand by disparaging the authority of the fathers of the first three centuries—'to whom Reformed Catholics are wont to make their chief appeal'—and on the other hand by arguing 'that oecumenical councils have the power of framing, or as Petavius says of settling and developing, new articles of faith'. However this might be, since Petau's work was 'most pleasing to modern Arians, who on this account with one consent look up to and salute him as their patron', the *Defensio Fidei Nicenae* was published in 1685 to show 'it to be manifestly repugnant to the truth, and most unjust and insulting to the holy fathers, whether those of the Council of Nicaea or those who preceded it'.[1] Ten years later Bull published his further work on *The Judgment of the Catholic Church on the Necessity of Believing that our Lord Jesus Christ is Very God*, which was directed to the same end. Both treatises, however, had been written primarily with an eye to soundness of doctrine amongst clergy of the Church of England; the *Defensio Fidei Nicenae* because its author had been informed that the works of Sandius 'were everywhere in the hands of our students of theology', and the *Judgment of the Catholic Church* (in refutation of the *Theological Institutes* of Episcopius) because 'during the last few years there have appeared in England several works, whose unprincipled authors have strained every nerve to weaken and overthrow the most important article of our faith, whereon certainly Christianity hinges', and to the defence of which Bull therefore rallied.[2]

The salient, if disquieting, characteristic of the domestic situation, to which Bull addressed his erudite patristic studies was, however, a marked decline of respect for the authority of the Fathers, a tendency parallel to, though differing from, contemporary trends in the Gallican church. 'In both churches, among a section of thinkers, the reputation of the Fathers was sliding downhill between 1680 and 1730. In England that section was the left-wing, the Latitudinarians, in France it was the right-wing, the anti-Gallicans.'[3] But the men of Latitude were themselves the *epigoni* of the Cambridge Platonists; and upon this school of divines must rest the initial responsibility for the new theological temper, which was to become dominant during the late seventeenth and early eighteenth centuries and was to sweep away the patristic defences of orthodoxy so laboriously constructed by Bull and Pearson. When Atterbury in his *Letter to a Convocation Man* resolved 'to look abroad and see how the wind stands from Holland', whence had been unloosed upon England a Pandora's box 'of Deists, Socinians, Latitudinarians, Deniers of Mysteries and pretending explainers of them to undermine and overthrow the Catholic Faith', the hyperbole of his language concealed a sober truth. Recent study has established not only 'a genuine connection between the aims of the Platonists in England and the Arminians in Holland', but also an intermittent corre-

---

[1] G. Bull, *Defensio Fidei Nicenae*: English translation in Library of Anglo-Catholic Theology (1851), pp. 9–12. R. Nelson, *Life of Dr George Bull*, pp. 280 *seq.*

[2] G. Bull, *Defensio*, pp. vii–viii; *The Judgement of the Catholic Church* (Library of Anglo-Catholic Theology, 1855), p. ix.

[3] W. O. Chadwick, *From Bossuet to Newman*, p. 58.

spondence carried on for more than two decades from 1667 to 1687 between the Dutch theologian Philippus van Limborch and two of the leading Cambridge Platonists, Henry More and Ralph Cudworth.[1] Furthermore this intercourse was continued with their Latitudinarian successors. When Burnet visited Holland in 1663, he found there, as elsewhere, that 'the moderate men had larger and nobler thoughts of God and of the design of the Christian religion than the zealots have'; and especially he

> was well acquainted with the Remonstrants, particularly Poelemburgh.
> . . .They were the men I saw in all Holland of the clearest heads and the best tempers; they had an excellent sense of the practical parts of religion (particularly of love and peace), and expressed great readiness to reunite with the Calvinists whenever they should come to cease from their imposing of their doctrines upon them; and thought that in these and many other points there ought to be more mutual forbearance. This they extended even to the Socinians; but they assured me they were not Socinians themselves, yet they did not like the subtleties of the Fathers and Schoolmen in mysterious points.[2]

Amongst Limborch's Anglican correspondents (in addition to Burnet) were Bishops Richard Kidder, William Lloyd, Edward Stillingfleet and Archbishop Tillotson; whilst Jean Le Clerc also dedicated some of his books to Burnet, and others to Archbishops Sharp and Wake.[3]

The Platonist school of English churchmen spanned the gulf dividing the earlier Stuart period from its post-Restoration successor. They were, as Burnet stated,

> generally of Cambridge, formed under some divines, the chief of whom were Drs Whichcote, Cudworth, Wilkins, More and Worthington. Whichcote. . . being disgusted with the dry systematical way of those times, studied to raise those who conversed with him to a nobler set of thoughts, and to consider religion as a seed of a deiform nature (to use one of his own phrases). In order to this, he set young students much on reading the ancient philosophers, chiefly Plato, Tully and Plotin, and on considering the Christian religion as a doctrine sent from God, both to elevate and sweeten human nature, in which he was a great example as well as a wise and kind instructor. Cudworth carried this on with a great strength of genius and a vast compass of learning. Wilkins was of Oxford, but removed to Cambridge. . . .At Cambridge he joined with those who studied to take

---

[1] R. L. Colie, *Light and Enlightenment: A Study of the Cambridge Platonists and the Dutch Arminians* (1957), chs. I–III *passim* for evidence of this correspondence.

[2] H. C. Foxcroft, *A Supplement to Burnet's History*, p. 92. Arnold van Poelemburgh was Professor of Theology at the Remonstrant Seminary at Amsterdam.

[3] R. L. Colie, *Light and Enlightenment*, pp. 30, 35.

men off from being in parties, or from narrow notions, from superstitious conceits and a fierceness about opinions. He was also a great observer and a promoter of experimental philosophy, which was then a new thing and much looked after.... More was an open-hearted and sincere Christian philosopher, who studied to establish men in the great principles of religion against atheism, that was then beginning to gain ground, chiefly by reason of the hypocrisy of some and the fantastical conceits of the more sincere enthusiasts.[1]

The omission of the name of John Smith stamps Burnet's list as imperfect, but his description of the Cambridge Platonists is just and fair. At the outset their chief characteristic as noted by contemporaries was an inflexible opposition to the central dogma of Calvinism, that of absolute predestination and reprobation. Like John Hales at the Synod of Dort, they 'bade goodnight to Calvin' on this crucial issue.

But their theological system parted company with traditional doctrines on more points than this. An outstanding principle was their appeal to reason and their ascription to it of an authority in religion second only to that of the Bible. 'To go against reason is to go against God; it is the selfsame thing, to do that which the reason of the case doth require and that which God himself doth appoint; reason is the divine governor of man's life; it is the very voice of God.' This avowal of Whichcote could be reinforced by quotation from all the Platonists. Nor did they admit any divorce between the rational and the spiritual. 'Sir', retorted Whichcote to Tuckney, 'I oppose not rational to spiritual; for spiritual is most rational.'[2] From this exaltation of reason there followed that devotion, remarked by Burnet, to Plato and Plotinus, in whom they found pedagogues to lead men to Christ. Christianity indeed could confirm and enlarge the wisdom of the ancients, but their witness so far as it went, was complementary, not contradictory, to that of revelation. To More, 'the Christian religion rightly understood' was truly 'the deepest and choicest piece of philosophy that is'; and he held 'that the image of God is the royal and divine Logos, but the image of this image is the human Intellect'.[3] Reason indeed, though supplemented by revelation, was itself the judge of the authenticity and content of what was revealed. 'The *written* word of God', observed

---

[1] G. Burnet, *History of My Own Time*, vol. I, pp. 321–2.

[2] Whichcote, *Aphorisms*, no. 76, cited in J. Tulloch, *Rational Theology and Christian Philosophy in England in the Seventeenth Century*, vol. II, pp. 77, 100.

[3] *Ibid.* pp. 353–4.

Whichcote, 'is not the first or only discovery of the duty of man. It doth gather, and repeat, and reinforce and charge upon us the scattered and neglected principles of God's creation, that has suffered prejudice and damnation by the defect and apostacy of man.'[1] But the Cambridge Platonists were no mere rationalists. They insisted that reason embraced conscience and mystical insight as well as ratiocination. For them the moral consciousness of man was a sure guide to salvation. 'The moral part of religion never alters', remarked Whichcote again. 'Moral laws are laws of themselves, without sanction by will; and the necessity of them arises from the things themselves. All *other* things in religion are *in order to* these. The moral part of religion does sanctify the soul; and is final both to what is instrumental and instituted.' Or again, 'The state of religion lies in a good mind and a good life; all else is about religion; and men must not put the instrumental part of religion for the state of religion.'[2] These precepts were not only a reply to Descartes and Hobbes, but the enunciation of a vital principle of Christianity. 'The Spirit of man is the candle of the Lord' was the foundation of Whichcote's mysticism; whilst Cudworth illustrated 'the Law of the Spirit of Life within us' by comparing man to a musical instrument; which was first 'played upon from without by the Musician's hand, who hath the theory and law of musick living within himself', and became next 'as if the soul of music should incorporate itself with the instrument and live in the strings'.[3] The uniqueness of this school of divines lay in their harmonious combination of reason, morality, mysticism and the study of natural phenomena with a profound faith in the fundamentals of Christianity. All save one of their company were members of Emmanuel College, whose pristine Calvinism was thus giving place to the milder temper of Christian Platonism. Moreover, their tradition was indigenous to Cambridge. When Burnet visited that university in 1663 he found 'the new philosophy was then much in all people's discourse, and the Royal Society was much talked of'; whilst coming next to Oxford he 'found ecclesiastical learning more in request'.[4]

The line dividing the Cambridge Platonists from their Latitudinarian successors is devious and difficult to draw. The relation-

---

[1] *Ibid.* p. 100.    [2] *Ibid.* pp. 106–7, 108.
[3] Cited in E. Cassirer, *The Platonic Renaissance in England* (trans. J. P. Pettigrove, 1953), p. 34. See also G. R. Cragg, *From Puritanism to the Age of Reason* (1950); F. J. Powicke, *The Cambridge Platonists*; and W. C. de Pauley, *The Candle of the Lord*.
[4] H. C. Foxcroft, *Supplement to Burnet's History*, pp. 46–7.

ship indeed was one of filiation. 'The most eminent of those who were formed under those great men', commented Burnet further, 'were Tillotson, Stillingfleet and Patrick', typical leaders of the Latitudinarians, who

declared against superstition on the one hand and enthusiasm on the other. They loved the constitution of the church and the liturgy, and could well live under them; but they did not think it unlawful to live under another form. They wished that things might have been carried with more moderation; and they continued to keep a good correspondence with those who had differed from them in opinion, and allowed a great freedom both in philosophy and divinity; from whence they were called men of latitude. And upon this, men of narrower thoughts and fiercer tempers fastened upon them the name of Latitudinarians. They read Episcopius much. And the making out the reasons of things being a main part of their studies, their enemies called them Socinians.[1]

The term 'Latitudinarian' indeed covered a wide diversity of opinion and outlook. Sheldon, for example, was one of Burnet's *bêtes noires;* yet the character given of him by his chaplain, Samuel Parker, bears evident affinities with the principles of the men of latitude.

He was a man of eminent piety; for though he was frequent and assiduous in prayers, yet he was not such an assiduous admirer of them as some are, nor did he so much regard the bare worship, as the use that was made of it; and therefore he judiciously placed the sum of religion in a good life. He used in his daily discourse to his family and friends to tell them that they should not think that all the service of God was confined within the cloisters and walls of the church, but rather that a great part of it was conversant abroad in the world and amongst societies of men; that if they lived justly, soberly and chastely, then at length and not before, they might think themselves pious; that otherwise it mattered not of what church or religion wicked men were; and therefore he greatly delighted himself with this saying, and always spake it with great exultation: 'Do well and be merry.'[2]

At the other extreme the Latitudinarian umbrella sheltered individuals of heterodox opinions, verging on Socinianism and Arianism. 'Certainly in our English Church', wrote Cudworth to Limborch in 1674, 'just as in Noah's Ark were all sorts of animals (if I may so express it), are all kinds of Protestants: Calvinists, Remonstrants, and I believe even Socinians, all dwelling here, united with no apparent discord in one and the same communion.'[3]

---

[1] G. Burnet, *History of My Own Time*, vol. I, pp. 323–4.
[2] S. Parker, *History of His Own Times* (trans. by T. Newlin, 1727), Book I, p. 42.
[3] R. L. Colie, *Light and Enlightenment*, p. 40; cf. *Letters of a Late Eminent Prelate* (to Hurd), p. 114, for Warburton's comparison of the Church to the Ark of Noah.

Between these two extremes stood the main body, whose principles were stated in the famous *Brief Account of the New Sect of Latitude-Men* by S[imon] P[atrick] of Cambridge to a friend at Oxford. They were first of all, episcopalians, who during the Interregnum had been aspersed by their enemies as 'men of a prelatical spirit, that had apostatized to the onions and garlick of Egypt because they were generally ordained by bishops', and whose names the Committee of Triers was believed to have recorded in 'a list of all those that were ordained by the Bishop of Norwich', of whom Patrick himself was one. Accordingly they were deeply attached to the order of their church.

Our Latitudinarians therefore are by all means for a Liturgy, and do prefer that of our own Church before all others, admiring the solemnity, gravity and primitive simplicity of it, its freedom from affected phrases, or mixture of vain and doubtful opinions; in a word they esteem it to be so good that they would be loth to adventure the mending of it for fear of marring it.

In respect of rites and ceremonies likewise they 'highly approve that virtuous mediocrity which our Church observes'; and equally 'they have a deep veneration of her government, which they stedfastly believe to be in itself the best, and the same that was practised in the times of the apostles'. With regard to

the doctrine of the Church, they do cordially adhere to it, as doth sufficiently appear by their willingness to subscribe to the Thirty-Nine Articles, and all other points of doctrine contained either in the Liturgy or Book of Homilies; and particularly (whatsoever may be privately whispered to the contrary) they do both devoutly adore the blessed Trinity in the Litany, and make solemn profession of their orthodox faith, both concerning it and other points, in the three Creeds, not excepting that which is commonly ascribed to Athanasius, nor is there any article of doctrine held forth by the Church, which they can justly be accused to depart from, unless absolute reprobation be one, which they do not think themselves bound to believe.

Such a profession of orthodoxy would have satisfied Bull; who would have been equally gratified by the further affirmation that they derived their doctrines

from the sacred writings of the apostles and evangelists, in interpreting whereof, they carefully attend to the sense of the ancient Church, by which they conceive the modern ought to be guided; and therefore they are very conversant in all the genuine monuments of the ancient Fathers, those especially of the first and purest ages.

Far from being just objects of suspicion to the Church of England, 'they seem to be the very chariots and horsemen thereof'; and therefore let no man accuse them of hearkening too much to their own reason, since their reason steers by so excellent a compass, the ancient Fathers and Councils of the Church. For Reason is that faculty whereby a man must judge everything, nor can a man believe anything except he have some reason for it; whether that reason be a deduction from the light of nature and those principles which are the candle of the Lord, set up in the soul of every man that hath not wilfully extinguished it; or a branch of divine revelation in the oracles of holy Scripture; or the general interpretation of genuine antiquity, or the proposal of our own Church consentaneous thereto; or lastly the result of some or all of these; for he that will rightly make use of his reason, must take all that is reasonable into consideration. And it is admirable to consider how the same conclusions do naturally flow from all these several principles; and what in the faithful use of the faculties that God hath given, men have believed for true, doth excellently agree with that Revelation that God hath exhibited in Scripture, and the doctrine of the ancient Church with them both.[1]

To one novelty they rejoiced to plead guilty:

that they have introduced a new philosophy. Aristotle and the Schoolmen are out of request with them.... They embrace a method of philosophy which they think was as much ancienter than Aristotle, as you conceive Oxford was before Cambridge.

This 'new and free philosophy' rested upon the admitted fact

that the theatre of nature is much enlarged since Aristotle's time, and there is no part of the world wherein there are not some notable new phenomena lately discovered, that must needs be of great account in natural philosophy.

Therefore the old systems must vanish; for

is it possible that so many new appearances should not alter the frame of philosophy, nay rather hazard the pulling down of the old ruinous house, that had too narrow foundations, that it may be built again with more magnificence?

Nor should this prospect dismay churchmen.

Methinks I hear some men say, all innovations are dangerous. Philosophy and Divinity are so interwoven by the Schoolmen that it cannot be safe to separate them; new philosophy will bring in new divinity; and freedom in the one will make men desire a liberty in the other.

To this it must be answered that

true philosophy can never hurt sound divinity. Christian religion was never bred up in the Peripatetic school, but spent her best and health-

[1] *A Brief Account of the New Sect of Latitude-Men, together with some Reflections upon the New Philosophy* (1662), pp. 5–10.

fullest years in the more religious academy amongst the primitive Fathers.
...let her old loving nurse the Platonic philosophy be admitted again into
her family.[1]

Established thus, as Joseph Glanvill concurred, 'on the grounds of
Scripture, right Reason and the best and purest Antiquity',[2] and
equipped further with the armoury of the new philosophy, the
Latitudinarians might hope to emulate the achievement of the instructed scribe who brought out of his treasure-store things new and
old. Granted the soundness of their postulate that 'truth lies in a
little compass and narrow room, vitals in religion are few',[3] they
might aspire to preserve the fundamentals of faith and to reconcile
the old beliefs with the new learning. Unhappily this optimism
proved unjustified. Within the Church of England there arose,
instead of Patrick's reluctance to amend its Liturgy for fear of
marring it, the radical revision set forth by Samuel Clarke and copied
by his followers in more extreme measure; instead of willing subscription to the Articles of Religion, a demand for subscription only
to a general formula affirming belief in the inspiration of the
Scriptures; instead of a devout adoring and solemn profession of
faith in the orthodox doctrine of the Trinity, the Arianism of Clarke
and Blackburne; and instead of respectful acceptance of the authority
of the Fathers, the contemptuous rejection of their testimony by
Hoadly, Middleton and Watson. The men of Latitude in truth were
called upon to face both a revolutionary change in the intellectual
outlook of educated Englishmen and a condition of post-Restoration
society characterised by a disregard for morality and the restraints
of good conduct. Against this dual challenge they struggled with
courage, sincerity and ability; and if the degree of their success in
both spheres was partial and qualified, the difficulty of their task
should be remembered in extenuation of their failures.

The charge has often been levelled against the Latitudinarians
that they reduced Christianity to a prudential, self-regarding moral
code. The Cambridge Platonists had insisted that 'the state of
religion lies in a good mind and a good life'; but they had suffused
their preaching of morality with a mysticism markedly lacking in
their prosaic successors. Yet the task of teaching the duty of morality

---

[1] *Ibid.* pp. 14, 20, 21, 22, 24.

[2] J. I. Cope, *Joseph Glanvill, Anglican Apologist* (Washington University Studies, 1956), p. 75.

[3] J. Tullock, *Rational Theology*, vol. II, p. 108, citing Whichcote's *Aphorisms*.

and of exhorting their hearers to the practice of virtue was laid upon the Latitudinarians by the conditions of their age. The Restoration epoch has become indeed a byword for immorality and profaneness. In reaction against the strictness of the Commonwealth regime and against puritan attempts to make men virtuous by acts of parliament, the Caroline court and society threw off nearly all moral restraints. Similarly in reaction against 'enthusiasm' and the 'spiritual' preaching of many divines during the Interregnum, the post-Restoration pulpit sought to restore the balance by its proclamation of a simple, homespun, but practical version of 'the whole duty of man'. Thus far the obligation of 'moral preaching' was imperative and justified. But it is undeniable that in discharging it, the men of Latitude often spoke in terms of worldly wisdom and merely prudential morality. Perhaps the *differentia* between the Cambridge Platonists and their Latitudinarian disciples in this respect can be best illustrated by a comparison of John Smith's discourse on 'The Excellency and Nobleness of True Religion' with Tillotson's sermons on 'The Wisdom of Being Religious', 'The Advantages of Religion to Society' and 'The Advantages of Religion to Particular Persons'. Smith observed that

religion is no such austere, sour and rigid thing as to affright men away from it. No, but those that are acquainted with the power of it, find it to be altogether sweet and amiable....Religion is no sullen Stoicism or oppressing melancholy, it is no enthralling tyranny exercised over those noble and vivacious affections of love and delight;...but it is full of a vigorous and masculine delight and joy, and such as advanceth and ennobles the soul, and does not weaken or dispirit the life and power of it. ...Another particular wherein men mistake religion is, *a constrained and forced obedience to God's commandments*....Those servile spirits which are not acquainted with God and his goodness, may be so haunted by the frightful thoughts of a Deity, as to scare and terrify them into some worship and observance of him. They are apt to look upon him as...an hard master; and therefore they think something must be done to please him and to mitigate his severity towards them....The spirit of true religion is of a more free, noble, ingenuous and generous nature....Nor does God charge any duty upon man without consulting first of all with his goodness; which being the original and adequate object of a good man's will and affections, it must needs be that all the issues and effluxes of it be entertained with an answerable complacency and chearfulness. This is the hinge upon which all true religion turns, the proper centre about which it moves.[1]

[1] John Smith, *The Excellency and Nobleness of True Religion*, cited in E. Cassirer. *The Platonic Renaissance in England*, pp. 163–5.

Tillotson likewise believed that

one of the great prejudices which men have entertained against the Christian religion is this, that it lays upon men heavy burdens and grievous to be borne, that the laws of it are very strict and severe, difficult to be kept and yet dangerous to be broken....For the removal of this prejudice I have chosen these words of the apostle, which expressly tell us the contrary, that the commandments of God are not grievous....Upon this account it will be requisite to take some pains to satisfy the reason of men concerning this truth, and if possible to make it so evident that those who are unwilling to own it, may yet be ashamed to deny it. And methinks I have this peculiar advantage of the argument that I have now undertaken, that every reasonable man cannot but choose to wish me success in this attempt, because I undertake the proof of that which it is every man's interest that it should be true. And if I can make it out, this pretence against religion will not only be baffled, but we shall gain a new and forcible argument to persuade men over to it.[1]

Similarly in proclaiming his favourite doctrine of the benevolence of God, Tillotson asked,

is it not really desirable to every man that there should be such a Being as takes particular care of every one of us, and loves us, and delights to do us good, as understands all our wants, and is able and willing to relieve us in our greatest straits when nothing else can?...Is it not every man's interest that there should be such a Governor of the world as really designs our happiness, and hath omitted nothing that is necessary to it, as would govern us for our advantage, and will require nothing of us but what is for our good, and yet will infinitely reward us for the doing of that which is best for ourselves?...And we have reason to believe God to be such a Being, if He be at all.[2]

Such preaching not unnaturally provoked the satirical riposte from Anthony Collins in his *Discourse of Freethinking*, 'what a charming idea does he give us of the Deity; it is alone sufficient without any further argument to make the atheist wish there were a Deity, and by silencing his prejudices, dispose him to conviction'.[3] Equally illustrative of the possibility of descent into bathos were Tillotson's principle that 'all the duties of the Christian religion which respect God are no other but what Natural Light prompts men to, excepting the two sacraments and praying to God in the name and by the mediation of Christ'; and his precept concerning the priority of natural duties, 'for I think myself obliged to deal plainly and to be so faithful to mothers as to tell them that nursing

---

[1] Tillotson, *Sermons*, vol. I, p. 56 (*Works*, 3 vols. 1752).
[2] *Ibid.* vol. I, p. 19.
[3] A. Collins, *A Discourse of Freethinking* (1713), Section III, 19.

their own children is a natural duty and of a more indispensable obligation than any positive precepts of revealed religion'.[1] Here again the preacher laid himself open to the devastating retort from the mordant pen of Swift: 'As a priest and prelate, he was obliged to say something of Christianity; but pray, observe, sir, how he brings himself off;...because mothers' nursing their children is a natural duty, it is of more moment than the two sacraments or than praying to God in the name and by the mediation of Christ.'[2] It was abundantly evident from such exchanges that Tillotson was representative of a Latitudinarian tradition, which, although inheriting from the Cambridge Platonists the vision splendid, had suffered it to no inconsiderable degree to fade into the light of common day.

But the shortcomings of the men of Latitude should not disguise the complexity of the problems presented to defenders of orthodoxy by the changing intellectual temper of their times. The chief element in this revolution was the nascent scientific movement. During the latter half of the seventeenth century the astronomical discoveries of Newton and Keppler were debated and assimilated, the microscope was discovered by Malpighi and the barometer by Torricelli, the telescope also was added to the armoury of man, and Boyle perfected the thermometer. With such a galaxy of novelties, an entire generation of educated Europeans revelled in this most wonderful of all ages, in which, as Pope proclaimed,

> Nature and Nature's laws lay hid in night,
> God said, 'Let Newton be', and all was light;

and in which also, as Addison believed,

> The spacious firmament on high,
> With all the blue ethereal sky
> And spangled heav'ns, a shining frame,
> Their great Original proclaim...
> In reason's ear they all rejoice
> And utter forth a glorious voice,
> For ever singing as they shine,
> 'The hand that made us is divine.'

At this distance of time, it is difficult to understand imaginatively the revolutionary effects of these inventions upon human thought. Hitherto the world had been generally conceived as the stage upon which innumerable spirits, both malign and good, practised their

---

[1] Tillotson, *Sermons*, vol. I, p. 491; vol. II, p. 310.
[2] Jonathan Swift, 'Mr Collins' Discourse of Freethinking' (*The Prose Works of Swift*, ed. Temple Scott, vol. III, p. 191).

arts to ensnare or edify man, and by which they maintained a reign of caprice and hazard. Henceforth the visible universe became the impressive scene of unvarying order and uniformity, in which all created things were obedient to the appropriate laws imposed upon them by their Creator. Moreover these discoveries induced a sense of exhilaration and freedom. Man alone of the creatures of the universe could understand the principles of creation, and by his new knowledge could co-operate with the Creator in the furtherance of his beneficent designs. The discovery of the magnitude of the universe and of the laws of its operation dignified rather than depressed the status of man; and moreover the principal authors of these scientific investigations affirmed the result of their endeavours to be the proof of the existence, power and wisdom of God, and were themselves firm believers in the Christian revelation. Not only were Boyle, Ray and Newton conspicuous for their personal piety, but all agreed that the new natural philosophy provided powerful evidence and support of religion. Boyle indeed by his will endowed the lectures bearing his name 'for proving the Christian religion against notorious infidels', and amongst the early lecturers on his foundation Bentley delivered a *Confutation of Atheism* and Clarke a *Demonstration of the Being and Attributes of God*. Locke in his *Essay Concerning Human Understanding* held the existence of God to be 'the most obvious truth that reason discovers', and its evidence to 'be (if I mistake not) equal to mathematical certainty'. Equally important was the process by which this conviction was attained; for 'from the consideration of ourselves, and what we infallibly find in our own constitutions, our reason leads to the knowledge of this certain and evident truth, that there is an eternal, most powerful and most knowing Being'; so that it was plain that 'we have a more certain knowledge of the existence of a God, than of anything our senses have not immediately discovered to us. Nay, I presume to say that we more certainly know that there is a God, than that there is anything else without us'.[1] The emphasis upon 'mathematical certainty' was significant, for mathematics enjoyed a high prestige, and not a few attempts were made to state Christianity in mathematical terms, as in *Theologiae Christianae Principia Mathematica* of John Craig, prebendary in succession of Durnford and Gillingham Major in Salisbury Cathedral, or William Derham's Boyle lectures on *Physico-Theology*, followed by his *Astro-Theology*.

[1] J. Locke, *Essay Concerning Human Understanding*, IV, 10: 1 and 6.

Concurrently with the scientific movement, there went an assault on the dominance of Aristotle and the schoolmen in the philosophical teaching of the universities. The author of the *Brief Account of the new sect of Latitude Men* depicted them as having bidden as final a goodnight to Aristotle as to Calvin; and evidence of revolt against the old philosophy was ubiquitous. Bishop Hacket, for example, although at the university he was 'much addicted to school learning, ...afterwards grew weary of it, and professed he found more shadows and names than solid juice and substance in it'. Indeed as a bishop he lamented that 'his principal study were cases of conscience, canon law and the liturgies of the ancient church,... [and] would often complain he found this last an unlearned study and much against his own nature, who was a lover of philology and rationality'.[1] Burnet at Aberdeen university 'went through the common methods of the Aristotelian philosophy', then 'fell violently into another study which had almost undone me, I went through several bodies of School Divinity, and read about twenty volumes in folio of these writers and grew fond of them', though later they seemed to him but 'cobweb stuff'. For in Edinburgh, the minister of the abbey church 'put books of another sort in my hand than those I had formerly dealt in. Smith's *Select Discourses* and Dr H[enry] More's works were the first. He recommended also the reading of Plato and the Platonists'; from which Burnet was led to 'apply himself to philosophy and mathematics', and to 'run through Descartes and Gassendi'. When he came to England therefore he 'easily went into the notions of the Latitudinarians', though soon quitting both the universities, 'fully undeceived of the high opinion he had formerly of them', even if 'Cambridge answered his expectation more' than Oxford, thanks to the men of latitude.[2] At a later date Joseph Butler, coming to Oxford from the Dissenting Academy of Mr Samuel Jones at Gloucester and Tewkesbury, complained to Clarke that 'we are obliged to mis-spend so much time here in attending frivolous lectures and unintelligible disputations, that I am quite tired out with such a disagreeable way of trifling'; and accordingly he contemplated transferring to Cambridge, though 'if I can't be excused from these things at Cambridge I shall only just keep term there'.[3]

---

[1] T. Plume, *A Century of Sermons*, pp. xl, li.
[2] H. C. Foxcroft, *Supplement to Burnet's History*, pp. 454–5, 460–1, 463–4.
[3] Butler to Clarke, Letter VII; 30 September 1717. *The Works of Bishop Butler*, ed. J. H. Bernard, vol. I, p. 332 (2 vols. London, 1900).

It is usually accounted to the credit of the Dissenting Academies that, thanks to their freedom from academic tradition and to their correspondence with divines of the Netherlands, they were pioneers in the movement to dethrone Aristotle in favour of Descartes and Ramus. But the old and the new in philosophy and science existed incongruously side by side in both ancient universities and modern academies. Thomas Secker gained little profit from Mr Timothy Jolly's Dissenting Academy at Attercliffe near Sheffield because 'only the old philosophy of the schools was taught there, and that neither ably nor diligently'; and it was during his residence in London in the house of the father of Mr John Bowes, later Lord Chancellor of Ireland, that he was introduced to Locke's *Essay Concerning Human Understanding*, and consequently, after his removal to Gloucester to Samuel Jones' Academy found 'many doubts had risen in his mind concerning conformity and many other religious matters'.[1] *Per contra* the University of Cambridge as late as 1669 presented Cosimo de' Medici with a dissertation condemning the Copernican astronomy, in the very year in which Oxford established a Botany Chair, followed by one in Chemistry in 1683; whilst at Cambridge the Lucasian professorship of Mathematics was founded in 1663, to be followed by Chairs of Chemistry in 1702 and of Astronomy and Experimental Philosophy in 1704. Moreover Addison's poem in praise of the witness of the universe to its great Original could still refer to the celestial bodies in pre-Copernican terms:

> What though in solemn silence, all
> Move round the dark terrestrial ball.

With the sinister spectre of Hobbes in the background, it was natural that churchmen should welcome the alliance offered by scientists in support of the fundamentals of faith. Indeed the Royal Society rejoiced in the championship of leading divines. Bishop Wilkins of Chester was a member, Sprat of Rochester its official historian and Ward of Sarum its supporter, whilst Glanvil also rallied to its defence against criticism. The last-named maintained that the Society 'deals in the plain objects of sense, in which, if anywhere, there is certainty; and teacheth suspension of assent till what is proposed is well proved; and so is equally an adversary to scepticism and credulity'.[2] Sprat claimed that

of our churchmen, the greatest and most reverend, by their care and passion and endeavours in advancing this institution, have taken off the

---

[1] Secker, Memoirs, ff. 4, 5.      [2] J. I. Cope, *Joseph Glanvill*, p. 61.

unjust scandal from natural knowledge, that it is an enemy to divinity. By the perpetual patronage and assistance they have afforded the Royal Society, they have confuted the false opinions of those men who believe that philosophers must needs be irreligious.

In return, however, the natural philosophers respected the proper territory of theology. 'They meddle no otherwise with divine things than only as the power, and wisdom and goodness of the Creator is displayed in the admirable order and workmanship of the creatures.'[1] At first also the new Cartesian philosophy was received kindly by some of the Cambridge Platonists. More indeed conducted an early correspondence with Descartes in which he referred in superlative terms to the latter's philosophy. Further, he was largely responsible for introducing its teaching into the university of Cambridge. But soon churchmen began to realise the dangerous possibilities for theology latent in both the new science and philosophy. On the one hand the conception of the universe as governed by a series of unvarying and irrefragable laws seemed to relegate God to the position of an external spectator of the machine which he had created; whilst on the other hand the Cartesian philosophy appeared to result in a deterministic system, and from this standpoint provoked the resolute contradiction of More and Cudworth. The dual prospect of a denial of the freedom of God in relation to the world and of Man in the sphere of morality awakened defenders of Christianity to the perils of their position.

Two lines of defence suggested themselves, the establishment of the existence of incorporeal spirits and the demonstration of the truth of miracles. 'Too many deny witches', wrote Glanvill, 'because they believe there are no Spirits; and they are so persuaded because they own no Beings in the world but matter, and the results of motion, and consequently can acknowledge nothing of a God.'[2] Locke allowed the existence of 'that intellectual world, wherein are infinite number and degrees of spirits out of the reach of our ken or guess';[3] and Cudworth likewise argued that 'if there be once any invisible ghosts or spirits acknowledged as things permanent, it will not be easy for any to give a reason why there might not be one supreme ghost also, presiding over them all and the whole world'.[4] From this it was a short step to belief in witches, and in the power

[1] T. Sprat, *History of the Royal Society* (4th ed. 1734), pp. 82, 132.
[2] J. I. Cope, *Joseph Glanvill*, p. 62.
[3] J. Locke, *The Reasonableness of Christianity*, *Works*, vol. II, pp. 571–2 (2 vols. 1740).
[4] J. Tulloch, *Rational Theology*, vol. II, p. 260.

of evil spirits to take possession of men. Alike in Glanvill, More and John Aubrey old superstitious beliefs concerning the reality of witch-craft survived side by side with the new scientific spirit, which Sprat praised for its deliverance of mankind from the fear of demons. For 'from the time in which the real philosophy has appeared, there is scarce any whisper remaining of such horrors; every man is un-shaken at those tales at which his ancestors trembled. The course of things goes quietly along in its own true channel of natural causes and effects.'[1]

But if credulity concerning witches was a weak prop for the sup-port of spiritual idealism, miracles were almost universally admitted to be crucial to Christianity. In the long controversy between the champions of revelation and the defenders of natural religion, the proof of miracles was one of the disputed points. For if revelation made known truths inaccessible to unaided reason, how otherwise could the authenticity of such a revelation be established save by the test of miracles? As Moses' declaration of the law in the Old Covenant was attested by signs and wonders, so the claim of Jesus to be the Messiah was vindicated by miraculous events. 'Now what conviction can there be to any sober mind concerning Divine Authority in any person, without such a power of miracles going along with him, when he is to deliver some new doctrine to the world to be believed, I confess I cannot understand', observed Stillingfleet.[2] Similarly Locke in his reduction of Christianity to belief in Jesus as the Messiah, affirmed that the truth of his divine mission 'had been attested by miracles', which by their character were suited to commend his teaching to unlettered followers. At a later date also Richard Watson, whilst prepared to jettison all speculative doctrines of Christianity, held fast to the miracles of the Virgin Birth and Resurrection of Christ.

The truth of the Christian religion depends upon testimony; now man is competent to judge of the weight of testimony,...and I consider the testimony concerning the resurrection of Jesus Christ (and that fact is the entire cornerstone of the Christian church) to be worthy of entire credit.

Accordingly,

whoever professes to believe the canonical books of the New Testament, virtually professes to believe that Jesus Christ did not come into this world according to the ordinary course of nature; that he voluntarily

---

[1] T. Sprat, *History of the Royal Society*, p. 340.
[2] Cited in G. R. Cragg, *From Puritanism to the Age of Reason*, p. 69.

sealed his mission with his blood; that he did not, like the rest of mankind, continue subject to death, but became the first-fruits of the resurrection.[1]

In addition to the challenge from science and philosophy, the church was faced by the impact of ethnic religions upon Christianity. Geographical discoveries, the increase of travel, colonial expansion and the contact of missionaries with other faiths were combining to raise complex problems of the relationship of Christianity to other religions. Moreover the age was bemused by the cult of the Noble Savage, uncorrupted by either priestcraft or statecraft, and enjoying the primitive simplicity of natural religion and of society without the state; whilst travellers published idealistic accounts of the religion and civilisation of ancient Egypt and Persia, and even of the faith of Mahomet. Most significant of all perhaps was the scandal created by Jesuit missionaries in China, who were accused by their rivals of assimilating the teaching of Christ to the tenets of Confucius and conflating the superstitions of Chinese religion with the rites of the Church, in order to win easy converts. In particular Fathers le Comte and Gobien published certain volumes, 'Nouveaux Mémoires sur l'état présent de la Chine', Histoire de l'édit de l'Empereur de la Chine', and 'Lettre sur les cérémonies de la Chine', in which they affirmed that the people of China had preserved for nearly two thousand years the knowledge of the true God and a pure morality, notwithstanding their ignorance of Christianity. For their boldness the authors incurred the formal censure of the Sorbonne on the ground that

si tous ceux qui ont vécu selon la raison, soit Juifs, soit Gentiles, ont été véritablement et proprement Chrétiens et en état de salut, comme ceux qui ont eu la foi et à qui Jésus Christ a été révélé, on peut donc se sauver par les forces de nature, et la foi en Jésus-Christ Médiateur n'est nulle-ment nécessaire.

The issue posed for defenders of Christianity by the existence of other religions and of races which had never heard its Gospel, was one of increasing gravity. In Dryden's *Religio Laici*, the salvability of 'Indian souls and worlds discover'd new' was, from the stand-point of revelation,

of all objections, chief
To startle reason, stagger frail belief.

---

[1] *Anecdotes of the Life of Richard Watson* (ed. R. Watson, 1818), vol. I, p. 24. R. Watson, *Miscellaneous Tracts* (1815), vol. II, p. 13.

A solution was sought by recourse to the Epistle to the Romans, which, having done yeoman service in exposition of Predestination, Justification by Faith and the relations of church and state, was now discovered to have also the key to this enigma.

For when the Gentiles, which have no law, do by nature the things of the law, these, having no law, are a law unto themselves; in that they show the work of the law written in their hearts, their conscience bearing witness therewith and their thoughts one with another accusing or else excusing them.

But whereas hitherto, 'since the time of Augustine (*De Spiritu et Littera*, c. 27) the orthodox interpretation had applied this verse either to the Gentile converts or to the favoured few among the heathen who had extraordinary divine assistance',[1] it was now elevated into an universal principle. So Dryden concluded that

> Not only charity bids hope the best,
> But more the great Apostle has express'd:
> That if the Gentiles, whom no law inspired,
> By nature did what was by law required;
> They, who the written rule had never known,
> Were to themselves both rule and law alone:
> To Nature's plain indictment they shall plead,
> And by their conscience be condemned or freed.
> Most righteous doom! because a rule reveal'd
> Is none to those from whom it was conceal'd.
> Then those who follow'd reason's dictates right,
> Lived up, and lifted high their natural light,
> With Socrates may see their Maker's face,
> While thousand rubric-martyrs want a place.

This was calling in a new world to redress the balance of the old with a vengeance! For it now became an open, and certainly much-debated, question not only whether natural religion without revelation might not be all-sufficient for salvation, but even whether revelation had merely confused the simple truths of natural religion by elaboration and mystery. Many tendencies conspired to emphasise the appeal of natural religion. If the witness of creation, as Addison wrote,

> Publishes to every land,
> The works of an Almighty Hand,

was it not more cogent and credible than the testimony of a pretended revelation, the knowledge of which had been denied alike to ancient peoples and to the natives of 'worlds discovered new'?

---

[1] Romans ii. 14–15; Mark Pattison, 'Tendencies of Religious Thought in England, 1688–1750'; in *Essays and Reviews* (1861), p. 273.

Moreover the 'scandal of particularity' attaching to such a revelation was paraded with wearisome repetition. It had been confined to one race, the Jews—not the most civilised of ancient nations—to one place and to one particular period of ancient history. Furthermore its record was written in dead languages, no longer understood by the generality of men, and contained in works whose interpretation was much disputed even amongst professed believers and scholars. How could such a revelation be held universally necessary to salvation, so that only one Name had been given under heaven by which men could be saved? The religious and theological implications of the scientific movement were now becoming evident; and its support to Christianity was, to say the least, less emphatic and more equivocal than had been at first expected. For if by contemplation of the starry heavens above and recognition of the moral law within (in accordance with the five fundamental principles which Lord Herbert of Cherbury believed to be innate ideas), men could attain a sufficient knowledge of their duty towards God and their neighbour, what need was there of any further revelation? Hence the cult of natural religion and the consequent reduction of God to a mathematical First Cause or to the Supreme Being of Deism. The vogue of such concepts may be seen in surprising quarters. Alexander Pope, a Roman Catholic in an age when such religious profession was scorned and temptations to apostasy were many and powerful, nevertheless gave almost complete expression to the theology of Deism. His *Essay on Man* has been described as *une profession de foi, éclatante, pour la première fois le déisme devenait poésie*; and his *Universal Prayer* as *la prière du déiste*.[1] It would be difficult indeed to conceive a more thoroughly deistic theology than that of this latter poem. Beginning with an invocation of 'the great First Cause' as

> Father of all, in every age,
> In every clime ador'd,
> By saint, by savage, and by sage,
> Jehovah, Jove or Lord,

it continued through several verses of impeccable deism to the concluding address,

> To Thee whose temple is all space,
> Whose altar, earth, sea, skies,
> One chorus let all Being raise,
> All Nature's incense rise.

[1] Paul Hazard: *La Pensée Européenne au XVIIIème Siècle* (1946), vol. II, pp. 170, 172–3; cf. the same author's *La Crise de la Conscience Européenne (1680–1715)* (1935).

Similarly Dryden (a convert to the Roman Church), in his endeavour to find a way of salvation for 'Indian souls and worlds discovered new', had said 'Goodnight' emphatically to Athanasius.

> For though his creed eternal truth contains,
> 'Tis hard for man to doom to endless pains
> All who believed not all his zeal required,
> Unless he first could prove he was inspired.
> Then let us either think he meant to say,
> This faith, where publish'd, was the only way;
> Or else conclude that, Arius to confute,
> The good old man, too eager in dispute,
> Flew high; and as his Christian fury rose,
> Damn'd all for heretics who durst oppose.

If complete surrender were not to be made to natural religion, the champions of revelation must square accounts with it by an accommodating reconciliation. Two conditions would need to be satisfied if such an endeavour were to promise success. First, Christianity must be represented as the necessary completion and complement of natural religion; and secondly, it must itself be simplified and purged of all save the fundamental articles of faith. But though revelation might supplement, it must not contradict natural religion. John Wilkins' treatise *Of the Principles and Duties of Natural Religion* aimed to demonstrate the basis of natural religion 'in the nature and reason of mankind', and the function of revelation 'so agreeable to the dictates of natural light', by baptising the former into Christianity after a distinctly perfunctory conversion.

And although before God was pleased to make this revelation of His will to mankind, men were obliged to the practice of the moral duties by the law of nature, and as the apostle speaks, 'having no law, are a law unto themselves, in that they show the work of the law, written in their hearts'; yet now that God hath in so much mercy revealed His will so plainly to mankind, it is not enough for us who enjoy this revelation to perform those moral duties which are of natural obligation, unless we also do them in obedience to Christ as our Lord and Lawgiver.[1]

So slight a change, however, seemed inadequate ground for the special dispensation of the Old and New Testaments. Orthodox defenders therefore argued that, thanks to the dimming of man's natural reason by the Fall, his apprehension of the nature of God and his capacity to obey the moral law had been enervated, so that further aid was necessary and this was supplied by revelation. Not

---

[1] John Wilkins, *Of the Principles and Duties of Natural Religion*, Book II, c. 9.

only could South dismiss an Aristotle as 'but the rubbish of an Adam', but Glanvill also believed that 'whereas we patch up a piece of philosophy from a few industriously-gathered, and yet scarce well-observed or digested experiments, Adam's knowledge was completely built upon the certain extemporary notice of his comprehensive, unerring faculties'.[1] Revelation therefore made clear what had become obscured; and in particular by its proof of the power of God afforded by the miracles of Christ, especially by his resurrection, and by its consequent establishment of the reality of a future life, ensured that divine sanctions in the shape of eternal rewards and punishments would enforce the moral distinctions between right and wrong. Christianity was therefore a republication of the law of nature, with a new law-giver, and with impressive inducements to well-doing and penalties for the reverse.

Thus presented moreover it might expect good results when preached to peoples of other religions. 'Nothing ought to be taught among them', wrote William Stevenson, chaplain at Fort St George of the native 'Indian Souls', to Henry Newman, secretary of S.P.C.K.

but the plain, unquestionable articles of the Christian faith in the same manner and as far as possible in the same words that the apostles used.... As it [the Christian faith] is in itself most agreeable to the reason and unprejudiced sense of mankind, so it ought to be set forth to the heathens in the same advantageous light; in that primitive simplicity and plainness of speech which we find used in Scripture; and unclouded with the arbitrary impositions and explications that have been made of our Christian faith since the days of the apostles.

Granted this simplicity,

the reasonableness of the Christian religion gives me great hopes that it will meet with a ready reception among the heathen. For seeing that the great design of the Gospel is to teach men the most perfect system of morality and such other important truths as reason alone could not have discovered; to enforce the practice of all virtue and piety by the most moving considerations, the greatest rewards and the most terrible punishments; a scheme of religion that is so agreeable to the natural notions of mankind, and containing nothing but what reason must approve and acquiesce in, which gives such just and worthy thoughts of almighty God, the dignity of human nature, and the great end and design of our life; I say, such a scheme of doctrine as this, which is so rational and noble, consistent in itself, and is supported by the most convincing proofs that moral facts are capable of, bespeaks the regard and attention of mankind,

---

[1] J. I. Cope, *Joseph Glanvill*, p. 60.

and powerfully insinuates itself even upon a prejudiced spirit. Indeed the necessity of moral obligations and the practical duties of the Gospel have been so clearly demonstrated from the light of Nature, and the proofs of the Christian revelation have been set in so clear a light, and may be offered with such irresistible evidence, that I am apt to believe, miracles are not now necessary for the conversion of these people; the want of a wonderful power being in a great measure supplied by that surprising light and perspicuity which in these last ages have been given to all the precepts and truths of the Gospel.[1]

Concordant with this opinion was the testimony of Governor Collet to Newman:

I should be glad to see our instructors in general keep to plain Christianity as it is found in the New Testament, whose native simplicity outshines all the pompous additions of the cathedral, and is much more substantial as well as easy than all the subtleties of the schools. On this subject I will propose one thing to you; that some judicious person would undertake to write a short and plain catechism, containing the principles of natural religion and so much of Christianity as is necessary and agreed to by all parties. Such a piece may easily be extracted from Dr Clarke's second volume of sermons at Mr Boyle's lecture. This catechism to be translated into the Portuguese language and sent hither. The essentials of Christianity lie in a very little room, I mean so far as it is a divine revelation superadded to natural religion.[2]

Equally urgent therefore was the need for the simplification of Christianity. In view of the alleged simplicity of natural religion (a generally accepted and uncriticised assumption of its champions), it was imperative that some short statement of the essentials of Christian belief should be set forth, which would be as comprehensive in scope as Newton's law of gravity in the scientific field. Moreover such an epitome should address itself not to the expert but to the ordinary man, and must justify itself before the new tribunal of reason. The task was essayed by John Locke, 'the title of whose treatise *The Reasonableness of Christianity* may be said to have been the solitary thesis of Christian theology in England for the greater part of a century'.[3] Locke had already laid down the relationship between reason and revelation.

Reason is natural revelation, whereby the eternal Father of Light and Fountain of all knowledge, communicates to mankind that portion of truth which he has laid within the reach of their natural faculties. Revela-

---

[1] W. Stevenson to H. Newman, 27 December 1716. Arch. W. Epist. 28, f. 33.
[2] Governor Collet to Newman, 19 September 1717, Arch. W. Epist. 24, f. 106.
[3] M. Pattison, *Essays and Reviews*, p. 258.

tion is natural reason enlarged by a new set of discoveries communicated by God immediately, which reason vouches the truth of by the testimony and proofs it gives that they come from God.[1]

To ascertain the content of revelation therefore Locke went to the Bible, because the prevailing systems of divinity were unsatisfactory and inconsistent. In fact he directed his attention chiefly to the New Testament (deeming the Old Testament serviceable only in so far as it was necessary for the understanding or proof of the New), and therein almost exclusively to the Gospels and the Acts. The Epistles were of secondary importance; for

I do not deny, but the great doctrines of the Christian faith are dropt here and there, and scattered up and down in most of them. But 'tis not in the Epistles we are to learn what are the fundamental articles of the faith, where they are promiscuously and without distinction mixed up with other truths in discourses that were only. . .occasional. We shall find and discern those great and necessary points best in the preaching of our Saviour and the Apostles, to those who were yet strangers and ignorant of the faith, to bring them in and convert them.[2]

The outcome of his investigation was that Christianity could be reduced to one single article: 'the faith required was, to believe Jesus to be the Messiah, the Anointed'; the truth of whose mission was authenticated by prophecy and miracle. Of course the doctrine of the apostles contained 'a great deal more, but that concerned practice and not belief'; and Locke was emphatic in his insistence on the indispensability of good works and right conduct as the fruits of repentance. The startling novelty of his exegesis however was its definition of belief as solely the acceptance of Jesus as the Messiah, on the twin evidence of predictive prophecy and of miracles. The Cambridge Platonists had recognised that the fundamentals were few; but Locke had reduced them almost to vanishing point. At the same time he expressed the utmost respect for the authority of the Bible, averring that 'it has God for its author, salvation for its end and truth without any mixture of error for its matter'; and that he would 'condemn and quit any opinion' so soon as 'I am shown that it is contrary to any revelation in the Holy Scripture'.

> Yet, lady, still remember, I maintain
> The Word in needful points is only plain,

---

[1] J. Locke, *Essay Concerning Human Understanding*, IV, 19, 4.
[2] J. Locke, *The Reasonableness of Christianity* (1740), *Works*, vol. II, pp. 582–3.

the *Panther* had remarked to the *Hind*; but Locke had carried simplification to an unprecedented degree.

It was evident that the first casualty of the process would be the orthodox doctrine of the Trinity. For though Locke, in obedience to the witness of Scripture, had spoken of God the Creator, the Son or Messiah and the Holy Ghost, if the matter were to be left there, the Athanasian doctrine of the Trinity would receive little support. An appeal to 'the Bible only' had been characteristic of the Arians of the fourth century and the Socinians of recent times, both of whom claimed to be defenders of the primitive Scriptural belief against the infiltration of concepts borrowed from Greek, that is pagan, philosophy. As the *Hind* retorted to the *Panther*:

> For did not Arius first, Socinus now
> The Son's eternal Godhead disavow?
> And did not these by Gospel texts alone
> Condemn our doctrine and maintain their own?
> Have not all heretics the same pretence
> To plead the Scriptures in their own defence?

Moreover during the latter half of the seventeenth century Socinian opinions were being propagated vigorously in England, as Dr H. J. McLachlan has shown,[1] though the attempt to affiliate them with 'the Oxford School of Rational Theologians' gathering in Falkland's house at Great Tew or with the Cambridge Platonists is unsound. A not inconsiderable controversy concerning the Trinity was kindled in the Church of England by Stephen Nye, rector of Little Hormead, Hertfordshire, in which both South and William Sherlock burned their fingers, and which led to the issue of royal directions in 1695 to the archbishop and bishops to suppress both preaching and publishing on this theme. The remedy, however, proved ineffective; and fuel was added to the fire by the appearance of Clarke's *The Scripture Doctrine of the Trinity* in 1712, the significance of which lay in the author's resolution to discover the New Testament doctrine as contrasted with the credal, and in the thoroughness of his investigation. For, after examining 1251 texts he reached the conclusions that the Father only is the supreme God, to whom alone supreme worship is to be paid, that the Son, although existing from eternity, is a subordinate being, who may be worshipped only as mediator, and that the Holy Ghost is also a subordinate being, for the worship of whom there is no clear Scriptural warrant. The

[1] H. J. McLachlan, *Socinianism in Seventeenth-Century England* (1951).

influence of the work was widespread. Secker, after leaving the Dissenting Academy at Tewkesbury in 1714,

'studied various theological subjects, with various fluctuations and changes of mind; particularly the doctrine of the Trinity, in which for some time I agreed very much with Dr Clarke; the inspiration of Scripture, on which I inclined to the *Sentimens de quelques Théologiens de Holland*, and subscription to the Thirty-Nine Articles concerning which I had afterwards a long correspondence with Mr Butler'. In view of his uncertainty of opinion—for 'though I was less inclined to some singularities of opinion than I had been, yet I continued favourable to others, nor could I be sure how soon or indeed in what manner, my judgment might fix'—he resolved to pursue for the time being the profession of medicine, 'yet never totally intermitting Divinity, much less doubting of the truth of religion, natural and revealed'.[1]

The conjunction of Clarke's *Scripture Doctrine of the Trinity* with the question of subscription to the Articles of Religion raised another difficult issue both of individual conscience and of ecclesiastical authority. It was evident that divines accepting the conclusions of Clarke could subscribe to the formularies of the Church of England and use its Liturgy only by placing an unnatural interpretation upon creeds and articles on the one hand and on the Book of Common Prayer on the other hand. Clarke himself indeed, in addition to producing a revised version of the Prayer Book to accord with his own Trinitarian beliefs, came to the conclusion that he could not accept any further preferment involving subscription to the Articles of Religion, though he would be willing to submit to consecration to the episcopate (a promotion not requiring such subscription) in order to press for an official revision of the prescribed ecclesiastical formularies.[2] The gravity of the situation was emphasised further when Hoadly in his famous Bangorian sermon on *The Nature of the Kingdom or Church of Christ* denied the competence of the church to impose any theological tests other than those expressly laid down by Christ himself. The implications of this claim to complete freedom of belief alarmed Wake, who held that here, and in the several publications of writers defending Hoadly, 'new principles of wicked insincerity and prevarication have been openly advanced in the point of subscription, according to which an Arian may subscribe

---

[1] Secker, Memoirs: MSS. ff. 6–7; cf. Jean Le Clerc, *Sentimens de Quelques Théologiens de Hollande sur l'Histoire Critique du Vieux Testament* (Amsterdam, 1685, English transl. 1697).

[2] Thomas Emlyn, *Memoirs of the Life and Sentiments of Dr Samuel Clarke* (1748), pp. 26–8.

both to our Liturgy and Articles as well as the most orthodox Christian'. More moderate divines, whilst not claiming exemption from all tests, demanded that subscription should be required only to the Bible and not to any confessional standards. 'Some of our divines have openly espoused the Arian notions', complained Wake further.

> Others are fallen into other gross heresies. Now to cover their particular sentiments, a new notion of libertinism is set up, that there ought to be no confession of faith, no subscription to anything but the truth of the holy scriptures, required to qualify any man to be a pastor, a dignitary or even a bishop of the established church; and that 'tis usurpation upon the peculiar authority of Christ for any one to require such subscriptions to be made to any confessions of faith whatsoever.[1]

The controversy continued apace, until it culminated in the Feathers Tavern Petition of 1772, which requested that subscription be required only to a formula recognising the authority of the Bible as a repository of divine truth without any definition of the sense in which it was to be interpreted. The acute conflict of conscience involved was illustrated by the circumstance that, after the rejection of the petition, Archdeacon Francis Blackburne of Cleveland, author of *The Confessional* (the chief work advocating relaxation of subscription), remained within the established church, whilst his son-in-law Theophilus Lindsay, vicar of Catterick, resigned his preferment and embraced a formal Unitarian profession.

The dilemma facing disputants in the Trinitarian controversy was that stated by the late bishop of Oxford, Dr Kirk; namely that 'the evidence of the New Testament is singularly disconcerting. Read in the light of the later faith of the Church, it presents an almost explicit Trinitarianism. Read apart from that light—as modern theology attempts to read it—it presents an almost inextricable confusion of ideas.'[2] But Clarke and his followers were determined to discount the later faith of the church. It was not that the eighteenth-century lacked powerful defences of the traditional doctrine of the Trinity. Waterland's *Vindication of Christ's Divinity* and his *Critical History of the Athanasian Creed* assembled magisterially the arguments for orthodoxy in reliance on the Fathers as authentic interpreters of Scripture, and contended for the principle that 'Scripture and antiquity (under the conduct of right reason) are what we ought

---

[1] N. Sykes, *William Wake*, vol. II, pp. 176, 181–2.
[2] K. E. Kirk, 'The Evolution of the Doctrine of the Trinity', in *Essays on the Trinity and the Incarnation*, p. 199 (ed. A. E. J. Rawlinson, London, 1933).

to abide by, in settling points of doctrine'. The lie direct was given by Conyers Middleton's *Free Enquiry into the Miraculous Powers which were supposed to have subsisted in the Christian Church*:

Dr Waterland, who was supposed to speak the sense of our present rulers, seldom appeals to the Scriptures in his controversial writings without joining antiquity to them, or the authority *of the three first centuries at least*, that *golden age of Christianity*, as he calls it. . . . Here we see antiquity joined as a necessary and inseparable companion to the Scripture and put even upon a level with it, by this eminent advocate of the Christian Faith. But since this seems to be a flat contradiction to the principles of the Reformation, and dangerous to the general credit and interests of the Protestant religion, it may be worth while to consider a little, from what particular motives and circumstances so inconsistent a practice should happen to prevail more remarkably in this than in any other Protestant Church.[1]

Hoadly also in his *Plain Account of the Nature and End of the Sacrament of the Lord's Supper* insisted on confining himself to the evidence of the New Testament and rejecting later authority.

The writers of the New Testament, being the earliest of all upon this subject and the most certainly acquainted with it (whether they be considered as witnesses to the institution itself, or instructed by those who were so, or as afterwards receiving what they taught from Christ himself) must be the best, or rather the only, writers for us to depend upon. Others who followed, whether sooner or later, have no pretences to the same regard from us. A very few years make a great alteration in men's notions and language about such points of religion; and the difference of many years makes a still greater alteration; whilst men of various opinions and strong imaginations are continually going on to comment and enlarge upon such subjects. The New Testament, therefore, in this case, is alone to be depended on.[2]

Perhaps the most unequivocal declaration, however, was that of the regius professor of Divinity at Cambridge, Richard Watson.

I reduced the study of divinity into as narrow a compass as I could, for I determined to study nothing but my Bible, being much unconcerned about the opinions of councils, fathers, churches, bishops and other men as little inspired as myself. . . . I never troubled myself with answering any arguments which the opponents in the divinity-schools brought against the Articles of the Church, nor ever admitted their authority as decisive of a difficulty; but I used on such occasions to say to them, holding the New Testament in my hand, *En sacrum codicem*. Here is the fountain of truth, why do you follow the streams derived from it by the sophistry, or polluted by the passions of man?[3]

[1] C. Middleton, *A Free Enquiry* (1749), Introductory Discourse: pp. xcix–ci.

[2] B. Hoadly, *A Plain Account* (1735), p. 8.

[3] *Anecdotes of the Life of Richard Watson*, ed. R. Watson, vol. I, pp. 62–4.

There could be little surprise therefore that he desired the omission of the *Quicunque Vult* from the Liturgy, on the express ground that

> we do not object to the doctrine of the Trinity because it is above our reason and we cannot comprehend it; but we object to it because we cannot find that it is either literally contained in any passage of Holy Writ, or can by sound criticism be deduced from it.

Indeed

> was I compelled to receive a creed of *human* composition, I would more willingly in these enlightened times receive one from such men as Locke, Clarke or Tillotson, than from either Athanasius or Arius, or even from hundreds of contentious or political bishops, assembled in solemn council at Nice, Antioch or Ariminum.[1]

Thus was the axe laid sharply to the root of the tree of patristic study and the authority of the Fathers; and such was the unhappy declension from the confident affirmation of Simon Patrick concerning the men of latitude, that in interpreting the apostles and evangelists, 'they carefully attend to the sense of the ancient Church, by which they conceive the modern ought to be guided'.

It remained to be seen whether the two other strands of that three-fold cord of reason, scripture and tradition, which Patrick had believed to be firmly knit together, could hold fast without the witness of the ancient church. The trial of their strength was applied by the complex and amorphous movement of Deism, which combined the assaults on traditional Christianity launched by natural religion, the comparative study of religion, deductions from the scientific movement and an incipient rationalistic criticism of the Bible itself. The first attack was begun by John Toland's *Christianity not Mysterious* in 1696. Toland, a layman who had been in his youth a Presbyterian exhibitioner at the university of Utrecht, argued that the Gospel afforded 'the most illustrious examples of close and perspicuous ratiocination conceivable',[2] and therefore could contain nothing mysterious in the generally accepted sense of the word. In the New Testament indeed *mustērion* signified something which, formerly hidden, had now been made plain.[3] Starting from the premise that 'the true religion must necessarily be reasonable and intelligible', he proceeded to demonstrate 'that these requisite conditions are found in Christianity'.[4] The mysteries disfiguring it

---

[1] Richard Watson, *Miscellaneous Tracts*, vol. II, pp. 108, 115.
[2] John Toland, *Christianity Not Mysterious* (1696), p. 46.
[3] *Ibid.* Preface, pp. xxvii–xxviii.          [4] *Ibid.* p. 91.

were borrowed from Jewish and pagan sources; and in pure Christianity there was nothing contrary to reason nor even above it. Revelation therefore was simply an additional 'mean of information', combining certitude with perspicuity.[1] This line of argument was repeated at the interval of a generation in Matthew Tindal's *Christianity as Old as the Creation*, published in 1730, which took as its basis the persuasion that natural religion 'differs not from revealed, but in the manner of its being communicated; the one being the internal, as the other the external revelation of the same unchangeable will of a Being, who is alike at all times infinitely wise and good'.[2] Christianity therefore must be simply 'a republication or restoration of the Religion of Nature'.[3] Since the nature of God was eternally the same and the nature of Man alike in all ages, it was to be expected that all mankind should agree 'in owning the sufficiency of the Law of Nature to make men acceptable to God; and that the primitive Christians believed there was an exact agreement between Natural and Revealed Religion, and that the excellency of the latter did consist in being a republication of the former'.[4] Within these austere limits both Toland and Tindal adopted a respectful attitude towards Scripture; but Locke's emphasis on prophecy and miracle as authenticating the mission and teaching of the Messiah led to further and more damaging examination of its reliability.

Anthony Collins' *Discourse of the Grounds and Reasons of the Christian Religion*, published in 1724, whilst professing agreement with the orthodox contention that the argument from prophecy was essential to the proof of Christianity, turned the flank of this position by contending that literal fulfilment cannot be maintained, and therefore an allegorical interpretation must be accepted; whereby of course any interpretation demanded by the exigencies of any situation could be extracted from any prophecy. To Collins,

if any one Christian fact be true, it is that Christians in all ages and times, and more especially in the primitive times, have both understood the apostles to have argued allegorically from the prophecies cited by them out of the Old Testament, or have themselves argued allegorically from the prophecies they themselves cited out of the Old Testament.

From which it followed that

the whole Gospel is in every respect founded on type and allegory; that the apostles in most, if not in all cases, reasoned typically and allegorically;

---

Toland, *op. cit.* pp. 38, 43.
[2] M. Tindal, *Christianity as Old as the Creation* (1730), p. 2.
[3] *Ibid.* p. 176.        [4] *Ibid.* pp. 385, 387.

and that if the apostles be supposed to reason always after the rules used in the schools and if their writings be brought to the test of those rules, the books of the Old and New Testament will be in an irreconcilable state, and the difficulties against Christianity will be incapable of being solved.[1]

Predictive prophecy therefore was ruled out of consideration and literal fulfilment could no longer be sustained. Collins' argument was developed further in his *Scheme of Literal Prophecy Considered*, in 1727; and its novelty naturally provoked a series of replies (mainly along conventional lines), in defence of the traditional position.

Thomas Sherlock, however, in *The Use and Intent of Prophecy* published in 1725, adopted a more liberal interpretation, abandoning the attempt to force prophecy on the Procrustean bed of literal and detailed prediction and even allowing for a progressive understanding of divine purpose in the Old Testament. Admitting the 'difficulties in particular predictions and in the application of them made by writers who lived many hundred years ago', he replied that nevertheless

'tis not so easy a matter to shew, or to persuade the world to believe, that a chain of prophecies, reaching through several thousand years, delivered at different times, yet manifestly subservient to one and the same administration of Providence from beginning to end, is the effect of art and contrivance and religious fraud.[2]

Accordingly

the argument from prophecy for the truth of the Gospel does not rest upon this, that the event has necessarily limited and ascertained the particular sense and meaning of every prophecy; but in this, that every prophecy has in a proper sense been completed by the coming of Christ.[3]

Sherlock indeed reduced the issue to one simple point:

Is Christ that Person described and foretold under the Old Testament, or no? Whether all the prophecies relating to him be plain or not plain, whether all the ways used by the Jews of arguing from the Old Testament be convincing to us, it matters little. The single question is, Is there enough plain to shew us that Christ is the Person foretold under the Old Testament?[4]

The demand that each of the prophecies applied to Christ should have 'some express character and mark of Christ plainly to be under-

[1] A. Collins, *A Discourse of the Grounds and Reasons of the Christian Religion* (1724), part II, pp. [268], [270].
[2] Thomas Sherlock, *The Use and Intent of Prophecy in the Several Ages of the World* (1735), Preface, p. [2].
[3] *Ibid.* p. 33.          [4] *Ibid.* p. 43.

stood as such antecedently to his coming', was illegitimate.[1] Further, Sherlock was able to find evidence of a progressive development in this sphere. The first word of prophecy made to Adam and Eve when expelled from Eden, 'was proportioned to the wants and necessities of the world and sufficient to maintain religion after the Fall of Man'; whilst with the call of Abraham, 'we are now advancing to times of greater light, to clearer and more distinct prophecies, and more nearly relating to God's great dispensation of mercy and goodness to mankind, manifested by the revelation of his Son'.[2] But for the Gentile converts to Christianity, prophecy remained a secondary matter. St Paul at Athens deemed it 'quite ridiculous to offer proofs from prophecies. The appeal therefore, before them, is made to sound and clear principles of natural religion, and to the miracles of the Gospel'. In fine, 'to the Jew, prophecy was the first proof, to the Gentile it was the last. The Jew believed in Christ because foretold by the Prophets; the Gentiles believed the Prophets, because they had so exactly foretold Jesus Christ.'[3] Evidence of the welcome accorded to this interpretation by ecclesiastical authority was given in Wake's comment to Turrettini, that

at this distance of time it is hard to answer all the difficulties that may be raised against the explication or application of some particular prophecies. But take the whole course of the predictions of the Old Testament and compare them with their accomplishment in the New,...and no one who is not wilfully blind will be able to doubt either of the interpretation or the fulfilling of them. This therefore I think is the true way of answering these men; let them cease to cavil upon points which neither of us understand, and take the whole view of the two Testaments (the Old and the New) together, and then judge whether the former does not speak of what was performed under the latter, and both together prove the divine revelation of one another.[4]

A parallel assault to that of Collins on prophecy was mounted against miracles, and especially against the resurrection of Jesus, by Thomas Woolston's *Six Discourses on the Miracles of our Saviour* *(1727–9)*. Here the enemy was threatening a more vital bulwark of orthodoxy. Miracles in general seemed essential as evidence of the freedom of the Creator to regulate his creation, and in particular as authenticating the claims of revelation. Locke had accepted them without question as a necessary part of the reasonableness of

---

[1] Sherlock, *op. cit.* p. 67.     [2] *Ibid.* pp. 72, 105.     [3] *Ibid.* p. 161.
[4] N. Sykes, *William Wake*, vol. II, p. 170 (Wake to Turrettini, 28 November 1728).

Christianity; and even Toland had concurred that Christ 'proves his authority and Gospel by such works and miracles as the stiff-necked Jews themselves could not deny to be divine', and had affirmed their credibility, since there was not 'any miracle mentioned in the New Testament but what served to confirm the authority of those that wrought it, to procure attention to the doctrines of the Gospel, or for the like wise and reasonable purposes'.[1] Accordingly Woolston's contention that the miracles should be interpreted allegorically, to the exclusion of their historical truth, struck at the core of Christianity. Accepting the challenge of orthodoxy to 'reduce the controversy to a narrow compass', namely to the resurrection of Jesus, he declared it 'to be the most notorious and monstrous imposture, that ever was put upon mankind', and a 'monstrous and incredible miracle'; and he exhorted Christians to seek the only credible solution by going 'along with me to the Fathers for their mystical interpretation of the whole story of Jesus' Resurrection'.[2] This onslaught provoked the expected volume of replies, typifying that 'Old Bailey theology' described by Dr Johnson, 'in which the apostles are being tried once a week for the capital crime of forgery'. Once again Thomas Sherlock rallied to the defence, and his *Trial of the Witnesses of the Resurrection of Jesus*, published in 1729, represented 'the concentrated essence of eighteenth-century apologetic theology'.[3] His argument was simple: that 'here must be a real miracle or a great fraud'; that neither Jesus nor his disciples were guilty of fraud; and therefore their testimony must be accepted. Accordingly, when the judge put to the jury the question: 'Are the Apostles guilty of giving false evidence in the case of the resurrection of Jesus, or not guilty?', the foreman answered 'Not guilty'.[4] But although on evidential grounds the orthodox defended New Testament miracles successfully against the Deists, Conyers Middleton's denial of all miracles outside the narrow confines of the apostolic age placed the gospel signs and wonders in a position of perilous, if splendid, isolation. Not only did he 'hand over the primitive Church, lock, stock and barrel, to the Roman Catholic Church',[5] thereby compassing the transient

---

[1] J. Toland, *Christianity Not Mysterious*, pp. 47, 153.
[2] T. Woolston, *A Sixth Discourse on the Miracles of our Saviour* (1729), pp. 4–5, 43.
[3] L. Stephen, *History of English Thought in the Eighteenth-Century* (1876), vol. I, p. 243.
[4] T. Sherlock, *The Tryal of the Witnesses of the Resurrection of Jesus* (1729), p. [109].
[5] W. O. Chadwick, *From Bossuet to Newman*, p. 76.

conversion of the youthful Gibbon to that church; but he also embarrassed Protestants to no inconsiderable extent, since, as Gibbon reasoned, if 'miracles are the test of truth', then 'that church must be orthodox and pure, which was so often approved by the visible interposition of the Deity'.[1]

The long controversy of orthodoxy against Deism was inconclusive and indecisive, largely because both parties lacked the key to the solution of their problems. On the one hand the Deists assumed the existence of an universal, simple, sufficient creed of Natural Religion, accepted by the *Bon Sauvage* of the pre-historic past and present alike, and free from mysteries and dark corners. This illusion was shattered by Butler's *Analogy of Religion, Natural and Revealed to the Constitution and Course of Nature*, in which he tore the veil from the face of Natural Religion and showed it to be as full of mystery and shadows as revelation. On the other hand, the orthodox were hampered by the strait-jacket of a static conception of the Biblical revelation and its record. Either the apostles and evangelists were forgers or else all their record was true. In regard to the Old Testament indeed Sherlock had pointed the way to the concept of a progressive revelation, which was to resolve the puzzle in later times; but with respect to the New Testament, apologists advanced only tentatively and gingerly towards such a revolutionary theory. Butler allowed that

as it is owned, the whole scheme of Scripture is not yet understood; so, if it ever comes to be understood before the restitution of all things, and without miraculous interpositions, it must be in the same way as natural knowledge is come at; by the continuance and progress of learning and of liberty, and by particular persons attending to, comparing and pursuing intimations scattered up and down it, which are overlooked and disregarded by the generality of the world. For this is the way in which all improvements are made; by thoughtful men's tracing on obscure hints, as it were dropped us by Nature accidentally, or which seem to come into our minds by chance. Nor is it at all incredible that a Book, which has been so long in the possession of mankind, should contain many truths as yet undiscovered. For all the same phenomena and the same faculties of investigation, from which such great discoveries in natural knowledge have been made in the present and last age, were equally in the possession of mankind several thousand years before. And possibly it might be intended, that events as they come to pass, should open and ascertain the meaning of several parts of Scripture.[2]

---

[1] E. Gibbon, *Memoirs of My Life and Writings* (ed. G. B. Hill, 1900), pp. 67–9.

[2] Butler, 'Analogy', part II, c. III, § 10, in *Works* (1900), vol. II, pp. 171–2.

The suggestion was carried a step further by Edmund Law's *Considerations on the State of the World with Regard to the Theory of Religion*, the purpose of which was

to shew that Arts and Sciences, Natural and Revealed Religion, have upon the whole always been progressive, from the creation of the world to the present time, as also that they have been suited to each other, as well as to the circumstances of mankind during each period of their progression.[1]

Having surveyed the Old Dispensation in the light of this premise, Law went on,

the very same method might be shewn to be continued under Christianity itself....It was in its infancy in Christ's time, who communicated the things of it to his disciples by little and little, as they were able to bear them; beginning with the plainest and most obvious, laying the foundation and first principles of the doctrine during his ministry and conversation with them after his resurrection, and leaving the more full opening of it till the descent of the Holy Ghost, which likewise led them gradually into its several truths.[2]

From its 'childhood under the apostles', Christianity had advanced *pari passu* with other branches of human knowledge.

That perfect *Analogy* between religion and the common course of nature, which has been so beautifully displayed by a late excellent writer, holds no less true, I believe, in this respect; and that as all Arts and Sciences, every improvement in natural and civil life are still drawing nearer to perfection,...in short as every branch of knowledge has been all along enlarging and improving itself, and every successive age not only enjoys the discoveries of the foregoing, but adds still greater and more valuable ones of its own; so it is probable that the knowledge of Religion alone is not at a stand; but on the contrary, that as we continually advance in the study of God's Works, so we shall come to a proportionably better understanding of his Word. As by all these means human reason is still growing more perfect, so by the same means divine revelation will gradually clear up, and Christianity itself draw nearer to its fullness.[3]

For, as the knowledge of religion, both natural and revealed, 'will appear to have held pace in general with all other knowledge from the beginning', so 'if it has hitherto been really progressive, we find good reason to expect the same still farther'. Law indeed sought to safeguard himself from misunderstanding by explaining that

when I mention *improvements* in religion, I don't by any means intend a discovery of new points, or improving upon the original revelation itself in anything essential to the general doctrine of salvation; but only a more

---

[1] E. Law, *Considerations on the State of the World* (1745), Preface, p. 1.
[2] *Ibid.* p. 165.　　　　[3] *Ibid.* pp. 182–4.

perfect comprehension of what was formerly delivered; a view of the extent and excellence of this great mystery concealed from former ages, and which, though given almost all at once, yet was received perhaps but partially.[1]

To this end, contemporary advances in philosophy and the principles of criticism and interpretation applied to the Scriptures would dissipate the prejudice,

which makes us as it were afraid to look into them, and examine them with the same freedom that we do, and find we must do, every other book which we desire to understand: I mean the notion of an absolute, immediate inspiration of each part and period, even where the writers themselves most effectually disclaim it.[2]

Here the Age of Reason stood upon the very threshold of the doctrine of development and the rise of Biblical criticism, which were to characterise the thought of its successor.

The manner and extent to which contemporary theological controversies affected the religious life of the church are difficult to estimate. Law reckoned amongst the virtues of his times that

unprofitable austerities are rather changed for that more reasonable service and devotion, which renders the Deity amiable and the imitation of him useful to mankind; which makes each worshipper more happy in himself, and helpful to his fellow-creatures.[3]

There can be no doubt of the widespread vogue of this doctrine of Divine Benevolence. Tillotson's sermon on the text 'And His commandments are not grievous', became the general theme of his age. At times indeed it sunk to bathos. The solitary 'scrap of my pulpit eloquence' included in the recently-published *Letters of Spencer Cowper, Dean of Durham*, sets forth

what I call my sovereign cordial in all difficulties and distresses, which (pardon the preacher) is this reflection: 'That every man must be finally happy, if he has not by his folly and ill conduct forfeited all title to be so; or otherwise no one can be finally miserable, whilst it is consistent with infinite goodness to make him otherwise'.[4]

Moreover, the popularity of Tillotson's sermons resulted in much adulteration of their doctrine when adapted to the ears of rustic auditors. The sermons of Anthony Hastwell, incumbent of two small parishes in the North Riding of Yorkshire, Kildale and Great Ayton, in the latter half of the eighteenth-century, illustrated the

---

[1] Law, *op. cit.* pp. 225, 247, 249–50.    [2] *Ibid.* p. 251.    [3] *Ibid.* p. 239.
[4] *Letters of Spencer Cowper, Dean of Durham*, no. LXXV, p. 53 (ed. E. Hughes, Surtees Society, 1956). For Dean Cowper, see c. VI, pp. 212–15.

prosaic and homespun character of such preaching. Borrowing the language of Tillotson, he argued that

when all things are considered, it will be found that as the way of God and virtue is much plainer and easier than that of vice and wickedness, so a man may take less pains to be very good than very bad; and will more consult his own ease, pleasure and satisfaction by living a religious than an irreligious life.

Indeed the demands made of man by God tempered the wind to the shorn lamb.

God almighty, in the laws he gave us by Christ, never intended to require an exact and unsinning obedience to them; but in the Gospel sense we are said to obey God's laws when we use our sincere endeavours to obey them; when in the main of our lives we live up to them; when we do not indulge ourselves in any known, wilful course of sin; but, as far as the weakness of our nature and the circumstances of our lives permit, we do as much as we can to mortify our corrupt affections and live holy and virtuous lives.

Therefore virtue

puts us to little bodily pain, brings no great weariness or consumption of spirits on us, is not contrary to, but exceedingly well agrees with the constitution and frame of our nature; and is, besides, such a design that whosoever undertakes it, may assuredly promise to himself success.... It will quicken our diligence and industry even as to the prosecution of our secular affairs.

From these arguments it followed that

every considerate man, from the evidence of truth, must be forced to acknowledge that, all things considered, 'tis more easy, safe, desirable and delightful to be good, to serve God, to live in obedience to his laws and discharge a good conscience, than to enjoy all the pleasures of sin which are but for a short season.[1]

The correspondences between Anthony Hastwell and James Woodforde in this respect are evidence of their common source and of the widespread use of Tillotson. Sermon no. 140 of Woodforde was preached from the same text, and borrowed extensively the *ipsissima verba* of Tillotson. The preacher aimed to show that both 'present pleasure and the assurance of future reward' attended the practice of Christianity; so that if men 'put both these together, the pleasures of religion and the reward of it, they cannot but appear to be a very great encouragement'. The same prosaic calculations were present in the copyist as in his exemplar. 'It is undoubtedly

[1] E. W. Watson, 'An Eighteenth-Century Clergyman', in *Church Quarterly Review*. vol. CV (January 1928), no. 210, pp. 255-71.

sufficient then to recommend religion to any considerate person that the advantages of it are greater than of any worldly design, and the difficulties of it not greater.' Indeed its commandments were truly not grievous: 'for to use our sincere endeavours is nothing else but to do as much as we can; and if we do that, we are sure of God's grace and assistance.' The conclusion therefore was that 'in a word, plain, easy and safe are the paths of religion, and which will always entertain us with pleasure in the course of our journey, and will crown us with happiness at its end'.[1] The counsels of Hastwell and Woodeforde were the pulpit counterpart of the series of prints, published by order of Parliament, in which the differing fortunes of two Charity-School boys were set forth pictorially so that all who ran might read. The one followed his apprenticeship with such sobriety, industry and piety as to marry his master's daughter, become magistrate and alderman, and finally to find himself acting as justice in the trial of his school-fellow. This latter had been an unworthy apprentice, frequenting gin-shops, falling into loose company, and contracting debts and finally was to end his life on the gibbet.

Echoes of the scientific themes of the age were also to find their place in the sermons of the clergy. Dean Cowper of Durham in considering the doctrine of the Incarnation, admitted that

our present more perfect insight into Nature, which extends the visible creation almost to the infinite, wherein sun rises upon sun, world upon world, and that reasonable and well-founded conclusion from thence, that these are all inhabited by intelligent beings, of equal, perhaps of much superior, excellence and more exalted perfections than we on this earth,... this better philosophy still increases the difficulty

of such a belief. *Per contra,*

excepting that more sure word of truth, the Scriptures, we have no other source of acquiring a knowledge of God and his perfections than that of the great volume of Nature....Here we see the same exertions of infinite power, the same traces of infinite goodness, the same signatures of un-erring wisdom....See the ample provision which God lays before us, and how all things are so ordered that they not only conduce to our service, but minister delight to the sons of men; and we shall be too apt to think that Man was his only care, and that all these exertions of power, wisdom and goodness had Man for their sole end.

[1] N. Sykes, 'The Sermons of a Country Parson: James Woodeforde in his Pulpit', in *Theology*, vol. XXXVIII, no. 224 (February 1939), and no. 227 (May), pp. 97–106, 341–52. I am gratefully obliged to Dr R. E. H. Woodforde of Winscombe, Somerset, for permission to read and to quote from these forty sermons.

Furthermore, 'what maintains the whole, maintains every part', and so 'by analogy between the Works and Word of God, between the God of the natural and moral world', the Incarnation becomes credible to men.[1] Parson Woodforde likewise discoursed to his rural congregation of the testimony of Nature to the existence and attributes of God. Sermon 155 bade them consider

what are all the nations upon this globe? What this globe itself when compared with the greatness of the works of God in this universe? Nay, what when compared even with this one solar system of ours? But what again is this system, what the sun with all the planets that attend him, when compared to the greatness of those works which fall ever under our notice?...But farther, how little is all which we can comprehend of the works of God, when compared with the immensity of space without any possible limit or bound: I say, how inconsiderable all the works of God, that we know anything of when compared with this immensity and that Being who fills it!

From this consideration of the inanimate universe, the preacher passed to 'the testimony of animate creation'; and particularly to 'the higher orders, who are endowed with intellectual, especially with moral, powers. Of this kind, though lowest in rank, is the human race, to whom this globe is given for an habitation.' But what of 'all the worlds which God hath made; are they without life, without inhabitants of the rational and moral kind? No, certainly. How inexpressible the number of them! How great that family of God! Who can number his hosts'? Therefore, in the most approved modern manner, Woodeforde concluded by appealing to the belief of the scientists of his own day in God.

It is pleasing to a good mind to think that this great article of our faith is established and confirmed by the best and highest improvements which have been made in reason and the knowledge and study of Nature; and that those who have made the greatest progress in their enquiries, ascribe activity only to the mind, as that in which matter hath no share; making it apparent that to speak of the powers of matter, and of a necessity under which they are, or a chance by which changes are produced in it, is a language which really has no meaning. God omnipotent reigneth; in His infinite mind the plan of this universe was formed, and by his power the glorious design was carried into execution.

In another sermon, no. 221, the Diarist averred

that too much cannot well be said of the excellency and use of the precepts of what is called Natural Religion, nor can the necessity of their observance

[1] Spencer Cowper, *Eight Discourses preached on or near the Great Festivals in the Cathedral Church of Durham* (1773), I, pp. 7–8, 10.

be too often and too warmly inculcated, if considered only in themselves, and not as exclusive of other duties. Christianity has established them on the firmest basis; and our modern advocates for the moral system in opposition to, or derogation from, the divine, must (if they will act consistently with their pretences) retain a great veneration and esteem at least for the Gospel, which has given us the only perfect scheme of moral laws, and bound them upon us by sanctions of infinitely greater force than the reason or authority of man could devise.[1]

The discovery of a manuscript volume containing six sermons of John Lloyd, vicar of Epping from 1710 to 1754 and rector in plurality of Stapleford Tawney from 1753, and chaplain to Bishop Charles Cecil of Bristol in 1733 (by which office he qualified for a dispensation for pluralism), bears additional testimony to the familiarity of these themes.[2] As with the sermons of Hastwell and Woodforde, those of Lloyd were repeated frequently and regularly. Lloyd also discoursed to his flock concerning the advantages of religion to the individual, since 'prudence would certainly oblige him to provide for those interests which are of greatest worth and value, and for that life which is most lasting and permanent'; and accordingly, 'upon an impartial view of things, it is certainly to be concluded that the greatest gain is godliness, and that true is the saying of the apostle, godliness is profitable for all things, having the promise of this life and of that which is to come'. Moreover, Lloyd, treating of the relationship of natural and revealed religion, expounded to his people 'the insufficiency of human reason fully to discover and apprehend the nature and attributes of God, and the necessity of forming our judgement concerning them by the sole intimations of revelation'. Even

concerning the objects of sensation, of which we have the best and clearest evidence, nothing more is discovered by our senses than a bare power of affecting them after such or such a manner; and what we are able to learn further of their nature from reasoning and experience, arises often no higher than opinion only and probability.

---

[1] N. Sykes, 'The Sermons of a Country Parson, in *Theology*, vol. XXVIII, no. 224, pp. 104–5.

[2] For permission to read, and quote from, this manuscript volume, bearing the inscription on the fly-leaf: 'Vol. 7 <sup>mum</sup> continens conciones', I am gratefully obliged to R. W. Johnson, Esq., of Pinner, Middlesex, who kindly loaned it to me and who had bought it for a few pence at a Shoreditch bookstall at the beginning of the present century. Epping vicarage was worth £230 per annum, and Stapleford Tawney about £160 per annum. The archbishop's licence for plurality to Lloyd is dated 10 March 1732/3.

Not that reason should be unduly depreciated.

This imputation of ignorance which we have charged upon mankind, ought not to be perversely improved, as if it had been asserted we had no certain knowledge of any things whatsoever. For a deficiency in any power doth by no means argue an absolute denial of such a power; and it were an absurd and unreasonable conclusion to infer, that because there are several things which we know not, there are therefore no things which we know.

Indeed reason could establish the existence of God.

That there is a supreme Being or God, who is the first cause and chief governor of all things, and who has a just right to our greatest veneration and worship, is a truth of which we have such certain evidence and knowledge, that it seems impossible for any thinking man to be either ignorant or doubtful of it.

Unaided reason however could go little farther than this in respect of knowledge of God.

The best notion of God we are capable to entertain is framed either by conceiving united in Him in an unlimited manner all the excellencies we observe dispersed among other beings; or else by separating from Him not only all faults, but also all manner of imperfections, which other things are subject to.

Even when this had been done 'by attributing to Him all manner of perfection whatsoever', the sum of our knowledge, as Clement of Alexandria, had said was 'no more than this, that we know what He is not, but know not what He is'. Revelation therefore was indispensable to the true knowledge of God; and its testimony should not be rejected.

Hence it is that the doctrine of the Trinity, the Incarnation and other mysteries of the Christian religion have suffered so much from the exceptions of captious and sceptical men. Some absolutely disbelieve them, because they are not agreeable to the dictates of their reason, and others endeavour so to interpret them as to make them conformable thereto; whereas the truth is that reason has nothing to do in the whole affair, but that the holy scriptures ought to be sufficient to secure them from the infidelity of the former, and their own mysteriousness from the explications of the latter.

Therefore,

the only end I proposed in shewing the insufficiency of reason, was thereby to evince the necessity of judging of the mysteries of our religion only by what is asserted of them in the sacred scripture. There alone they are contained, and thence alone are they to be interpreted.

Lloyd was here in full agreement with Swift's *Letter to a Young Clergyman*:

I do not find that you are anywhere directed in the canons or articles to attempt explaining the mysteries of the Christian religion. And indeed since Providence intended there should be mysteries, I do not see how it can be agreeable to piety, orthodoxy or good sense, to go about such a work. For to me there seems a manifest dilemma in the case: if you explain them, they are mysteries no longer: if you fail, you have laboured to no purpose. What I should think most reasonable and safe for you to do upon this occasion, is, upon solemn days, to deliver the doctrine as the Church holds it and confirm it by Scripture.[1]

It is interesting to observe that Woodforde also preached on this topic of the relationship of reason to revelation. In Sermon no. 86 he claimed that we have 'in the whole course of St Paul's preaching, the authority of that apostle for using our reason in matters of religion'; though it was necessary carefully 'to examine in what instances it is necessary to make use of our rational faculties in matters of religion, and in what instances we are to lay aside our reason and become implicit in our belief'. The function of reason in respect of revelation was 'in enquiring into the evidence upon which that revelation is supposed to be built'; and in particular to apply the test that 'we all know that God can reveal nothing that is either inconsistent with his own attributes of wisdom and goodness, or is impossible in itself, or implies a manifest contradiction'. To Woodforde, as to the majority of divines of his age, the irrefutable proof of a revelation lay in the power of its proclaimer 'to work miracles and alter the course of Nature'; so that 'we should think ourselves obliged to receive the doctrines of those who come with these powers, provided their doctrines be such as are worthy of the Divine Nature, and such as do not contradict any former revelation which God has given'. In another discourse the preacher followed this argument, as did Lloyd, by pointing out that if a revelation were thus authenticated, its content should be accepted even though beyond the capacity of reason to understand. 'If He [God] is pleased to reveal things of himself which we cannot comprehend, our want of comprehension is no just reason why we should reject such a revelation'; and in relation to the resurrection in particular, 'since almighty God has revealed this doctrine to us, it must be the indispensable duty of all who receive his Word to believe it'.[2]

[1] J. Swift, 'A Letter to a Young Clergyman' (*The Prose Works of Swift*, ed. Temple Scott, vol. III, p. 213).     [2] N. Sykes, in *Theology*, XXXVIII, no. 224, pp. 101–3.

Dean Cowper however rated prophecy more highly than miracles; since the latter were 'chiefly a testimony to those who beheld them (for the credit of them, when reported, rested entirely on the veracity and ability of the reporter)', whereas the former 'had this superior advantage that the completion of events, foretold ages before, added new strength to the evidence established on miracles; and time, instead of lessening, must continually increase this evidence, according as it shall bring to pass events foretold by the spirit of prophecy'. In his own age indeed, prophecy served 'for the establishing our faith in the historical evidence given by miracles to the divine mission of Christ'. Cowper had no doubts as to the force of this testimony. For 'we have in the prophetic writings, so many proofs of this foreknowledge in God as to make it an undeniable truth; for the conformity between history and prophecy is frequently so amazingly great, that the prophet often rather seems to be relating a past event than predicting a future one'. Nor should the obscurity of many alleged predictions be an argument against the truth of prophecy; for since their fulfilment often depended on human co-operation, they must 'be couched in such terms as should not too obviously mark out the persons concerned'. There was also 'no contradiction in the supposition that two persons at a great distance of time from each other may, by the providence of God, be placed in such circumstances that what is foretold of the latter, may coincide with what the former may have done or suffered'; and therefore the preacher concluded that the Holy Spirit 'moved the prophets to utter prophecies, in which were united the prediction of events of very different natures and of ages very remote from each other'.[1]

Belief in the existence of incorporeal spirits had seemed necessary as an antidote to scientific materialism and mechanism no less to Glanvill than to the Cambridge Platonists; and Lloyd made bold to instruct his congregation on this difficult subject. He was aware indeed of its pitfalls. 'It must be confessed that matters of mere speculation are not proper to be discoursed of in promiscuous assemblies, because they seldom directly tend to the two great purposes of religion, the fear of God and a holy life. But, there being in the sacred Scriptures...Such frequent mention of angels, and the things delivered concerning them being capable of eminently serving to the advancement of piety and virtue, I think among the

---

[1] Spencer Cowper, *Eight Discourses*, pp. 17, 18, 21-3, 29.

diverse subjects treated of in sacred places, it will not be unuseful to dedicate some time to the contemplation of those glorious and exalted spirits.' Care must be taken, however, not to bemuse his hearers 'with any of the various conjectures, idle and fanciful men have vented upon this obscure subject', which were 'for the most part begotten in a cloister, the issue of vigorous imaginations, heated by superstition or solitude'. The consideration of angelic beings must have an eye to 'some deductions drawn from them which may conduce towards the advancement of piety and virtue'. But first Lloyd broke a lance with sceptics; who would accept 'the prodigious velocity of the sun round his own centre', as was 'now generally embraced and acknowledged as a certain truth' though 'beyond the power of human imagination to apprehend', and yet refused to believe in supernatural beings. The analogy of nature was pressed into service; for if God had created ants, why not archangels? 'For if the great Creator has condescended to produce such great multitudes not only of animals without reason, but vegetables without sense and even beings without life; is it not rational to suppose He has much more exerted his power in the production of more noble beings, such as show greater evidences of his wisdom and power, and draw nearer a similitude to his own nature? Besides, of all the creatures here below, Man alone is endowed with faculties capable of reflecting upon the works of God and praising their almighty Maker; and can it be esteemed probable that among all his works God should make but one species of beings able to observe his wisdom and extol his glory?' If then, 'to those who impartially consider the nature of God and the works of creation', the existence of angelic beings is probable, 'to those who believe the authority of Scripture', probability will become certainty. The preacher therefore assembled the Biblical testimony in behalf of angels and drew the appropriate conclusions 'for the advancement of piety and virtue'. Belief in angels gave men a nobler conception of God and even inculcated the ubiquitous lesson of benevolence towards their fellow-men! 'Let therefore the beneficence of these blessed spirits remind and admonish us of the affections we owe to one another; let no distance in kindred or circumstances cause us to despise the interest of our fellow-creatures, since beings so much superior to us disdain not to act for our benefit; but, as it is more noble to give than to receive, let us by acts of charity and beneficence raise and advance our characters, and so make nearer approaches to those more noble and exalted creatures'. This blending of the sublime and the mundane was eminently characteristic of the age of reason, which in its own way and in a limited degree, was also a not inconsiderable age of faith.

But it should not be supposed that its preaching neglected the more practical, not to say prosaic, aspects and duties of life. Of the forty extant sermons of Parson Woodforde the great majority were concerned with pastoral counsels. Dean Cowper likewise discoursed of the virtues of humility as shown in seeking 'the good of our neighbour', of morality 'founded on the eternal difference' between right and wrong; and of truth, 'not bare, speculative truth, but truth as a virtue and principle of action'. Both Lloyd and Woodforde warned their flocks of the deceitfulness of riches and inculcated the stewardship of wealth. Woodforde also delivered on successive Sundays two sermons on the obligation and nature of prayer, which set forward a high standard of both public and private devotion in this respect, and exhorted his hearers to such a fervency as was 'a gentle, pleasing, heavenly flame, and not a headstrong and outrageous fire, which hurries men into enthusiasm'. He preached also on the duty of attendance at the public worship of God (conceived as 'the great and universal Benefactor'), and of regular reception of the Holy Communion.[1] Nor were his flock left without instruction concerning the relationship of their daily occupations to the teachings of religion. Agriculture 'ought to be done with a constant and habitual view to the glory of God, and it easily may, without any inconvenience or disadvantage to our secular designs'. He that holdeth the plough could at the same time learn wisdom, by reflecting 'what perfect art, what incomprehensible contrivance appear in the formation and structure of the vegetable world; what variety and uniformity, what order, symmetry and proportion of parts!' By daily contact with Nature, he could perceive how 'there is a necessity that these things should be all regulated according to a stated course and order, or the world would be utter confusion'; and could understand that 'the care of the Supreme Being, by which this general order or stated course of things is preserved, may not unfitly be called a General Providence'.

Generally speaking, these sermons breathed that spirit of optimism and confidence which inspired Addison's essay on 'Chearfulness' as

---

[1] N. Sykes, 'The Sermons of a Country Parson' in *Theology*, vol. XXXVIII, no. 227 (May 1939), pp. 341–52.

a 'constant habitual gratitude to the great Author of nature', and which was expressed in his praise of God, whose

> Bounteous hand with worldly bliss
> Has made my cup run o'er,
> And in a kind and faithful Friend
> Has doubled all my store.

If the theological controversies of the age caused many divines to make shipwreck of the proportion of the faith, in the sermons of Hastwell, Woodforde and Lloyd there was a simplicity of belief, aptly associated with a simplification of style which contemporaries such as Burnet and Evelyn noted as springing from the example of Tillotson's sermons. But the rustic congregations in Yorkshire, Norfolk and Essex received also full measure pressed down and running over, in the length of these discourses. Nor was the age of reason lacking somewhat incongruous survivals of former times, whether in the persistent belief in witchcraft, or in the curious collection of relics seen in York Minster in 1695 by Thomas Brockbank, which embraced, amidst sundry secular marvels, 'St Peter's sword, the cock, St Peter's well', from which he 'drank some of the water'.[1]

The outstanding feature of the doctrine of Divine Benevolence, however, was the stimulus given to philanthropy. Tenison observed justly of the age that 'practical Christianity was its talent and delight'; and Law affirmed of his contemporaries that 'we have certain virtues now in greater perfection, particularly more of true charity or universal benevolence, than ever since the time of primitive Christianity'.[2] Measured by the standard of the Epistle of St James, the age could challenge comparison with almost any epoch of Christian history. Its faith was abundantly fruitful in good works. On the one hand stood the foundation of the Societies for the Propagation of the Gospel and for Promoting Christian Knowledge, whose continuing achievement is writ large in the history of the Church of England, together with the several Religious Societies and the Society for the Reformation of Manners. On the other hand was the impressive testimony of the Charity School Movement, and of the ubiquitous hospital foundations in London, in the university towns and throughout the county towns of England. Dean Cowper

---

[1] *Diary and Letter Book of Thomas Brockbank (1671–1709)*, (ed. R. Trappes-Lomax, Cheetham Society, 1930), p. 101.
[2] E. Law, *Considerations on the State of the World*, p. 244.

even paid a visit to Newcastle (which he particularly detested) in order to be present with the bishop at the laying of the foundation stone of a new infirmary, and Parson Woodforde attended musical entertainments in Norwich cathedral in aid of the county hospital. Such good works were the fruit of, not the substitute for, piety. The Church of England moreover during the century from Sheldon to Secker nourished such faithful laymen as John Evelyn, Robert Nelson, Henry Newman and Samuel Johnson. If the accepted traditions of clerical duty as revealed in the *Diary* of James Woodforde and divers Visitation Returns seem somewhat exiguous and desiccated by modern standards, yet, as the sermons of Woodforde amongst other evidence testify, they could become the vehicle of a pastoral ministry not without worthy chracteristics. Perhaps the key to true religion as understood by the age may best be found in its favourite manual of devotion, *The Whole Duty of Man*, published in 1658 and enjoying an extraordinary vogue for the ensuing century. Here, in the seventeen chapters designed to be read thrice over on the Sundays of each year, was set forth 'The Practice of Christian Graces or the Whole Duty of Man', comprehending 'the Duty of Man by the Light of Nature, by the Light of Scripture', in 'the Three Great Branches of Man's Duty to God, Ourselves and our Neighbours'. Moreover the exposition was 'laid down in a plain way for the use of the meanest reader', and written in a popular directness of style so that he who ran might read. If William Cowper stigmatised it as a 'repository of self-righteousness', and George Whitefield classed its author with Tillotson as one who knew 'no more about true Christianity than Mahomet', it nevertheless constituted an abiding monument to the sober, rational piety of an age which believed firmly, in accordance with its title, in the injunction, 'Fear God and keep his commandments; for this is the whole duty of Man'.

# VI

## QUIETA NON MOVENDA

'The Revolution found the Church under an interim rather than an establishment.'[1] The prescient diagnosis of Archdeacon Reynolds emphasised the gravity of the failure of the ecclesiastical settlement in 1689 to undertake the needful measures of readjustment. The disastrous influence of the Non-juring schism on Sancroft's comprehension project has been already indicated. But the deprivation of the archbishop had other ill consequences, since he had drawn up a programme of practical reforms, which might have delivered the church from the paralysis induced by its static constitution in an age of rapid change. In a paper written in his own hand and headed 'For the Regulation of Ecclesiastical Affairs', he had sketched a scheme of reform.[2] Beginning with the oft-discussed problems of excommunication and commutation of penance, he rehearsed previous suggestions on these heads. He urged

that excommunication be made solemn, to which end that the sentence may be pronounced in open court, either by the bishop assisted by some of his clergy, or in the absence of the bishop, by some of the gravest clergy, for that purpose deputed by the bishop from time to time under his hand and seal; that the sentence of excommunication be pronounced only upon causes of blasphemy, apostasy, heresy, schism, refusing to have his or their child baptized, or to receive the Holy Communion as it is commonly used to be received in the Church of England, or to come to divine service now commonly used in the said Church of England, or errors in matters of religion or doctrine now received and allowed in the said Church of England, incontinency, extortion, simony, perjury in the ecclesiastical court, idolatry, refusing to bring their children and servants to be catechised.

In all other cases of contempt,

instead of the sentence of excommunication by the bishop, the sentence of contumacy may be pronounced in open court by the chancellor or his deputy;

and in accordance therewith,

he that is thus sentenced, may suffer all the temporal punishments and disabilities which now follow upon excommunication (but that he be not

---

[1] G. Reynolds, *An Historical Essay upon the Government of the Church of England*, p. 188.　　　　　[2] Tanner MSS. 300, ff. 143 *seq.*

excluded *a sacris*, prohibited Christian burial or suffer spiritual penalties); but that a writ *de contumaci capiendo* may issue out after the same manner, and proceedings be thereupon made, as it used to be in the writ *de excommunicato capiendo*; and that the writs *de excommunicato* and *de contumaci capiendo* may be issued out without any great trouble or charge.[1]

Similarly with regard to commutation, he desired that the sentence of absolution from excommunication should be pronounced with the like solemnity as the infliction of that sentence; and

that no commutation of penance be made by any chancellor, archdeacon or other officer without the allowance of the bishop of the diocese under his hand, nor the money taken to be expended otherwise than by the direction and approbation of the bishop, upon pain of suspension of the party offending, and in case of contumacy, upon pain of degradation.

In order to strengthen the judicial authority of the diocesan bishop, Sancroft proposed

that no bishop shall grant any patent to any Chancellor, Commissary or Official for any longer term than for the life of the grantee only; nor otherwise than with express reservation to himself and successors of power to execute the place, either alone or with the Chancellor, if the Bishop shall please so to do, saving always to the said Chancellor the fees accustomably taken for executing the said jurisdiction; and that patents so made hereafter may be good in law; [and] that in all such patents the Bishop shall keep in his own hands the power of censuring clergymen.

Furthermore, any such legal officers who were convicted before the bishop of malversation or corruption, should be liable to suspension for a period; and 'in cases of pertinacity and incorrigibility (viz. after two suspensions) to be deprived of their places'. An appeal should lie in case of such deprivation to the archbishop of the Province, 'sitting in person (or by a Bishop deputed in their stead) assisted by three Bishops and an Ecclesiastical Judge', whilst an appeal from deprivation by an archbishop should lie to the Court of Delegates; and their determinations should be final. By these means Sancroft sought to reinforce the authority of the bishops against their lay officers and to emphasise the spiritual basis of ecclesiastical jurisdiction.

The memorandum turned next to the ubiquitous and insoluble problem of pluralism; where it was proposed that

no person henceforth to be admitted to receive and hold together more than two ecclesiastical benefices with cure, and those to lie within the

---

[1] The section dealing with excommunication and contumacy is marked in the margin: *De his amplius deliberandum.*

distance of 20 miles; having a curate to be allowed by the archbishop of the province or bishop of the diocese under his hand and seal, the curate to be allowed either £40 per annum or a moiety of the benefice where he serves, public charges first deducted. No man to take henceforth and hold two dignities requiring residence in several churches.

The extent of pluralism amongst the higher clergy indeed vexed Sancroft exceedingly; and he did not hesitate to make his disapproval known when occasion offered. Thus he rebuked Humphrey Prideaux for holding together with his academic office in Oxford a prebend of Norwich cathedral, 'so far removed from the place of my usual residence, by reasons of the incapacity this distance puts on me of being serviceable in all the duties there required of me'.[1] Further, he exerted his utmost influence, though in vain, to prevent the appointment of John Sharp, rector of St Giles-in-the-Fields, to the deanery of Norwich in 1681; and told Sharp 'plainly when he came to me, that how great soever his merit might be otherwise, I could never think him fit for that dignity, till he could take up his parish of St Giles and set it down at the gates of Norwich', adding that he hoped to secure the preferment to the deanery of one of the clergy of the diocese, 'that would reside and attend the service of God in their cathedral'.[2]

But the gravest and most insuperable cases of pluralism arose from poorly-endowed benefices, which, not affording a sufficient stipend for a resident incumbent, must needs be held in plurality. In these cases the archbishop suggested an extension of the act of 37 Henry VIII, c. 21, permitting the union of churches 'whereof one doth not exceed £6 in the King's Book and not being distant above a mile', to include vicarages not exceeding £14 and rectories not exceeding £10 and distant two miles from each other. Additional steps to be taken should embrace the encouragement of bishops and of deans and chapters to augment poor benefices and curacies; and particularly the provision of an established maintenance 'in places absolutely impropriate, in the hands of the laity, where there is no competent allowance established for ministers to serve the cure (which are many times, large and very considerable parishes)'. These proposals, together with the further recommendation 'that all peculiar and exempt jurisdictions be submitted to the bishop in whose diocese they lie and a commission granted to some persons to make

---

[1] Tanner MSS. 36, f. 126, Prideaux to Sancroft, 2 October 1681.
[2] Ibid. f. 52. Sancroft to the Bishop of Norwich, 18 June 1681.

reasonable and just allowances to the persons concerned', were however only palliatives. The problem of pluralism was too intractable
to respond to such expedients; and nothing short of the extensive
recovery of lay impropriations (which not even the royal example of
Queen Anne's Bounty was able to effect), or of such a radical reform
of cathedrals and redistribution of their revenues as was to be
accomplished in the reign of Victoria, could avail to cure this
spreading cancer which destroyed the living tissues of a truly
pastoral ministry.

In regard to the punishment of scandalous clergy, Sancroft considered whether the hortatory 10th Canon of 1640, requiring those

to whom the government of the clergy is committed that...according
to the power with which they are entrusted, they diligently labour by
the execution of the above named canons and all other ecclesiastical
provisions made for this end, to reform all offensive and scandalous
persons,

should be reinforced by more specific regulations. He proposed
therefore

that the proceedings against clergymen for criminal causes may be by the
Bishop himself, assisted by two or more of the gravest and most understanding clergy, or by three such clergymen (in absence of the Bishop)
appointed by the Bishop under Commission under his hand and seal,
taking the Chancellor or other discreet person or persons to their assistance
if they see cause.

Furthermore, he recommended

that the proceedings in such cases be summary; *sine strepitu, et figura
Judici servata, tantum aequitate*; viz. that upon complaint or fame, it may
be lawful for the Bishop or his Commissioners (ut supra) to summon the
clerk and witnesses to appear before them, to examine them viva voce,
and forthwith to proceed to sentence of temporary suspension for the first
or second fault, or in heinous crimes or cases of incorrigibility, to deprivation....The suspension to continue till the offender reform, or be
acquitted by the *Judex ad quem*. In case of deprivation an appeal to lie
to the Archbishop of the Province, ut supra in case of Chancellor.

Further he desired

that no prohibition to the ecclesiastical courts be granted, unless the truth
of the suggestion be sworn; that where it shall appear out of the libel or
suggestion that a Consultation lies, that the Consultation be granted without putting the party to demurr to the suggestion; [and] that in suits for
tithes, no prohibition be granted after definitive sentence in the ecclesiastical
court.

Finally, he was of opinion that

in criminal causes of the clergy, no inhibition to be granted, nor censure inflicted taken off by the *Judex ad quem*, until the Archbishop upon sight of the processes of the inferior court shall give his Fiat.

Thanks to the fiasco of the Convocation of 1689, none of these projected reforms was considered; nor were the two immediate successors of Sancroft at Canterbury in a position to attempt bold changes. Tillotson's tenure of the primacy was too short, whilst Tenison was absorbed in the Convocation controversy and harassed by the political kaleidoscope of the reign of Anne. With the accession of Wake to the archbishopric, however, the opportunity for a firm policy seemed to have arrived; but his quarrels with the whig ministers concerning the repeal of the Occasional Conformity and Schism Acts and the abortive Blasphemy Bill frustrated the hopes which had attended his preferment. Not until Walpole and Townshend in 1723 called to their assistance as ecclesiastical counsellor Edmund Gibson, recently translated to London, did the church enjoy the prospect of a vigorous, reforming programme. Nor did the first-fruits of the partnership belie expectations; for the institution of Whitehall preacherships and the foundation of regius professorships of Modern History and Languages in the two universities were a foretaste of the boldness and ability of the new 'pope'. Gibson's intention was to follow these preliminary steps by a thorough-going scheme of ecclesiastical reformation; and a memorandum embodying his extensive projects testifies alike to the pressing need for changes and to the audacious character of the remedies suggested.[1]

At the outset Gibson realised the need for alteration in the size of dioceses, and, if possible, for an increase in the number of diocesan bishops. His own experience as bishop of Lincoln had convinced him of the unwieldy size of that diocese, and especially of the difficulty of providing adequate opportunities for the laity to receive the grace of Confirmation. His experiment of separating the work of Confirmation from that of Visitation, in order to give more time and solemnity to the religious rite and to reduce the number of confirmands to 300 or 400 at each place, was only a partial remedy; and even so, provoked criticism as detracting from the social importance of the episcopal visitation. His first thought therefore was to in-

---

[1] Secker MSS. 6, ff. 175 *seq.* 'Ecclesia Anglic: Bishop Gibson's thoughts concerning alterations in it.' Written in Secker's hand, with the note *ad finem*: 'Transcribed, or rather extracted from fol: book. Feb. 12, 1734/5.'

crease the number of dioceses; but objections soon multiplied to make this impossible. On the one hand, he was convinced that the laity would not contemplate an increase in the number of lords spiritual in Parliament; whilst on the other hand clerical opinion feared 'that to have any bishops not to sit in parliament will be [a] bad precedent'. Moreover, there were no endowments to provide the stipends of additional diocesan bishops. The next alternative therefore was the revival of suffragan bishoprics, the disappearance of which since the reign of Elizabeth I remains one of the baffling mysteries of Anglican history. The statute 26 Henry VIII, c. 14, had specified twenty-six suffragan sees (two of which, Gloucester and Bristol, later became diocesan bishoprics), in order to provide 'for the more speedy administration of the sacraments, and other good, wholesome and devout things and laudable ceremonies, to the increase of God's honour, and for the commodity of good and devout people'; and thereby to supply the places of those medieval bishops *ex partibus infidelium* whose services had supplied the deficiences of English diocesans. Accordingly sixteen suffragan bishops were consecrated during the sixteenth century, the latest of whom John Sterne, bishop of Colchester, was consecrated in 1592 and died in 1608. Thereafter the office of suffragan bishop lapsed. In Charles II's Declaration concerning Ecclesiastical Affairs of 25 October 1660, however, it was promised, in reply to repeated puritan requests, that 'because the dioceses, especially some of them are thought to be of too large extent, we will appoint such a number of suffragan bishops in every diocese, as shall be sufficient for the due performance of their work'; but once again no action was taken. Yet, as John Lewis, vicar of Margate, wrote in 1738,

one thing seems to make them necessary in our larger dioceses, and those in which the bishops themselves do not, or cannot, reside; and that is the due and regular performance of Confirmation, which ought to be celebrated once at least every year, and at such convenient distances that people may easily resort to it; whereas by the manner of its being performed now once in four or five years, and in so few places, and at such distances as fifteen or sixteen miles, the design is in a manner lost. Nor is this all. The diocesan bishops are absent from their dioceses, some altogether, and others the most part of the year.[1]

[1] *Bibliotheca Topographica Britannica*, no. XXVIII (1875). 'Some Account of Suffragan Bishops in England': being 'An Essay towards an account of Bishops Suffragan in England, occasioned by a Letter of the Rev. Thomas Brett', printed in Drake's *Antiquities of York*, p. 539; by the late Rev. John Lewis, Minister of Margate in Kent, written 1738.

These considerations were present to the mind of Gibson; but once again difficulties, both practical and theoretical, frustrated his endeavours. The Henrician legislation had made no financial provision for the stipends of suffragan bishops, and this problem still remained. Furthermore, the statute had restricted the royal choice of such bishops to the two names submitted by the diocesan bishop; and Gibson remarked the perplexing alternatives that

it will be thought hard they should not succeed in [the] bishoprick; and if they succeed, this puts [the] choice of a successor in [the] Bishop; or, if [the] King make suffragans entirely, they will be often disagreeable to [the] bishop.

An even more disquieting possibility, granted the prevailing social traditions, also suggested itself. 'By degrees, episcopal care will all devolve on suffragans; and younger sons of [the] nobility will be all the bishops and only attend parliament'—a disastrous dichotomy between the ecclesiastical and civil duties of the episcopate.

In face of these formidable obstacles, therefore, Gibson fell back on a bold and comprehensive scheme for the redistribution of diocesan boundaries and of episcopal sees, which might increase the efficiency of pastoral oversight without involving either an increase in the number of bishoprics or the revival of suffragan sees. His proposals were that

Carlisle, which hath not 100 parishes, should take in Cumberland and Westmorland, part of which are in Chester. York to part with Nottinghamshire, Lichfield with Derbyshire, and of these two [a] new Bishopric of Southwell. Norwich to keep only [the] deaneries of Lothingland, Wangford and Dunwich in Suffolk; [the] rest of that county to be added to Ely, which hath only 160 parishes. Lincoln to consist only of that county; and the bishop to have the deanery of Lincoln, with such share of [the] revenue of the bishopric as shall be thought proper. Peterborough to take Leicestershire. Huntingdon, Bedford, Buckinghamshire and Hertfordshire to make [a] Bishopric of Eton.

This was perhaps the most daring and revolutionary innovation; for Gibson's purpose was to make the bishop also provost of Eton and to convert the fellows into prebendaries, thereby using the revenues of the college to furnish part of the stipend of the new bishop and the entire emoluments of his cathedral chapter! In addition, however, the bishop was to have 'the house and manor of Buckden and part of the revenue of [the] bishopric' of Lincoln; and his jurisdiction was further to include the archdeaconry of St Albans, which was to be detached from the diocese of London. Other dioceses were to be dealt with equally cavalierly.

Canterbury to take in Rochester; Oxford to take Berkshire; Sarum, Dorsetshire; Worcester, half Gloucestershire, Bath and Wells, [the] other. Brecknock, where are Prebends, to take from St David's, Brecknockshire, Cardiganshire and Radnorshire. Each bishop to have in the parts given to him the patronage which [the] bishops of those parts now have. But all things to stand as they are during the lives of the present incumbents, archdeacons and officers.

Finally, those bishoprics which were to be extinguished, Rochester, Bristol and Gloucester, were to have their cathedrals converted into collegiate churches, and the 'incomes of those bishoprics applied to the new ones'. The scheme was of breath-taking audacity and thoroughness for its times, amounting to nothing less than a comprehensive revision of the territorial diocesan organisation of the Church of England. At the cost of the extinction of three sees (two of which were of Henrician creation) and the establishment of three new dioceses of Brecknock, Eton and Southwell, Gibson hoped to effect a practical solution of the most pressing problems of episcopal oversight and administration.

Furthermore, his project would help towards meeting the scandal of too frequent translation of bishops from one see to another. The reason for this growing practice was to be found in the wide inequality of income between the richer and poorer sees, which in turn led, as he noted, to the circumstance that 'bishops of poorer sees are strangers to them'. But, however cogent the practical case for translation, it was productive of much justifiable censure. 'Bishops in general seem worldly-minded, and their votes for the court seem to proceed from interest; and this multiplies commendams which are often inconvenient remedies.' Gibson was aware that his redistribution of diocesan boundaries would not meet this financial problem. Accordingly he suggested the 'paying £1500 a year from Durham and as much from Winchester to smaller bishoprics, [and] annexing four prebends of Westminster to four middling ones'. If, however, his project for the alterations in dioceses did not take effect, he proposed 'annexing the deanery of St Paul's to [the] bishopric of Bristol and that of Westminster to Rochester', expedients which were readily adopted during the eighteenth century; and 'another way of augmenting is by annexing such sinecures, or other promotions without cure of souls, as are in the patronage of sees', to the respective bishops. Finally it must be a consequent condition of these reforms that no bishop was 'to be translated in less than seven years and then but once'. The scandal of the frequent and rapid translations of Hoadly from Bangor to Hereford, thence to Sarum and finally to Winchester, was an apt contemporary illustration of the evils which Gibson sought to eradicate. Translation indeed was to remain, but within severe limitations; for 'every private patron thinks it reasonable to promote a clergyman that hath done his duty in a smaller living to a better; and without this, presbyters of figure and learning and good preferments will not be bishops of smaller sees'.

In view of the crucial situation of the episcopate as the cornerstone of effective ecclesiastical administration, the failure to implement Gibson's proposed reforms was of ill consequence for the church. It was little surprising, however, that the only item of his programme to be adopted was that of annexing the two metropolitan deaneries to two of the poorer sees, since the temper of the age was averse to radical measures. Indeed a century later when the increase of the diocesan episcopate was effected by the creation of new bishoprics at Manchester and Ripon, the objection to a corresponding increase in the number of bishops in the House of Lords was raised, and met at first by a proposal to unite the sees of Bristol and Gloucester and those of Bangor and St Asaph in order to allow of the establishment of two new northern dioceses without adding to the quota of parliamentary prelates. From 1836 to 1897 accordingly Bristol and Gloucester became one diocese, though the proposal in regard to the Welsh sees was never carried into operation. Furthermore the alternative possibility suggested by Gibson of the revival of suffragan bishoprics was not adopted until 1870, when Henry Mackenzie was consecrated as bishop of Nottingham, the first suffragan bishop since Sterne of Colchester in 1592. Nor was the inefficiency of episcopal oversight the only disadvantage resulting from the static situation of the episcopate. Translations continued to increase, and their refusal to be made a penal reprisal against bishops of independent views. On the one hand during the century after 1689 St Asaph was held by fifteen bishops, nine of whom were translated, Bangor by fourteen, of whom eleven were translated, St David's by sixteen, twelve of whom received the reward of translation, and Llandaff by eleven, of whom seven were translated. On the other hand Secker continued twenty-one years in the poor see of Oxford as the penalty for his independence in joining a 'formed opposition', whilst later in the eighteenth century Richard Watson was left as bishop of Llandaff for twenty-four years, thanks to his inveterate political idiosyncrasies. The power of granting or denying a translation became therefore a just object of censure; though when in 1731 a motion was made in the House of Commons for leave to bring in a Bill to prevent translation of bishops, the motive of its promoters was rather to embarrass the administration and its ecclesiastical adviser, Gibson, than to remedy the abuses which he had hoped to eradicate by his project for the reform of dioceses. Furthermore, the increasing demands of parliamentary attendance upon bishops withdrew them from their dioceses for the greater part of each year, and threw a greater responsibility for ecclesiastical administration upon their archdeacons, to whose position therefore Gibson next turned his attention.

Archdeacons have enjoyed a proverbially bad name, from the letter of John of Salisbury to Nicholas de Sigillo on the latter's appointment to the archdeaconry of Huntingdon in the mid-twelfth century to the aspiration of Burnet in the Conclusion of his *History of My Own Time* that 'when this matter is well looked into, I hope archdeacons, with many other burdens that lay heavy on the clergy, shall be taken away'. Nevertheless, the diligence and industry of Thomas Frank, archdeacon of Bedford, John Rogers of Leicester, and Thomas Greene, archdeacon of Canterbury, during Wake's tenure of the sees of Lincoln and Canterbury, and of Dr John Head, the 'very faithful and useful archdeacon' of Secker's primacy, together with the example of Gibson as archdeacon of Surrey, demonstrated the invaluable character and extent of the services which could be rendered by conscientious holders of the office to their absentee diocesans. Unfortunately some archdeacons, instead of supplying the defects arising from the absence of the bishops in London, followed their precedent by being non-resident also. Mr Lewis of Margate commented on this circumstance in his plea for the revival of suffragan bishops.

The archdeacons follow their bishops' example, and no wonder since the habitation or residence of so many of them is at two hundred miles' distance from their archdeaconries; whereas if any regard was had to the Church of Christ, such learned and good men would be made archdeacons as were beneficed in the several archdeaconries, and lived with and among the clergy whom they inspected. But this is unhappily prevented in the Province of Canterbury by the archbishop's making so many archdeaconries his Options, and disposing of them to his chaplains and favourites, however unqualified by their having cures at so great and unreasonable a distance from them.[1]

Archbishop Tenison indeed during his primacy had been so harassed by the controversies in Convocation as to seize every opportunity of making archdeaconries his Options, in order to increase the number of supporters of the bishops' cause in the Lower House. Gibson could not hope to prevent all the evils arising from injudicious archidiaconal appointments; but he proposed as a partial remedy that 'if archdeacons be not resident within [their] archdeaconry, or without licence under the bishop's hand and seal reside out of it more than three months in the year, [the] archdeaconry to be void'. In addition he desired them to be required to visit their entire archdeaconry parish by parish within the first three years of their office; and thereafter he commended a proposal put forward in Convocation in 1710 that they should visit parochially one rural deanery each year and the whole of their jurisdiction within six years. To this end he advocated that all bishops should appoint rural deans, where they were not already existent, and establish rural deaneries. Likewise he wished presentments of immorality to be made by the archdeacon directly to the bishop, instead of to the chancellor; so that the bishop 'can see to the prosecution, and it becomes more solemn, especially if the bishop himself would sit upon sentence of considerable causes'. To the same purpose of more efficient administration, he would have peculiars 'to be extinguished, or else regularly visited, [and] exemptions to be extinguished, except the king's chapels and palaces'.

In common with all reformers, Gibson was vexed by the insoluble problem of pluralism, amongst both dignitaries and the parochial clergy, and put forward suggestions for mitigating its evils since he could not hope to abolish it altogether. Since one of the chief causes of scandal was non-residence in cathedrals, he proposed that 'residence to be kept in cathedral and collegiate churches according to statute; and where statutes [are] of doubtful authority, or inconvenient, to be revised and confirmed'. Further, prebendaries were to be obliged 'to preach in person or exchange with each other', and deans 'to be obliged to longer residence, especially considering the necessary absence of the bishops'. Particularly, no person was to be allowed 'to hold dignities in two churches, nor above one living with

[1] J. Lewis, 'Some Account of Suffragan Bishops in England', p. 19.

a prebend-residentiary'. All cathedrals were to maintain schools, since this 'would so far shew the usefulness of them', and bishops 'should make greater use of their chapters'. In dealing with pluralism of benefices with cure of souls, Gibson wished to reduce the distance between livings held in plurality to fifteen miles, to require the holders to reside two months on each benefice and to preach thirteen sermons annually in each church, and to allow a higher salary to their curates than was paid by single-beneficed men. In addition no benefice exceeding £200 per year was to be held in plurality.

As bishop of Lincoln, Gibson had inherited from his predecessor a legacy of difficulties with his legal officers, and no part of episcopal administration seemed to him in greater need of reform. In the 'Introductory Discourse' to his *Codex Juris Ecclesiastici Anglicani* and again in the collection of papers published under the title *Of Visitations, Parochial and General*, he had set down his ideas concerning the necessary changes in these respects, which were summarised in his present programme. First, it was essential that chancellors, vicars-general, and officials should be 'persons able to perform their duties'. Moreover chancellors should reside at their consistories, and vicars-general in the diocese which they served. Most important was the separation of the offices of official and vicar-general, already advocated in Gibson's earlier publications; so that the one should be 'for contentious jurisdiction, in which perhaps it were best processes should go out in the king's name; the other for things relating to manners, visitations, institutions, licences, repairs of churches etc., called voluntary jurisdiction. The first [was] to enforce his orders by the writ *De contumaci capiendo*, the other by excommunication.' Abuses in relation to absolution and commutation should also be regulated. Commutation should be 'rare, public, signified to the congregation, and an account of the money given yearly to the bishop'. A form should be drawn up for denouncing and taking off excommunication; an uniform oath should be provided for churchwardens and a process should always be issued out against persons presented by them. In order to prevent irregular marriages, the ceremony should always be held in one of the churches where the parties dwelt, banns should only be published when the minister was satisfied that the parties were actually within the parish, and after inspection of a certificate of their respective ages and an affidavit made by the master of the house where they lived, that they were both parishioners.

Equally important, however, with the regulation of the conduct of the clergy after admission to holy orders was the ensuring of the sound education of those aspiring to the ministry. Many reformers had experienced the jealousy shown by the two universities towards any suggestion that their methods were inadequate or any proposal for improvement. Burnet indeed was convinced that

the greatest prejudice the Church was under, was from the ill-education of the clergy. In the universities they for the most part lost the learning they brought with them from schools, and learned so little in them that too commonly they came from them less knowing than when they went to them, especially the servitors, who if they had not a very good capacity and were very well disposed of themselves, were generally neglected by their Tutors. They likewise learned the airs of vanity and insolence at the university, so that I resolved to have a nursery at Salisbury of students in Divinity who should follow their studies and devotions till I could provide [for] them.

This experiment of a theological college was continued for five years at a cost to the bishop of £300 per annum, but since it aroused 'such hatred against me, especially at Oxford', it was finally dropped. Indeed 'those at Oxford looked on this as a public affront to them and to their way of education, so that they railed at me not only in secret, but in their Acts unmercifully for it'.[1] But criticism of the inadequacy of the universities' preparation for ordination did not proceed only from a native and graduate of Scotland like Burnet. Prideaux as an archdeacon had deplored

the excessive ignorance he had met with in such as offered themselves for ordination at their examinations....Young men frequently come to the universities without any knowledge or tincture of religion at all, and having little opportunity of improving themselves therein whilst undergraduates, because the course of their studies inclines them to philosophy and other kinds of learning, they are usually admitted to their first degree of B.A., with the same ignorance as to all sacred learning as when first admitted to the universities; and many of them as soon as they have taken that degree, offering themselves for Orders, are too often admitted to be teachers in the Church when they are only fitted to be catechumens therein. These considerations made the doctor often lament the loss of Dr Busby's benefaction, who offered to found two Catechetical Lectures, one in each university, with an endowment of £100 per annum each, for instructing the undergraduates in the rudiments of the Christian religion, provided all the said undergraduates should be obliged to attend these lectures, and none of them be admitted to the degree of B.A. till after having been examined by the Catechist as to their knowledge of the doctrines and

---

[1] H. C. Foxcroft, *Supplement to Burnet's History*, pp. 500–1.

precepts of the Christian religion and by him approved of. But this condition being rejected by both universities, the benefaction was rejected therewith, and the Church hath ever since suffered for the want of it.

Accordingly in 1715 Prideaux laid before Lord Townshend a comprehensive series of *Articles for the Reformation of the two Universities*; which included provisions, that

no person…shall in any exercise of Divinity to be performed in the schools of either of the said universities, quote any text out of the Old Testament in any other language than the Hebrew, or any text out of the New Testament in any other language than the Greek;

that

whereas great numbers of students of the said universities do, after taking the degree of B.A., leave the said universities, and taking Orders, enter upon cures, that all such may be the better qualified for the said profession, it be ordered that no person shall be admitted to the degree of B.A., till he shall have undergone an examination of his knowledge of the Christian religion, and be able to give a good account thereof, as taught and professed in the Church of England;

and

that in order thereto, the said universities shall take care, that an uniform system of Divinity be made by the Professor of Divinity in the said universities, or such other as they shall think fit to appoint, in which all undergraduates shall be instructed by their tutors and afterwards be examined before they take the said degree of B.A., and that till such a system of Divinity shall be composed, the said examination shall be made in the Church Catechism and the Articles of the Church of England, and no one be admitted to the said degree till he can give a thorough account of them and prove all particulars from Scripture.[1]

Similarly Wake as bishop of Lincoln had expressed the earnest desire that tutors at Oxford would 'read some system or body of divinity to their pupils and engage them to make them at least masters of the Greek of the New Testament'; and that as the basis of such teaching they would use some of the current expositions of the Catechism and Articles.[2] The reforms suggested by Gibson were in line with these recommendations; namely, that the

philological and philosophical studies in the universities to be finished and exercises for Bachelor to be performed in three years, the fourth to be spent wholly under a Divinity Tutor. The bishops to fix and signify to Heads of Colleges what kind and degree of knowledge they will insist on for Orders. Testimonials to express that the persons have been examined

---

[1] *Life of Humphrey Prideaux*, pp. 90–1, 227, 232–3 (Articles, XXXVIII, XLIX, L).
[2] N. Sykes, *William Wake*, vol. I, pp. 163–4.

before the Head, the Dean and Tutor. Those destined for Orders to be reminded of sobriety and devotion, [and] cautioned against too great freedom of life [since] these dispose them to be fond of gentlemen's tables and neglect poor parishioners.

Indeed Gibson was convinced that more care was taken in all other Protestant churches than in the Church of England to instruct their ministers in the duties of the pastoral cure; and that a beginning of reform should be made by the universities.

Finally, his project embraced a number of items, often canvassed before in Convocation and elsewhere; such as the revision of the Canons of 1603, the compilation of new terriers, the making of a new table of fees 'agreeably to the present times and rate of money', the authorisation of an Office for the consecration of churches and churchyards, of a form for admitting converts from the Church of Rome and of a form for the visitation of prisoners and condemned persons; the setting forth of a method for the quick and easy recovery of church rates, the preparation of one book of visitation articles for the whole kingdom, and (not without a touch of the amusing perhaps) 'organists and choir music too light'! Unfortunately none of his suggestions, whether major such as the redistribution of dioceses, or minor as the provision of a single form of visitation articles, was carried into effect. The fundamental reason for Gibson's failure in this respect, despite the vigour of his personality and the comprehensiveness of his projects, lay in the virulence of anti-clerical feeling in the whig party with which for political reasons he was driven to ally. 'For some years past', he complained in 1744, 'the excess of Church Power has been the great subject of conversation and writing, and it has been made matter of wonder how the Bishop of London has so long escaped parliamentary censure for advancing doctrines inconsistent with the king's supremacy'.[1] The strength of this anticlericalism was testified by the introduction into the House of Commons in 1730 of a Bill to prevent suits for tithes, where none, nor any composition for tithes, had been paid within a specified number of years, followed by a motion for permission to introduce a measure to prevent episcopal translations. These in turn were succeeded in 1733 by a Bill to regulate proceedings in the ecclesiastical courts (which was in effect a thorough-going attack on all branches

---

[1] E. Gibson, 'Thoughts on the Legality and Expedience of a Letter Circular from Archbishop Potter to the Bishops, on the Archbishop's dying before a new-elected Convocation met'. MSS. St Paul's Cathedral, 17. B. 15.

of their jurisdiction), by a Bill for settling church rates, and finally in 1736 by measures 'to restrain the disposition of lands whereby the same become inalienable', and to transfer suits against Quakers for non-payment of tithe from the church courts to the Justices of the Peace.

Such a persistent campaign against the church and clergy justified Gibson's complaint that 'it was not safe, if they could help it, to let anything come into parliament relating to either, lest some peevish or spiteful motion of one kind or another should be grafted on to it'. In particular Lord Chief Justice Hardwicke in the debate on the Mortmain Bill 'expressly said that there were many things in two books written by the Bishop of London, or by his order, contrary to law, and that in those books powers were asserted to be in the Church which did not belong to it'.[1] So fierce was the hostility to himself that Gibson did not venture to publish a long memorandum, which he wrote to refute the speech of Hardwicke in delivering judgment in the case of Middleton v. Crofts, on the point of the power of the Convocation to make canons which should bind the laity. Hardwicke had denied formally this power, whereupon Gibson assembled a massive corpus of evidence, stretching from the preamble to the Act of Appeals of 1533 to James I's confirmation of the Canons of 1603, to prove that the implied principle had been that Canons duly enacted according to the Submission of the Clergy Act were binding upon the laity as well as the clergy. From the legal and historical standpoints, his argument was of undoubted cogency; but he acknowledged that his plea stood no chance of acceptance in the temper of the times. On the other hand he refused to surrender the point of principle by adopting (as some voices counselled) the remedy of seeking parliamentary confirmation for ecclesiastical canons.

It is not to be supposed that the two houses of parliament would confirm a body of Canons without examination, merely because they had passed the two houses of Convocation and been confirmed by the king. But it may well be supposed that in these two great bodies there are those (how many I dare not say) who would not be over-favourable to a body of Canons as such; some who may be in judgment against any church establishment at all; others who may not be satisfied with the present establishment; and others who may think that if there must be an established church, the lay powers are more fit to be trusted with the settling and conducting of it than the bishops and clergy.

---

[1] N. Sykes, *Edmund Gibson*, p. 162.

Furthermore,

if the parliament should be applied to for a sanction of the Canons in such matters as concern the laity, this would be a virtual acknowledgement that all former Canons and Constitutions which affect the laity, however approved by the ablest lawyers in their respective times and thereupon confirmed by royal authority, were *ab initio* null and void; and after such a concession no more of the same kind would ever again be made or attempted in Convocation. Whereas a time may come, when these points may be reconsidered in the temporal courts, or in parliament, or both, and may then be possibly seen in a different light from that they have lately been. I do not expect to live to see that day, any more than to see a sitting and acting Convocation. But if in any future time, the consideration of the late Judgment shall be resumed, and the thought of a sitting Convocation revived, and these memorials which I leave behind me, be then found of any the least service to the cause of religion and the established church, it will be an abundant recompense for all the pains I have taken about them.[1]

From an entirely different standpoint from that of the ministers of state therefore Gibson was driven to acquiese in the maxim *quieta non movere* and to drop his reforming projects; and where so bold and resolute a champion of the authority of the church, alike in its judicial and deliberative capacities, was compelled to admit defeat, little hope of success could be entertained from other hands. The primacy of Potter indeed was a sore disappointment. Even less than Wake did he command the confidence of the king's administration, and, like his predecessor, he was overshadowed by the powerful figure of Gibson at Fulham. Moreover the latter was particularly critical of his failure to implement the king's statement that 'the royal licence might be easily obtained for that purpose whenever it should be likely to him [the archbishop] and other sincere friends of the church, that the Convocation might sit to good effect and unto the real benefit of this church'. Notwithstanding the fiasco of the short experiment of a sitting Convocation in 1741, Gibson wished the Upper House in 1744 to draw up a Representation of the present state of religion in the kingdom for presentation to the sovereign, and to this end urged that the primate should apply for a royal licence to sit and act.

Let it be supposed that the Licence were to be granted on the single account of the forementioned Representation; and (though general and in the usual form) not designed to be carried further, and so understood. Even this might have good consequences in some other respects. It would

---

[1] E. Gibson, 'The Mischievous Consequences of the late Judgment in the Court of King's Bench.' MSS. St Paul's Cathedral, 17. B. 13.

occasion frequent meetings of the bishops under a legal call and so without exception; and those meetings would lead them to consider what statutes or canons need to be actuated and a more strict observation of them enforced; what are the difficulties which particular bishops meet with in their own dioceses (all which they would have an opportunity to represent to their brethren in order to be favoured with their advice); how things may be bettered without the help of new statutes or new canons, by an unanimous exercise of the ordinary jurisdiction and authority and by mutual agreements among the bishops as to the methods of proceeding; with other deliberations of the like kind which such frequent meetings would naturally introduce.

Most especially was it of the utmost importance not to let slip any opportunity (such as that offered by the king's assurance to the primate) of revitalising Convocation.

In all points relating to the Convocation and the proper methods of putting it into motion, this should always be one consideration, if not the chief; that as to any motion or action besides the common forms of opening and proroguing, it has been already discontinued and laid asleep for seven and twenty years; and if the like discontinuance is to go on, the Convocation must sink more and more into a state of contempt, as an useless, insignificant body, and by degrees it will be no longer considered as a part of our ecclesiastical constitution.[1]

The paralysis of the ecclesiastical constitution was reflected in an especial manner in the frustration of all attempts to secure the consecration of bishops for the North American colonies. Much undeserved obloquy has been visited upon the church for its supposed indifference to this vital matter of the provision of episcopal offices for the Anglican congregations in the Plantations. In point of fact the responsibility attached solely to the ministers of state. So early as the reign of Charles II a project for the settlement of a bishop in the colonies had been framed, and Gibson, in the searches which he conducted into the origins of the jurisdiction of the Bishop of London in the Plantations, discovered the royal letters patent for the establishment of a bishop in Virginia, probably drafted by Sir Leoline Jenkins. 'How that design miscarried, appears not, unless it were that the whole endowment was to be out of the customs.'[2] Possibly the advent to power of the Cabal was partly

[1] E. Gibson, 'The Archbishop's Declaration to the Bishops'. MSS. St Paul's Cathedral, 17. B. 15.

[2] E. Gibson, 'Bishops in America'. Secker MSS. (Lambeth Palace Library) 6. f. 257. Endorsed in Secker's hand *ad finem*: 'Extracted March 1737/8, from a Memorial presented by the Bishop of London many years since, to the late Duke of Devonshire, when President of the Council.' William, 2nd Duke of Devonshire, was President from March 1725 to May 1730.

responsible also, since Sir Orlando Bridgeman, to whose good offices the matter had been entrusted, was dismissed from office thereby. During the reign of Anne a much more ambitious scheme was set forward by the S.P.G., which in 1712 approved a project for the settlement of no fewer than four bishops, two on the mainland, at Burlington, New Jersey, and Williamsburg, Virginia, respectively, and two for the islands, in Barbados and Jamaica, with salaries of £1000 per annum for the continental bishops and £1500 for those in the islands. It was proposed that the diocese of the bishop of Burlington should embrace the continent north and north-east of the Delaware river together with Pennsylvania on the other side of the river; whilst the see of Williamsburg should include the continent south and south-west of the Delaware river (excepting Pennsylvania). The choice of Williamsburg was influenced by the establishment there of William and Mary College, of which the bishop might well be appointed head in order to make it a serviceable seminary for the training of native clergy. In 1713 this programme was laid formally before the queen, and a reminder was given to her the year following by the Archbishop Sharp of York and Bishop Robinson of London, which produced her promise to 'direct the same to be referred to the proper persons to consider and make report thereof'; but unfortunately her death put an untimely end to the matter. Archbishop Tenison left by will £1000 to the S.P.G. to be paid within two months after the consecration of one bishop for the mainland and another for the islands, and to be divided equally between the two sees; and a new deputation waited upon George I in 1715 to reinforce the previous communication, receiving the assurance that he 'would favour and encourage the pious designs and undertakings of the Society'.[1]

Matters thus stood at a standstill when the translation of Gibson to the see of London in 1723 brought a new champion to the front. After investigating the origins and legal basis of his authority as bishop of the Plantations, he drew up his own project for the settlement of bishops there. It was somewhat more modest in scope than that presented to Queen Anne in 1713, since he would be content with one bishop for the islands, and, if necessary, with one for the mainland. In addition to Tenison's bequest another anonymous

---

[1] Secker MSS.; N. Sykes, *William Wake*, vol. II, p. 209; A. L. Cross, *The Anglican Episcopate and the American Colonies* (Harvard Historical Studies, IX, 1902); N. Sykes, *Edmund Gibson*, pp. 368–72.

benefaction of £1000 had been received, and there was good prospect of an annual grant of £100 from a charitable foundation; so that the sum of £2000 plus this annual income was available for the episcopal endowments. The stipend of the headship of the college in Virginia was £200 per annum; whilst the prospective establishment of Codrington College in Barbados would provide part of the salary of the bishop of that see; and if need be, the best benefices within their respective jurisdictions could be annexed to the bishoprics. A more delicate approach was needful to propose to ministers of state other possible sources of revenue; amongst which Gibson suggested the grant of a small part of the Crown customs, the mulcting the clergy of a tithe of their incomes, the appropriation of one prebend in each of the four cathedrals of which the Lord Chancellor was patron until other maintenance could be found (on the precedent of Anne's reign when such prebends had been attached to certain Headships of Houses in Oxford and Cambridge), the provision of English benefices in order to enable the first bishops (if sent from England) to 'purchase such conveniences of life as are not to be had, or very dear, in the Plantations'; and finally, 'an assignment in each province of a proper quantity of such crown lands as are not yet taken up, and a house to be built upon each, with a proper number of negroes, to be under a bailiff, which number the bishop shall be obliged to keep full and convey to his successors, as is practised in some parishes in the Plantations to good effect. Thus the bishop will be both more able and willing to visit each province frequently and live hospitably there.' None of these provisions, of course, would discourage voluntary donations from private persons, which would rather be stimulated by these evidences that the project was 'heartily espoused by the government'.

Gibson had little difficulty in enumerating and emphasising the advantages of bishops in the Plantations. Amongst the foremost and most obvious was the growth of an indigenous ministry. Not only were ordinands discouraged by the voyage to England 'and danger of small-pox which is very fatal to them on their arrival here'; but also the colleges already founded could not fulfil their function as ecclesiastical seminaries so long as these obstacles were interposed. Furthermore, with resident bishops, the churches 'would be supplied by persons of known good behaviour and life, not wanderers; by their own natives, to whom they will naturally be kinder than to strangers; by persons who would choose to exercise their ministry there, not who are driven to it and therefore stay only till they can repair their fortunes and get preferment here'. Indeed it was certainly to be expected that the colonists would subscribe more readily to the building and endowment of churches and parishes, if they were to be served by their own kin rather than by the unsuccessful or scandalous clerics from England. From the same standpoint too the laity would benefit by a regular and frequent episcopal visitation of the clergy, though Gibson was treading on thin ice when suggesting the application to the colonies of his favourite maxim of the propriety of giving to ecclesiastical persons judicial power of correction of the morals of the laity: 'to restrain immorality amongst the laity, so far as it may be found practicable and proper to extend the jurisdiction of the bishop to them'. More immediately beneficial to the laity would be the regular administration of the rite of Confirmation, which would also oblige the clergy 'to instruct their youth more carefully'. All these reasons were cogent; but it was a task of equal difficulty and delicacy to dispose of the objections to the establishment of episcopacy, which would certainly come from the colonies and particularly from those whose founders had fled from the oversight of bishops in England.

To the first anticipated objection, namely that the bishops 'will be able to make head against the civil governors', Gibson retorted by recommending that they should 'be allowed no share in the civil administration'; and to this end that they should 'be sent at first and by way of trial in the condition of Suffragans to the see of London, or any other, upon the foot of 26 Henry VIII [c. 14] which lays suffragans under the strongest restraints as to the exercise of their powers'. In regard to the certain protests from the dissenters, especially in New England and Pennsylvania, and to allay their alarm, 'it may be provided in the strongest terms that no persons or churches shall be under the jurisdiction of the bishop, but those who conform to the liturgy and worship of the Church of England'. In order to guard against the contingency of the bishop's sentence in judicial proceedings being the first and last judgment without appeal, provision should be made for appeals to the bishop of London or some other bishop in England, and thence to the archbishop and the Court of Delegates; 'or rather, considering the trouble, danger and expense of this, and what a discouragement it would be particularly of prosecuting irregular clergymen when they could evade punishment so long, in all causes in which the bishop is allowed to take cognisance, appeal may be to a standing Court of Delegates there, appointed by the king and to consist of the Governor, some of the Council, three or four of the clergy in each government; or to a standing Delegacy in England appointed for that purpose'. Finally, in reply to the gravest objection and possibility, that a native episcopate and clergy might foment rebellion amongst the colonists against rule from England, Gibson placed his finger unerringly upon the one, sufficient and indeed only safeguard against such danger (with or without bishops), 'because they cannot defend themselves against the French, Spaniards, Indians, nor indeed subsist, without protection and many necessaries from England. Nor will so many distinct governments combine to revolt, nor can they do it separately.' Moreover bishops would encourage loyalty. 'The bishops will always be appointed here, and so may be confided in to assist the government.'

Although Gibson concluded that 'this is therefore a groundless suggestion, and it would be very hard, if all the above-mentioned advantages must be lost on account of it', the administration took exactly the contrary view, and attached more weight to the danger of provoking rebellion amongst the colonists than to all the good effects of a colonial episcopate. Not even when ecclesiastical confusion in the Plantations was worse confounded by the appearance there of two Non-juring bishops, Talbot and Welton, did the ministry at home respond to the bishop of London's argument that 'if two or three suffragan bishops were regularly consecrated here, and sent to the Plantations to administer episcopal offices to the clergy and people of the established church before those two had spread their infection among them, this would be the most effectual way to put a stop to their attempts'. A decade later Gibson returned to the attack and sought to enlist the support of the new archbishop, Potter; whilst in 1741 Secker entered the lists with a sermon before the S.P.G., a circumstance which was made the ground of criticism of his promotion in 1758 to the primacy, as one who 'was a strong advocate (though not a very argumentative one) for the introduction of bishops into America'.[1] In 1745 a deputation waited on the duke of Newcastle to press the matter once more; but all efforts were unavailing, including the increase of donations by a benefaction of £1000 from Gibson himself and £500 from the Lady Elizabeth

---

[1] N. Sykes, 'The Duke of Newcastle as Ecclesiastical Minister', in *English Historical Review*, vol. LVII (January 1942), no. 225, pp. 68-9.

Hastings. When Sherlock succeeded to the see of London he presented to the Privy Council in 1749 a long and comprehensive survey of the position in 'Some Considerations humbly offered by Thomas, bishop of London relating to the Ecclesiastical Government in His Majesty's Dominions in America'; which evoked an equally lengthy and detailed rejoinder from Horace Walpole setting out the official grounds for rejecting all such appeals. Walpole emphasised the certainty of opposition from dissenters at home 'by the instigation and complaints of their brethren in the colonies', who would be exasperated and animated to make warm representations against it to the government here, as a design to establish Ecclesiastical Power in its full extent among them by degrees. Further, he reminded Sherlock of the suspicions aroused by his 'extraordinary zeal and desire to increase Ecclesiastical Power in this country'; and counselled him to 'let your spiritual zeal yield to your temporal prudence'.[1] Bishop Butler also published a short paper on the subject in 1750. The duke of Newcastle expressed to Sherlock the unvarying and unyielding opposition of the administration by reminding him twice during September 1749, that 'the appointing bishops in the West Indies was a great and national consideration, that had long been under the deliberation of great and wise men heretofore and had been by them laid aside', and again that it was 'a question which had been often agitated, and which the wisest and best men hitherto had not thought proper to determine in the way he proposed'.[2] So late as 1767 Secker, with Archbishop Drummond of York, waited on Lord Shelburne, Secretary of State, to recommend 'the appointment of Bishops in America', but 'could make no impression at all upon him'.[3] The truth of the situation had been succinctly stated in 1736 by Bishop Benson of Gloucester, that 'the united interest of the bishops here is not powerful enough to effect so reasonable and right a thing as the sending of some bishops into America'.[4] The major opposition indeed came from the colonies themselves; where, it is worthy of note, Bishop Richard Challenor during the same period met with such opposition to his design to provide episcopal supervision for Roman Catholics that finally an Anglican bishop was consecrated before a Roman Catholic.

[1] A. L. Cross, *op. cit.* Appendix XI, no. 6, and XII; E. F. Carpenter, *Thomas Sherlock*, ch. VII.
[2] N. Sykes, *Edmund Gibson*, p. 372.
[3] Secker, Memoirs, f. 74 (Lambeth Palace Library).
[4] A. L. Cross, *op. cit.* p. 106, n. 2.

The bogy of 'Church Power' might be a useful weapon for Lord Hardwicke to brandish against Gibson or Horace Walpole against Sherlock, but the reality of lay power over the church was a fact beyond dispute. When Thomas Herring followed Potter at Canterbury (styling himself to his friend Hardwicke as 'a very insignificant and pusillanimous man'), the duke of Newcastle disregarded him so completely in the matter of episcopal appointments as to provoke protests even from his intimate friends. His brother, Henry Pelham, admonished him within a year of Herring's promotion that 'I wonder you take so little notice of the archbishop in these vacancies; it makes him look little, and since you have placed him at the head, I think you should not yourself show you think him insignificant'; and in similar vein Hardwicke wrote to 'submit it to your consideration, whether in such a number of ecclesiastical preferments as come now to be disposed of at once, it will not have a wrong appearance not to show some regard to an archbishop of Canterbury so lately made and so entirely attached to you'.[1] Somewhat more considerate treatment was given at first to Secker, who related in 1766 how

the duke had often asked me about persons whilst I was B[isho]p of Oxford and still more after I was A[rchbisho]p, and paid some regard to what I said; but upon the whole took his own way. After his first resignation in this king's reign [George III], I was neither asked nor told anything by the king or any of his ministers; excepting that Mr Grenville once told me Dr Terrick was intended for B[isho]p of London and that he hoped I approved it. I said, I did, but thought they sh[oul]d consult some clergyman of figure and character about promotions; but that I did not desire to be that clergyman. For I believe neither L[or]d Bute, nor Mr Grenville consulted any clergyman; and in their time the king never said anything to me about any promotion; excepting that in 1761 he told me in the morning that he w[oul]d make Dr Squire B[isho]p of St David's, which everybody knew in the afternoon. After all, the duke of N[ewcastle] gave away livings without knowing my opinion of persons, and I often reproved him for his regard to recommendations of great men and members of parliam[en]t etc. No B[isho]p hath hitherto been made on my recommendation, unless Dr Lowth is to be excepted.[2]

This assertion of lay power over the church was the means of enabling the cadets of noble families to establish their claims to its wealthier dignities. 'Reckon upon it that Durham goes to some noble ecclesiastic', observed Warburton with his customary mordancy to Hurd on the vacancy of that see in 1752.

[1] N. Sykes: 'The Duke of Newcastle as Ecclesiastical Minister', in *English Historical Review* (January 1942), p. 63.   [2] Secker, Memoirs, f. 62 verso.

'Tis a morsel only for them. Our grandees have at last found their way back into the Church. I only wonder they have been so long about it. But he assured that nothing but a new religious revolution to sweep away the fragments that Harry the VIIIth left after banqueting his courtiers, will drive them out again. The Church has been of old the cradle and the throne of the younger nobility. And this nursing-mother will, I hope, once more vie with old imperious Berecynthia:

> Laeta Deum partu, centum complexa Nepotes,
> Omnes Caelicolas, omnes super alta tenentes.[1]

It was but a short step thence to the avowed maxim of Grenville that he considered bishoprics as of two kinds: bishoprics of business for men of abilities and learning, and bishoprics of ease for men of family and fashion. Of the former sort he reckoned Canterbury, and York, and London, and Ely on account of its connection with Cambridge; of the latter sort Durham, and Winchester, and Salisbury and Worcester.[2]

The classification might well have been extended to deaneries, as the career of Dean Spencer Cowper of Durham, illustrated in his recently published *Letters*, abundantly testified.

Being the second son of Lord Chancellor Cowper, Spencer had to obtain a competence either in the church, or Parliament, or by a wealthy marriage; and to his elder brother he confided whilst at Exeter College, Oxford, in 1736, his equal reluctance to embrace any of these possibilities. Averring his unwillingness to 'putting on the Gown...for many reasons needless to mention, if I knew of any better way of adding some increase to my present fortune', he reflected that

if I put on the Gown, very probably I might get a considerable addition to my present fortune, but there, if I expect to rise to any height of prefer-ment in the Church, self-interest must be my guide, and entire submission to command, especially if I hope for a seat in the Bench in your house, nay, after I have it, if I intend to make it worth my while the sitting there; but in that way I had no such views; I had rather content myself with a moderate preferment in the Church, and be my own master, than do anything disagreeable, or be the humble slave of any one for the best mitre on the Bench.

Accordingly he concluded that 'the gown is the last resort'.[3] Two years later however he decided 'to take the Gown', though still with grave reservations.

---

[1] *Letters of a Late Eminent Prelate*, no. XLVII (to Hurd), p. 118.

[2] 'Life of Dr Thomas Newton', in *Lives of E. Pocock, Z. Pearce, T. Newton and P. Skelton*, vol. II, p. 154.

[3] *Letters of Spencer Cowper, Dean of Durham 1746–74*, ed. E. Hughes (Surtees Society, vol. CXLV, 1956), no. VII, p. 6.

Indeed I had objections to it and have still, but what in time may wear off. The disrepute the profession is in at present, the fear of not being lookt on in the same light by our own friends, which is the unavoidable consequence of the former, the difficulty of behaving so as not to give offence to those of the same order who make it their business to scan every word and action, nay misrepresent both, if they can have any prospect of jockeying you out of your expected preferment, these are all objections, but the principal remains behind. The great difficulty I shall have to bring myself to preach, indeed I think it is unsurmountable. The nonsense I hear weekly at St Mary's convinces me that the talent of talking sense is given but to very few, and I have not vanity enough to think I should be an exception where the exceptions are so few, and not courage enough to undertake what I have so small a prospect of succeeding in. But there are preferments which do not require it, as prebends and canonries, which would be more suitable preferment for me till I am better qualified or more used to the business of preaching (if ever I do use myself to it) than any parish living.[1]

In August 1738 therefore, at the age of twenty-five, as he reported to his brother, 'next Sunday I...undergo the first Ordination', and after three weeks 'must go through the ceremony once more. I dont enjoy the happiest hours at present, but I hope time and custom will make things easier to me.'[2] In the following December his friends were already soliciting the duke of Newcastle for an anticipated vacancy of a canonry of Christ Church; and in the next year were canvassing Walpole likewise, 'that the first prebend or canonry where he is not engaged, he would let Spencer have it'.[3] In April 1742 Cowper accepted the rectory of Fordwiche in Kent, in the gift of his elder brother, who in the previous month had asked Newcastle for the deanery of Exeter for him, on the ground that 'he took Orders by the late Queen's express commands and with a promise to provide for him, yet nothing was done for him before her majesty died, nor since'.[4] Although this endeavour was unsuccessful, in May 1742 Spencer was appointed prebendary of the fifth stall in Canterbury cathedral, within four years of ordination; and had to be restrained by his friends from applying forthwith for a royal dispensation for non-residence, since, 'as the king may misunderstand the nature of the request, and it may give him an ill impression of me, I by no means ought, especially at present, desire it, but rather be contented with all its inconveniences'.[5] For the next four years therefore the young divine divided the winter months between

---

[1] *Ibid.* no. XVIII, p. 13.    [2] *Ibid.* no. XX, p. 15.
[3] *Ibid.* no. XXII, p. 16 and Appendix I, p. 212.
[4] *Ibid.* Appendix VI, p. 215.    [5] *Ibid.* no. XXVIII, p. 19.

Canterbury and London, employing a curate at Fordwiche, and enjoying the family house in Hertfordshire in summer; until in 1746 his brother prevailed upon the duke of Newcastle to procure the deanery of Durham for him, at the age of thirty-three and within eight years of his entering into Holy Orders.[1]

On 21st July 1746 he was installed by proxy as Dean of Durham, 'so I shall have no occasion to be there long before Michaelmas';[2] and in September with undisguised reluctance he set out on the journey northwards. His first impressions of Durham were distinctly unpleasing; the city he found 'nasty and disagreeable', the deanery residence, although having a noted Hall and Great Room, 'the others are some of them good rooms but awkwardly disposed, others so dark and dismal you cannot see your hand in them'; whilst even the cathedral itself

has so little beauty in it that it is no improvement to the prospect. The inside is very clumsy. The Great Isle is filled with heavy massive pillars out of all proportion. The Choir very small but neat, not bigger than a College Chapel, but ornamented in the Gothic way very richly. A very fine organ, a good organist and tolerable good voices. The Copes...meer frippery and scandalous....By what I find...it will be difficult to get rid of them, some of my brethren are so attached to them and pleased with their finery. How they can be so fond of playing the popish priest, unless they have a secret bias that way, I can't imagine.[3]

Not unexpectedly therefore he restricted his visits to Durham to the minimum, residing there usually from the beginning of September to mid-December (though once in 1749 he stayed for Christmas), and spending nine months of the year in Hertfordshire and the south. In accordance with the fashion of his times, he was greatly devoted to musical assemblies, and 'early in his career, had a new organ built in the cathedral and was untiring in his efforts to make Durham a musical centre'.[4] Each year he celebrated the king's birthday with a huge rout at the deanery, exchanged social visits with leading personages of the county, and paid his respects to successive Bishops of Durham at Auckland Castle. The single member of the chapter in whose company he appears to have taken pleasure was Martin Benson, bishop of Gloucester, of whom he observed at the outset that 'he is my only comfort at present and I believe will always be my greatest'.[5] Although Cowper was by no means fastidious in

---

[1] *Letters of Spencer Cowper*, no. LXXXIII, p. 57.
[2] *Ibid.* no. LXXXIV, p. 58.
[3] *Ibid.* no. LXXXVIII, pp. 61–2.
[4] *Ibid.* Introduction, p. viii.
[5] *Ibid.* no. LXXXVII, p. 61.

matters ecclesiastical, he professed the strongest antipathy to the process of electing a new bishop on the death of Butler. 'The Congé d'Élire is just arrived, and we have fixed the election for Thursday next', he informed his brother on 3 November 1752.

I observed on reading it, it begins with a lie, 'according to your humble Petition', and 'in regard to your humble Prayer and request made known to us', though the Dean and Chapter never even preserves the form of making one for a new election; and the Letter Mandatory ventures as long a bow, when it expatiates on the known wisdom, piety and the great gravity of the person recommended, though thanks to the greater wisdom of our ministry, it preserves some degree of veracity this bout. The whole form of the election is as ridiculous as this summons to it, and in one of the Instruments returned to the Crown, it usually runs into downright profaneness, for it was there said that it was according to the *special motion of the Holy Ghost*, but that we were all unanimous in the last to omit.[1]

The portrait of an unreservedly secular careerist derivable from Cowper's letters, must be qualified by Professor Hughes' observation that

we should do him a great injustice if we took these intimate, personal letters as a picture of the whole man; we have to read his simple, unaffected sermons and his *Letter* to his niece, Lady Caroline, on first taking the sacrament, to realise that he was a sincere and devout Christian, albeit without 'enthusiasm' which he mistrusted.[2]

By and large, however, his career and outlook on the clerical profession are closely paralleled by those of scions of such noble families as the Ashburhams, Keppels, Barringtons and Cornwallis, whose plaintive or indignant demands for preferment fill the embarrassed pages of the correspondence of the duke of Newcastle. Indeed the general effect of this ubiquitous assertion of lay power in the Church may be aptly summarized in the surprised comment of Cowper on learning that Dr Edward Crane, prebendary of Westminster, had refused the see of Exeter in 1762: 'this is so unusual a piece of self-denial that it requires a man of full as much veracity as Dickens to support its credibility.'[3]

From Sheldon to Secker, therefore, the Church of England witnessed a century of kaleidoscopic changes in the constitutional, political and religious condition of the nation, whilst remaining

---

[1] *Ibid.* no. CLXXXIV, p. 156. The new bishop was Dr Richard Trevor.

[2] *Ibid.* Introduction, p. xi.

[3] *Ibid.* no. CCXXX, p. 209. Dr Samuel Dickens was prebendary of the twelfth stall at Durham.

itself unchanged in respect of its Canons, Liturgy and judicial administration and yet forfeiting the services of Convocation. The contrast indeed between the circumstances of their respective primacies is striking. Sheldon entered upon office as one of the principal architects of the Restoration church settlement in its hour of triumph over dissenters, armed with formidable means for the suppression of Nonconformity. Secker, himself the son of a dissenting father and intended for the dissenting ministry, gave reassurances to the duke of Newcastle before his appointment to Canterbury concerning 'his conduct towards the Dissenters', and that 'he is well with Dr Avery and Dr Chandler';[1] whilst later in his archiepiscopate he 'desired the favour of the acquaintance' of 'Mr Amory, a noted Dissenting minister', since he had no friends 'left amongst the Dissenting ministers and thought it was convenient I should have some'.[2] This revolution in the position of Protestant dissenters after 1689 was perhaps the most influential single circumstance affecting also the situation of the established church. Thanks to the uneasy equilibrium created by the repeal of the Occasional Conformity and Schism Acts combined with the refusal to remove the Test and Corporation Acts, the Whig administrations of the first two Hanoverian sovereigns did not venture to allow any increase of power to the Church of England which would provoke the jealousy of the dissenters. Hence the continued silencing of Convocation, the refusal to introduce the ecclesiastical reforms desired by Gibson and the denial of bishops for the Plantations. Hence also the artificially-stimulated outcry against 'Dr Codex' and the ominous comparisons between himself and Laud, and (as Gibson complained) the 'trying times when bishops are less respected and their actions narrowly watched by enemies, and Church Power is openly complained of as a national grievance'.[3] In such conditions the episcopate could only struggle to maintain its traditional methods of oversight, by visitation, confirmation, ordination and pastoral counsel to the clergy in the discharge of their parochial ministry.

In all these respects Secker exemplified the zeal and diligence of the Caroline prelacy which earned the eulogy of Gwatkin.[4] During

---

[1] N. Sykes, 'The Duke of Newcastle as Ecclesiastical Minister', in *English Historical Review* (January 1942), p. 68.  [2] Secker, Memoirs, f. 74 verso.

[3] E. Gibson, 'Thoughts on the Legality of a Circular Letter from Archbishop Potter to the Bishops of his Province'. St Paul's Cathedral MSS. 17. B. 15.

[4] For Secker, see Secker Memoirs (MSS.); Beilby Porteus, *The Works of Thomas Secker, with his Life*; A. W. Rowden, *The Primates of the Four Georges*.

his brief episcopate at Bristol from 1735–7, he held a visitation of Dorsetshire in the August of 1735, confirming at fifteen centres, and in the following month completed his circuit in his see city. Despite the shortness of his tenure of the see he left behind a 'Parochial Account of the Diocese' for the use of his successors, which Bishop Thomas Newton found of great service. After his translation to Oxford he developed the methods begun at Bristol. He held constantly three ordinations each year, and arranged frequent Confirmations, at times and places other than those of his regular triennial visitations; noting that in 1738 'at Bloxham I confirmed six hours without ceasing, the numbers I know not, as I had not then begun to use tickets', and later that 'wherever I confirmed, I sent religious tracts for the ministers of each parish within the district to distribute, and after a while Confirmation tickets also, finding no other way effectual to keep the people orderly'.[1] In his visitation Charge of 1741 he pledged himself that 'so long as it pleased God to continue his health and strength, Confirmations should be frequent in every part of the diocese', and added that 'for this purpose when Confirmations were on a Sunday, which was the time he would usually pitch upon for the convenience of the people, excepting at the places of his visitation, they might omit for that day the morning or evening prayers as they saw occasion'.[2] At Oxford, as previously at Bristol, he left for his successor 'a large quarto Parochial Book, and all the notices relative to the temporalties and spiritualties that he could procure', remarking the contrast with his predecessor, Potter, who did not 'set down above two or three things in writing for the use of his successor in the see during the whole time that he held it'.[3]

In his oversight of the much smaller diocese of Canterbury, in the year of his translation, 1758, he conducted his primary visitation and in eighteen days held fifteen confirmations, assisted by Bishop Yonge of Bristol. Moreover he was particularly careful to ensure that the archiepiscopal peculiars were not neglected in the matter of confirmations. He 'followed the custom of confirming one year at Bow church and the next year at one of the others; but altered the hour from that of Evening to that of Morning Prayer'.[4] In 1761 'he visited and confirmed at Cliffe in Sussex and confirmed at Buxted;

---

[1] Secker, Mcmoirs, ff. 25 verso, 49–50.
[2] Secker, *Charges* II, *Works*, vol. V, pp. 337–9.
[3] Secker, Memoirs, f. 50.     [4] *Ibid.* f. 54 verso.

and visited and confirmed at Bocking, and confirmed at Hadleigh'. Indeed he made it a particular care 'to visit as many as I could conveniently of my Peculiars, because scarce any memory was left that any a[rch]b[isho]p had visited them personally....Nor could I find that any a[rch]b[isho]p had confirmed in his Peculiars, excepting in London and at Croydon.'[1] His eight published Visitation Charges (five at Oxford and three at Canterbury) testified to his earnest concern with all branches of the episcopal office, and constitute still a rich mine of information relating to the pastoral standards of his age in such points as the performance of divine service, the frequency of celebrating the Holy Communion, the duty of catechising, the administration of Baptism, the care of church fabrics and ornaments, and the maintenance of Rogationtide perambulations. The recently published *Articles of Enquiry addressed to the Clergy of the Diocese of Oxford at the Primary Visitation*[2] of Secker in 1738 together with the replies made by the several incumbents, confirm the impression given by the similar Returns to Archbishop Herring's Visitation Articles at York in 1743 that the general standards of churchmanship had changed little since Caroline times. The ideal aimed at was that of Divine Service twice each Sunday, with a sermon in the morning and in the afternoon an exposition of the Catechism at least, whilst the celebration of Holy Communion was usually quarterly, rising to a monthly Sacrament in the chief parishes. Pluralism and non-residence, however, gravely interfered with the efforts of bishops to ensure even this modest observance, and many churches had only one service and sermon each Sunday. Secker strove to raise the average attainment by exhorting his clergy to read Divine Service reverently, with especial care to the singing of psalms, to catechise throughout the summer months and not only in Lent, to read prayers publicly on Wednesdays, Fridays and Holydays particularly on Good Friday and Christmas Day, and to interpose a celebration of the Holy Communion at Michaelmas as a harvest thanksgiving, bridging thereby the long interval between Whitsuntide and Christmas, with the hope that 'if afterwards you can advance from a quarterly communion to a monthly one, I make no doubt but you will'.

Between the primacies of Sheldon and Secker also the church had

[1] Secker, Memoirs, f. 56.
[2] Edited by H. A. Lloyd Jukes and published by the Oxfordshire Record Society, 1957.

to face the full and multifarious assault of a theological revolution, comprising the impact of science and philosophy, the vogue of Deism and natural religion and the revival of Arianism and Socinianism. If Sheldon in his younger days had been associated with the circle of Lord Falkland at Great Tew, and if the character drawn of him by Samuel Parker retained distinct lineaments of this Latitudinarian tradition, Secker in his youth at the Dissenting Academies had been deeply tinctured with the fashionable liberalism in respect of 'the doctrine of the Trinity, in which for some time I agreed with Dr Clarke, and the inspiration of Scripture, on which I inclined to the *Sentimens de Quelques Théologiens de Holland*'.[1] When he 'had come to a soberer way of thinking about theological matters',[2] and had been ordained, he became an indefatigable defender of orthodoxy both in his own person and by encouraging others. He was of assistance to Butler in the publication in 1726 of the first edition of his *Sermons*, taking 'much pains in making his meaning easier to be apprehended', and again, in preparing the *Analogy* for the press in 1736, 'I was somewhat serviceable to him in the method and thoughts of this book, but very much in making the language of it more accurate and intelligible, which cost me a great deal of time and pains'.[3] He encouraged Dr Thomas Church, prebendary of Chiswick in St Paul's cathedral, to write a *Vindication of the Miraculous Powers which subsisted in the First Three Centuries of the Church*, in reply to Middleton in 1751, and an *Analysis of the Philosophical Works of the late Viscount Bolingbroke* in 1755, to which he contributed 'some corrections and additions'.[4] Not only did he encourage Dr William Bell, prebendary of Westminster, to write *A Defence of Revelation in General and the Gospels in Particular, in Answer to a Late Book subscribed 'A Rational Christian'*; but 'after he had written it once over, I induced him to throw it into a new form, suggested to him innumerable corrections, additions and improvements, and wrote the last chapter almost entirely'.[5] His chief concern however was with Archdeacon Francis Blackburne's *The Confessional*, published anonymously in 1766 and setting forth the aims of the movement for relaxation of the terms of subscription required of the clergy. Secker took especial care to procure an answer from the pen of Dr Gloster Ridley, prebendary of Teynton Regis in Salisbury cathedral, in the shape of 'Three Letters to the

---

[1] Secker, Memoirs, f. 6.  [2] *Ibid.* f. 9.  [3] *Ibid.* ff. 15, 22.
[4] *Ibid.* f. 47 verso.  [5] *Ibid.* f. 63 verso.

Author of *The Confessional*', observing that 'I wrote a great part of each of them and furnished him with all the help that was in my power. And some things having been published against him in the newspapers on account of them, I defended him in two publications in the *London Chronicle*, one anonymous, the other signed Oxoniensis.'[1] Since Blackburne had cast incidental aspersions on archbishop Wake's correspondence with Gallican divines as a plot to introduce popery into the Church of England, Secker collected from Mr Osmund Beauvoir at Canterbury the letters which had passed between his father William, as chaplain to Lord Stair in Paris, and Wake, together with extracts from Wake's correspondence preserved at Christ Church, Oxford; and sent them to Dr Richardson, chaplain to Sir Joseph Yorke at the Hague 'to be communicated to Mr Maclaine for the foundation of his defence of the archbishop, which he proposed to subjoin to the 2nd edition of his translation of Mosheim's Ecclesiastical History, and which I have advised him to print separately'.[2] Maclaine took the advice and published this material as Appendix III to his 1768 edition of Mosheim. Indeed Secker might be thought in some ways to have anticipated the functions of a modern Church Defence and Press and Publications Board, for he recorded in 1766 that 'I had at different times and under different names for several years before put Articles in the papers relative to Church Matters, as Briefs, and the Repair of Churches, American Bishops[3] etc., which, if I have leisure, I may perhaps collect together. For, as we are frequently attacked in News papers, I think we should defend ourselves there; and am sorry that scarce any one besides myself hath done it.'[4]

When Secker's primacy ended in 1768 two of the major problems which were to vex the established church during the latter half of the eighteenth-century had run a considerable part of their course, whilst a third was yet below the horizon. His death occurred thirty years after the conversion of John Wesley, when the Methodist revival had already made a marked impact upon both church and nation; whilst the Feathers' Tavern Petition, the logical outcome of *The Confessional*, was presented to the House of Commons in 1772, as the culmination of a movement noted earlier with apprehension by Herring as aiming at 'a reformation of our establishment in its

[1] Secker, Memoirs, f. 94.     [2] *Ibid*. f. 71.
[3] E.g. 'An Answer to Dr Mayhew's Observations on the Charter and Conduct of the S.P.G.', 1764.     [4] *Ibid*. f. 72–3.

doctrines, discipline and liturgy'. On the other hand the social revolution which, by its transference of population from the south to the new industrial towns of the north and midlands, presented a challenge of unprecedented gravity to the church in respect of the provision of new churches and parishes to minister to the needs of the people, had not yet manifested its nature or proportions. To none of these challenges was the church able to make a wholly effective response. Despite the powerful and weighty defences of orthodoxy from the pens of Waterland and Butler, the heterodox campaign increased in momentum. In 1771 Richard Watson was advanced to the regius professorship of Divinity at Cambridge and proceeded to advocate the new theological opinions from his chair, supporting the Feathers' Tavern Petition and arguing for the adoption of Dr Samuel Clarke's Liturgy in place of the Book of Common Prayer. Even after the defeat of this Petition, Beilby Porteus, the faithful chaplain and biographer of Secker, approached Archbishop Cornwallis in 1773 as a member of a deputation (which believed itself to represent 'the wishes of a very large proportion both of the clergy and the laity'), to request 'the bishops to promote a review of the Liturgy and Articles in order to amend in both, but particularly the latter, those parts which stood in need of amendment'. The primate after consulting his brethren severally, reported 'the opinion of the bench in general that nothing in prudence can be done'.[1] In the Irish parliament, already in 1756 Bishop Robert Clayton of Clogher had moved for the omission of the Nicene and Athanasian creeds from the Prayer Book of the Irish Church, though the question was dropped with his death two years later; but the project was ensured of an episcopal champion in England when Watson became bishop of Llandaff in 1782.

Meantime the flank of the heterodox movement was being turned by the Methodist revival, which, instead of essaying a direct assault by theological argument, was preaching the doctrine of Man's sinfulness and depravity and his desperate need of redemption, which could be effected only by One who was truly Son of God. Soteriology thereby came to the rescue of orthodoxy, but at the risk of creating a further schism in the church. John and Charles Wesley indeed received not inconsiderable kindness, sympathy and understanding at first from such bishops as Gibson and Potter. Moreover Secker's charges to his diocese of Canterbury contained repeated pastoral

[1] R. Hodgson, *Life of Beilby Porteus* (1811), pp. 38–40.

counsels in regard to the Methodists, that 'the only way is for the clergy to imitate and emulate what is good in them, avoiding what is bad', together with warnings that 'we have in fact lost many of our people to sectaries by not preaching in a manner sufficiently evangelical', and that 'those who are now forming new separations gain and preserve a surprising influence amongst their followers by personal religious intercourse'; and also exhortations that 'the only complete vindication of ourselves will be to preach fully and frequently the doctrines which we are unjustly accused of casting off or undervaluing'.[1] But individual acts of exhortation, and even of encouragement, were no substitute for a corporate and articulated policy on the part of the episcopate towards the rapidly expanding Methodist societies. Moreover, when the freedom of the Methodists from the fetters of parliamentary control enabled them to respond to the needs of shifting populations by building meeting-houses in the new industrial towns, whilst the established church was hamstrung by the supposed legal necessity of a private Act of Parliament to create each new ecclesiastical parish, the stranglehold of lay power became as oppressive as evident.

It must remain a moot point how far the suspension of Convocation accentuated the failure of the church to formulate an agreed and coherent policy towards the Methodist revival, and to respond to the challenge of the social problems resulting from the industrial revolution. Occasional gatherings of the episcopate at dinner at Lambeth during the holy days after Christmas, before paying their New Year compliments to the sovereign, or during Easter week, were no adequate substitute for regular synodical deliberation. Gibson at least had been convinced that the continued suppression of sitting and acting Convocations could only lead to disaster for the bishops and clergy, and to an increasing assertion of the control of the laity. It was significant that the Feathers' Tavern Petition was introduced into the House of Commons and defeated there by the eloquence of Burke. In an *Oratio Synodalis*, composed by Secker for delivery in the first Convocation to meet after the accession of George III, but not delivered owing to indisposition, he dealt at length with the question of the advisability of seeking a royal licence and Letters of Business. Observing that much ridicule was evoked by the spectacle of a formal summons to Convocation without allowing it to do

---

[1] Secker, *Charges* VI, VII, VIII, *Works*, vol. V, pp. 441, 443, 461–2, 480 (ed. B. Porteus, 6 vols., 1811).

business, and emphasising the valuable part played by Convocation at the Reformation and its indissoluble connection with the temporal constitution of the realm, he set himself to reply to those who urged the resumption of sitting Convocations as a means of restoring the discipline of the church. Pointing to the multitude of different enemies of the church, atheists, deists, heretics, papists and Protestant dissenters, he argued that the surest way to unite them in a common hostility to the established church would be to revivify Convocation. Furthermore, if the results of formal deliberation in Convocation were small, further contempt would ensue; if great, much time would be required for important matters, and opposition would be provoked; *quoquo nos vertamus, gravem offensionem concitabimus.* There was also the danger (with a backward glance at the not distant past) of divisions within the church in consequence of a sitting Convocation, so that the last state of both church and synod would be worse than the present. Accordingly he accepted the maxim of *quieta non movenda*; and devoted the remainder of his intended allocution to exhorting his brethren of both houses to strive earnestly by pastoral methods for the edification of the church and the defeat of its enemies.[1] Between the counsels of Gibson and Secker therefore there was a great gulf fixed; and the history of the church from the death of Secker to the age of reform would seem to justify Gibson's apprehensions of the loss to its corporate life from the silencing of Convocation.

During the century which divided the primacies of Sheldon and Secker it was the habit of eminent divines to speak the praises of the *Ecclesia Anglicana* in superlative terms. To Sancroft

if there be now in the world a Church to whom that eulogium, that she is as a lily among thorns, is due and proper, it is this Church of which we are members, as it stands reformed now and established amongst us; the purest certainly upon earth, as being purified from those corruptions and abuses which the lapse of times, the malice of the devil and the wickedness of men had introduced insensibly into the doctrine and worship and government of it.[2]

Joseph Glanvill also rejoiced that

by the blessing of God we enjoy a Constitution, Apostolical in its Doctrine; Primitive in its Government; decent in its ceremonies; grave and pious in

---

[1] 'Oratio quam coram Synodo Provinciae Cantuariensis anno 1761 convocata habendam scripserat, sed morbo praepeditus non habuit, Archiepiscopus' (T. Secker, *Works*, vol. v, pp. 508–25).

[2] G. D'Oyly, *Life of Sancroft* (1821), vol. I, pp. 166–7.

its Liturgy: We have the Scriptures, the Creeds, the Sacraments, the main Ordinances and Duties of the first and purest times; we are freed from the Idolatries, Superstitions, and other corruptions of the Roman Church on this hand; and clear from the vanities and Enthusiasms that have overspread some Protestants on that; our Church hath rejected the painted bravery of the one; and provided against the sordid slovenliness of the other.[1]

Before the eyes of his foreign correspondents both of the Gallican and Protestant churches, Wake likewise set forth a picture of the Church of England so staunchly orthodox in faith that 'whatever other Churches adhere firmly to the Vincentian canon, the Church of England is pre-eminent among them, nor will ever repudiate anything which has been believed everywhere, always and by every one'; and equally catholic in regimen, preserving 'the episcopal polity, duly moderated and divorced from all unjust dominion, as it stands amongst us, and as it has been received in the Church since the times of the Apostles'.[2] Similarly Archdeacon Basire avowed that 'I have surveyed most Churches, Eastern and Western, in fifteen years' ecclesiastical pilgrimage (during my voluntary banishment for my religion and loyalty), and I dare pronounce the Church of England, what David said of Goliath's sword, "There is none like it", both for Primitive Doctrine, Worship, Discipline and Government'.[3] To the historian who, like the watchman on the tower, sees that 'the morning cometh and also the night' as he looks backward upon the chequered epoch from Sheldon to Secker, the measured words of R. W. Church, written of the sombre days of 1845, may well seem a more apt and accurate characterisation.

The English Church was after all as well worth living in and fighting for as any other; it was not only in England that light and dark, in teaching and in life, was largely intermingled, and the mixture had to be largely allowed for. We had our Sparta, a noble, if a rough and incomplete one; patiently to do our best for it was better than leaving it to its fate, in obedience to signs and reasonings which the heat of strife might well make delusive. It was one hopeful token, that boasting had to be put away from us for a long time to come.[4]

*Respice in servos tuos et in opera tua: et dirige filios eorum.*

---

[1] J. I. Cope, *Joseph Glanvill*, p. 83.
[2] N. Sykes, *William Wake*, vol. I, p. 282; vol. II, p. 3.
[3] J. H. Overton, *Life in the English Church 1660–1714*, citing Basire, p. 44.
[4] R. W. Church, *The Oxford Movement*, pp. 401–2 (London, 1891).

# SELECT BIBLIOGRAPHY

*Books are listed under their authors' and editors' names, and also
under the names of those of whom they treat*

### MANUSCRIPT SOURCES

Secker MSS. (Lambeth Palace Library).
Tanner MSS. (Bodleian Library).
B. 14, 15 Linc. (Bodleian Library).
Wake, Autobiography (privately owned).
Wake: Letters to Lord Cowper (County Record Office, Hertford).
Forty Sermons of James Woodforde (privately owned).
Sermons of John Lloyd (privately owned).
Gibson MSS (St Paul's Cathedral Library).
Lambeth Act Books, IV.
House of Lords MSS., published in Historical Manuscripts Commission,
IXth Report, Part II, Appendix.

### PRINTED SOURCES

*Acts of the Parliament of Scotland, 1593–1707*, ed. T. Thomson and
C. Innes (12 vols. Edinburgh, 1814–75).
BATE, F. *The Declaration of Indulgence, 1672: a Study of the Rise of
Organised Dissent* (London, 1908).
BAXTER, R. *Reliquiae Baxterianae*, ed. M. Sylvester (London, 1696).
BEBB, E. D. *Nonconformity and Social and Economic Life, 1660–1800*
(London, 1935).
BENNETT, G. V. *White Kennett, Bishop of Peterborough* (London, 1957).
BENZ, E. *Bischofsamt und Apostolische Sukzession im Deutschen Pro-
testantismus* (Stuttgart, 1953).
BERNARD, J. H. (ed.). *The Works of Bishop Butler* (2 vols. London, 1900).
BIRCH, T. *The Life of Archbishop Tillotson* (2nd ed. London, 1753).
BOSHER, R. S. *The Making of the Restoration Settlement* (London, 1951).
BOSSUET, J. B. *Œuvres* (12 vols. Paris, 1836).
—— *Correspondance de Bossuet*, ed. Ch. Urbain and E. Levesque (15 vols.
Paris, 1909–25).
—— *Le Gallicanisme de Bossuet*, by A. G. Martimort (Paris, 1953).
—— 'Bossuet, ses Relations avec Angleterre', by Abbot F. Cabrol, in
*Revue d'Histoire Ecclésiastique* (1931), vol. XXVII.
—— *Bossuet, Historien du Protestantisme*, by A. Rébelliau (Paris, 1891).
BREWER, J. S. (ed.). *Church History*, by T. Fuller (6 vols. Oxford, 1845).
BRINKWORTH, E. C. R. *Episcopal Visitation Book for the Archdeaconry of
Buckingham* (Buckinghamshire Record Society, 1947).
BROCKBANK, T. *Diary and Letter Book of Thomas Brockbank*, ed. R.
Trappes-Lomax (Cheetham Society, no. 89, new series, 1930).
BUDÉ, E. DE. *Lettres Inédites addressées de 1686 à 1737 à J. A. Turrettini*
(3 vols. Paris, 1887).

BULL, BISHOP G. *The Life of Dr George Bull*, by R. Nelson (London, 1713).
—— *Difensio Fidei Nicenae* (Eng. trans., Library of Anglo-Catholic Theology, 1851).
—— *Judicium Ecclesiae Catholicae* (Eng. trans., Library of Anglo-Catholic Theology, 1885).
BURNET, BISHOP G. *A History of My Own Time, with Notes by the Earls of Dartmouth and Hardwicke, and Speaker Onslow*, ed. M. J. Routh (6 vols. Oxford 1823).
—— *A Supplement to Burnet's History of My Own Time*, by H. C. Foxcroft (Oxford, 1902).
—— *Vindication of the Orders of the Church of England* (London, 1677).
—— *The Letter Writ by the Last Assembly General of the Clergy of France to the Protestants* (London, 1683).
—— *A Letter to Mr Thevenot, containing a Censure on Mr le Grand's History of King Henry VIII's Divorce to which is added a Censure of M. de Meaux's History of the Variations of the Protestant Churches* (London, 1689).
BUTLER, BISHOP J. *Works*, ed. J. H. Bernard (2 vols. London, 1900).
CABROL, ABBOT F. 'Bossuet, ses Relations avec Angleterre', in *Revue d'Histoire Ecclésiastique* (1931), vol. XXVII.
CALAMY, E. *An Historical Account of My Own Life*, ed. J. T. Rutt (2 vols. London, 1829).
CARDWELL, E. *Documentary Annals of the Reformed Church of England* (2 vols. Oxford, 1844).
—— *Synodalia* (2 vols. Oxford, 1842).
CARPENTER, E. F. *Thomas Sherlock* (London, 1936).
—— *Thomas Tenison* (London, 1948).
—— *The Protestant Bishop, Henry Compton* (London, 1956).
CARTWRIGHT, BISHOP T. *The Diary of Thomas Cartwright*, ed. J. Hunter (Campden Society, 1843).
CASSIRER, E. *The Platonic Renaissance in England*, trans. J. P. Pettigrove (London, 1953).
CHADWICK, W. O. *From Bossuet to Newman* (Cambridge, 1957).
CLARK, W. N. *A Collection of Letters addressed by Prelates and Individuals of High Rank in Scotland to Archbishop Sancroft* (Edinburgh, 1848).
CLARKE, S. *Memoirs of the Life and Sentiments of Dr Samuel Clarke*, by T. Emlyn (London, 1748).
COBBETT, W. *Parliamentary History*, vol. IV.
COLIE, R. L. *Light and Enlightenment: a Study of the Cambridge Platonists and the Dutch Arminians* (Cambridge, 1957).
COLLINS, A. *A Discourse of Freethinking* (London, 1713).
—— *A Discourse of the Grounds and Reasons of the Christian Religion* (London, 1724).
COMPTON, H. *The Protestant Bishop, Henry Compton*, by E. F. Carpenter (London, 1956).
—— *Episcopalia, or Letters of Henry Compton, Bishop of London, to the Clergy of his Diocese 1686*, ed. S. W. Cornish (Oxford, 1842).

COPE, J. I. *Joseph Glanvill, Anglican Apologist* (Washington University Studies, St Louis, 1956).

CORNISH, S. W. *See* Compton.

COSIN, BISHOP J. *The Correspondence of John Cosin*, ed. G. Ornsby (2 vols.). Surtees Society, vols. LII, LV (Durham, 1869).

COWPER, SPENCER. *Letters of Spencer Cowper, Dean of Durham*, ed. E. Hughes (Surtees Society, vol. CLXV, 1956).

—— *Eight Discourses preached on or near the Great Festivals in the Cathedral Church of Durham* (London, 1773).

CRAGG, G. R. *From Puritanism to the Age of Reason* (Cambridge, 1950).

CREWE, NATHANIEL, LORD. *Nathaniel, Lord Crewe, Bishop of Durham*, by C. E. Whiting (London, 1940).

CROSS, A. L. *The Anglican Episcopate and the American Colonies* (Harvard Historical Studies, vol. IX, 1902).

CROSS, F. L. *Patristic Study at Oxford: Presidential Address to the Oxford Society of Historical Theology* (Blackwell, 1948).

CUMING, G. J. 'The Making of the Durham Book' and 'The Prayer Book in Convocation, 1661', in *Journal of Ecclesiastical History*, vol. VI, 1, and vol. VIII, 2.

DALTON, H. *Daniel Ernst Jablonski* (Berlin, 1903).

DICKINSON, W. C. and DONALDSON, G. *A Source Book of Scottish History*, vol. III, '1567–1707' (Edinburgh, 1954).

D'OYLY, G. *The Life of William Sancroft Archbishop of Canterbury* (2 vols. London, 1821).

DUPPA, BISHOP B. *The Correspondence of Bishop Brian Duppa and Sir Justinian Isham* (Northamptonshire Record Society, vol. XVII, 1956).

ELRINGTON, C. R. (ed.) *The Whole Works of Archbishop J. Ussher* (17 vols. Dublin, 1847–64).

EMLYN, T. *Memoirs of the Life and Sentiments of Dr Samuel Clarke* (London, 1748).

*Episcopalia, or Letters of Henry Compton, Bishop of London, to the Clergy of his Diocese*, ed. S. W. Cornish (Oxford, 1842).

EVANS, T. S. *Life of Robert Frampton, Bishop of Gloucester* (London, 1876).

EVERY, G. *The High Church Party, 1688–1718* (London, 1956).

FIRTH, C. H. *See* Macaulay.

FOXCROFT, H. C. *A Supplement to Burnet's History of My Own Time* (Oxford, 1902).

FRAMPTON, BISHOP, R. *Life of Robert Frampton, Bishop of Gloucester*, by T. S. Evans (London, 1876).

FULLER, T. *Church History*, ed. J. S. Brewer (6 vols. Oxford, 1845).

GIBBON, E. *Memoirs of My Life and Writings*, ed. G. B. Hill (London, 1900).

GIBSON, E. *Codex Juris Ecclesiastici Anglicani* (2 vols. 2nd ed. 1761).

—— *Of Visitations, Parochial and General* (London, 1717).

—— *Edmund Gibson, Bishop of London*, by N. Sykes (Oxford, 1926).

GILL, H. and GUILFORD, E. L. (eds.) *The Rector's Book of Clayworth, Notts.* (Nottingham, 1910).

GLANVILL, J. *Joseph Glanvill, Anglican Apologist*, by J. I. Cope (Washington University Studies, St Louis, 1956).

GRANVILLE, D. *The Remains of Dennis Granville*, ed. G. Ornsby (Surtees Society, 2 vols. 1860, 1865).

GREENWOOD, O. *See* Manning.

HACKET, BISHOP, J. *A Century of Sermons preached by Dr John Hacket, with an Account of the Life of the Author*, by T. Plume (London, 1675).

HAZARD, P. *La Crise de la Conscience Européenne, 1680–1715* (3 vols. Paris, 1935).

—— *La Pensée Européenne au XVIIIme Siècle* (3 vols. Paris, 1946).

HICKES, G. and NELSON, R. *A Complete Collection of the Works of John Kettlewell, with his Life* (2 vols. London, 1719).

HILL, G. B. (ed.). *See* Gibbon.

Historical Manuscripts Commission, *IXth Report*, Part II, Appendix, House of Lords MSS.

HOADLY, B. *A Plain Account of the Nature and End of the Sacrament of the Lord's Supper* (London, 1735).

HOCKLIFFE, E. (ed.). *Diary of Ralph Josselin* (Camden Society, 3rd series, vol. XV, 1908).

HODGSON, R. *Life of Beilby Porteus* (London, 1811).

HUGHES, E. (ed.). *Letters of Spencer Cowper, Dean of Durham* (Surtees Society, vol. CXLV, 1956).

HUNT, N. C. *Sir Robert Walpole, Samuel Holden and the Dissenting Deputies* (Dr Williams's Lectures, no XI, Friends of Dr Williams's Library, Oxford, 1957).

HUNTER, J. (ed.). *Diary and Correspondence of Ralph Thoresby* (4 vols. London, 1832).

—— *The Diary of Thomas Cartwright* (Camden Society, 1843).

ISHAM, SIR G. *The Correspondence of Bishop Brian Duppa and Sir Justinian Isham* (Northamptonshire Record Society, vol. XVII, 1956).

JABLONSKI, D. E. *Daniel Ernst Jablonski*, by H. Dalton (Berlin, 1903).

*Journals of the House of Lords.*

*Journals of the House of Commons.*

JOSSELIN, R. *Diary of Ralph Josselin*, ed. E. Hockliffe (Camden Society, 3rd series, vol. XV, 1908).

KEMP, E. W. *An Introduction to Canon Law in the Church of England* (London, 1957).

KENNETT, WHITE. *A Register and Chronicle, Civil and Ecclesiastical* (London, 1728).

—— *White Kennett, Bishop of Peterborough*, by G. V. Bennett (London, 1957).

KETTLEWELL, J. *A Complete Collection of the Works of John Kettlewell, with his Life*, by G. Hickes and R. Nelson (2 vols. London, 1719).

LAW, E. *Considerations on the State of the World with Regard to the Theory of Religion* (London, 1745).

LE COURAYER, F. P. *Dissertation sur la Validité des Ordinations des Anglais* (2 vols. Nancy, 1723).

LEWIS, J. 'Some Account of Suffragan Bishops in England', in *Bibliotheca Topographica Britannica*, no. XXVIII (J. Nichols, London, 1785).

LIGHTFOOT, J. B. *The Apostolic Fathers* (2nd ed. London, 1889).

*Lives of E. Pocock, Z. Pearce, T. Newton and P. Skelton* (2 vols. London, 1740).

LLOYD JUKES, H. A. (ed.). *See* Secker.

LOCKE, J. *The Reasonableness of Christianity* and *Essay Concerning Human Understanding*, in *Works* (2 vols. London, 1740).

MACAULAY, T. B. *History of England*, ed. C. H. Firth (6 vols. London, 1913).

MAGRATH, J. R. *The Queen's College, Oxford* (2 vols. Oxford, 1921).

MANNING, B. L. *The Protestant Dissenting Deputies*, ed. O. Greenwood (Cambridge, 1952).

MARTIMORT, A. G. *Le Gallicanisme de Bossuet* (Paris, 1953).

MATTHEWS, A. G. *Calamy Revised*. (Oxford, 1934).

McLACHLAN, H. J. *Socianism in Seventeenth-Century England* (Oxford, 1951).

MIDDLETON, C. *A Free Enquiry into the Miraculous Powers which were supposed to have subsisted in the Christian Church* (London, 1749).

MORIN, J. [MORINUS]. *Commentarius de Sacris Ecclesiae Ordinationibus* (Paris, 1655; Amsterdam, 1695).

NANKIVELL, J. W. H. 'A Survey of the Attempts at Religious Comprehension in the Church of England during the XVIIth century, with special reference to the period from the Restoration to the Revolution' (Oxford, B. Litt. thesis).

NEESER, M. *Grandeur d'Ostervald* (Neuchâtel, 1938).

NELSON, R. *Life of Dr George Bull* (London, 1713).

NEWLIN, T. *See* Parker.

NEWTON, T. *Lives of E. Pocock, Z. Pearce, T. Newton and P. Skelton*, (2 vols. London, 1816).

ORNSBY, G. (ed.) *See* Cosin.

PARKER, M. *Life of Matthew Parker*, by J. Strype (London, 1711).

PARKER, S. *History of His Own Time in Four Books* (trans. from the Latin by T. Newlin, London, 1727); *De Rebus sui temporis Commentariorum libri quatuor* (London, 1726).

PATRICK, BISHOP S. *Works*, ed. A. Taylor (9 vols. Oxford, 1858).

—— *A Brief Account of the New Sect of Latitude-Men, together with some Reflections upon the New Philosophy*, by S. P. (London, 1662).

PATTISON, M. 'Tendencies of Religious thought in England, 1688–1750', in *Essays and Reviews* (London, 1861).

PEARCE, Z. *Lives of E. Pocock, Z. Pearce, T. Newton and P. Skelton* (2 vols. London, 1816).

PLUME, T. *A Century of Sermons preached by Dr John Hacket, with an Account of the Life of the Author* (London, 1675).

POCOCK, E. *Lives of E. Pocock, Z. Pearce, T. Newton and P. Skelton* (2 vols. London, 1816).

PORTEUS, B. *The Works of Archbishop Secker, with his Life* (6 vols. London, 1811).

—— *Life of Beilby Porteus*, by R. Hodgson (London, 1811).

PRIDEAUX, H. *Life of Humphrey Prideaux* (London, 1748).
RÉBELLIAU, A. *Bossuet, Historien du Protestantisme* (Paris, 1891).
REYNOLDS, ARCHDEACON, G. *An Historical Essay upon the Government of the Church of England* (London, 1743).
—— *A Letter to the Reverend Dr Lisle, Prolocutor of the Lower House of Convocation* (London, 1742).
RUTT, J. T. (ed.). *See* Calamy.
SACHEVERELL, H. *The Tryal of Dr Sacheverell* (Dublin, 1910).
—— *The Bishop of Lincoln's and the Bishop of Norwich's Speeches in the House of Lords at the opening of the Second Article of the Impeachment of Dr Sacheverell* (London, 1710).
SANCROFT, ARCHBISHOP W. *The Life of William Sancroft, Archbishop of Canterbury*, by G. D'Oyly (2 vols. London, 1821).
—— *A Collection of Letters addressed by Prelates and Individuals of High Rank in Scotland to Archbishop Sancroft*, ed. W. N. Clark (Edinburgh, 1848).
SECKER, ARCHBISHOP T. *The Works of Archbishop Secker, with his Life*, by B. Porteus (6 vols. London, 1811).
—— *Articles of Enquiry addressed to the Clergy of the Diocese of Oxford*, ed. H. A. Lloyd Jukes (Oxfordshire Record Society, 1957).
SHARP, ARCHBISHOP J. *See* Sharp, T.
SHARP, T. *Life of John Sharp, Archbishop of York* (2 vols. London, 1825).
SHELDON, G. *Life of Gilbert Sheldon*, by V. Staley (London, 1913).
SHERLOCK, BISHOP T. *The Use and Intent of Prophecy in the Several Ages of the World* (3rd ed. London, 1735).
—— *The Tryal of the Witnesses of the Resurrection of Jesus* (London, 1729).
—— *Thomas Sherlock*, by E. F. Carpenter (London, 1936).
SKELTON, P. *Lives of E. Pocock, Z. Pearce, T. Newton and P. Skelton* (2 vols. London, 1816).
SPRAT, BISHOP T. *History of the Royal Society* (London, 4th edition, 1702).
STALEY, V. *Life of Gilbert Sheldon* (London, 1913).
STEPHEN, L. *History of English Thought in the XVIIIth Century* (London, 2 vols. 1876).
STOUGHTON, J. *A History of Religion in England* (8 vols. 2nd ed. London, 1911).
STROMBERG, R. N. *Religious Liberalism in Eighteenth-Century England* (Oxford, 1954).
STRYPE, J. *Annals of the Reformation* (London, 1709).
—— *Life of Matthew Parker* (London, 1711).
—— *Life of John Whitgift* (3 vols. Oxford, 1822).
SWIFT, J. *Prose Works*, ed. Temple Scott (vols. III and IV, London, 1898).
SYKES, N. *William Wake, Archbishop of Canterbury* (2 vols. Cambridge, 1957).
—— *Edmund Gibson, Bishop of London* (Oxford, 1926).
—— 'The Duke of Newcastle as Ecclesiastical Minister', in *English Historical Review*, vol. LVII, no. 225 (January 1942).
SYLVESTER, M. *Reliquiae Baxterianae* (London, 1696).
TAYLOR, A. (ed.). *The Works of Bishop Patrick* (9 vols. Oxford, 1858).

THORESBY, R. *Diary and Correspondence of Ralph Thoresby*, ed. J. Hunter (4 vols. London, 1832).

THORNDIKE, H. *The Theological Works of Herbert Thorndike* (Library of Anglo-Catholic Theology, Oxford, 1854).

TILLOTSON, ARCHBISHOP J. *Works* (3 vols. London, 1752).

—— *The Life of Archbishop Tillotson*, by T. Birch (2nd ed. London, 1753).

TINDAL, M. *Christianity as Old as the Creation* (London, 1730).

TENISON, T. *Thomas Tenison*, by E. F. Carpenter (London, 1948).

TOLAND, J. *Christianity Not Mysterious* (London, 1696).

TRAPPES-LOMAX, R. *See* Brockbank.

TULLOCH, J. *Rational Theology and Christian Philosophy in England in the Seventeenth Century* (2 vols. 2nd ed. Edinburgh, 1874).

TURRETTINI, J. A. *Letters Inédites addressées de 1686 à 1737 à J. A. Turrettini*, ed. E. de Budé (3 vols. Paris, 1887).

URBAIN, CH. and LEVESQUE, E. (eds.). *See* Bossuet, *Correspondance*.

USHER, R. G. *The Rise and Fall of the High Commission* (Oxford, 1913).

USSHER, ARCHBISHOP J. *The Whole Works of Archbishop J. Ussher*, ed. C. R. Elrington (17 vols. Dublin, 1847–64).

WAKE, ARCHBISHOP W. *William Wake, Archbishop of Canterbury*, by N. Sykes (2 vols. Cambridge, 1957).

WARBURTON, BISHOP W. *Letters from a Late Eminent Prelate* (2nd ed. London, 1809).

—— *The Alliance between Church and State* (London, 1736).

WATSON, E. W. 'An Eighteenth-Century Clergyman', in *Church Quarterly Review*, vol. CV, no. 210 (January, 1928).

WATSON, R. (ed.). *See next entry.*

WATSON, BISHOP R. *Anecdotes of the Life of Richard Watson, Bishop of Llandaff*, ed. R. Watson (2 vols. London, 1818).

—— *Miscellaneous Tracts* (2 vols. London, 1815).

WEISS, CH. *Histoire des Réfugiés Protestants de France depuis la Révocation de l'Edit de Nantes* (2 vols. Paris, 1853).

WHITEMAN, E. O. A. 'The Re-establishment of the Church of England, 1660–1663', in *Transactions of the Royal Historical Society*, 5th series, vol. V (1955).

—— 'The Church of England, 1542–1837', in *Victoria County History of Wiltshire*, vol. III, ed. R. B. Pugh (Oxford, 1956).

WHITGIFT, J. *Life of John Whitgift*, by J. Strype (3 vols. Oxford, 1822).

WHITING, C. E. *Nathaniel, Lord Crewe, Bishop of Durham* (London, 1940).

WILKINS, BISHOP, J. *Of the Principles and Duties of Natural Religion* (London, 2 vols. 1675).

WOOLSTON, T. *Six Discourses on the Miracles of our Saviour* (London, 1729).

# INDEX